Michele Elliott is a teacher, psychologist and mother of two boys. She has worked with children and families since 1968, and is on the Advisory Councils of ChildLine and the NSPCC. She has chaired World Health Organisation and Home Office working groups, and has been awarded a Winston Churchill Fellowship. She is the author of thirteen other books, including *Keeping Safe: A Practical Guide to Talking with Children, Feeling Happy, Feeling Safe*, a colour picture book for young children and the series *The Willow Street Kids*, for primary aged children. She is often on the television and radio discussing issues about children and writes a regular column for *Family Circle* magazine. In 1984 Michele founded the children's charity KIDSCAPE, which works to keep children safe from bullying, abuse and other dangers.

501 WAYS TO BE A GOOD PARENT

Michele Elliott

Hodder & Stoughton

First published in Great Britain as a paperback original in 1996
by Hodder & Stoughton
A division of Hodder Headline PLC

10 9 8 7 6 5 4 3 2

British Library Cataloguing in Publication Data

Elliott, Michele
501 Ways to be a Good Parent
I. Title
306.874

ISBN 0340 64903 8

Typeset by Phoenix Typesetting, Ilkley, West Yorkshire

Printed and bound in Great Britain by
Cox and Wyman Ltd, Reading

Hodder and Stoughton Ltd
A Division of Hodder Headline PLC
338 Euston Road
London NW1 3BH

Acknowledgements

John Hadjipateras told me that my next book should be a 'How To' kind, and so the idea for *501 Ways* took hold. John has also helped the KIDSCAPE charity, and without his support I don't think any of the work on protecting children would have been done. He is a great friend and the father of four wonderful children.

It has been a pleasure to write for *Family Circle* magazine and they have supported the publication of this book from the start. Some of the chapters started life as *Family Circle* articles and then grew. Special thanks to Deborah Murdock, Gilly Batterbee and Gill Adams for their great patience, excellent editing and cajoling.

The KIDSCAPE staff put up with my writing and long periods away from the office, which I think they quite enjoyed. A big thanks to Jane Kilpatrick, Linda Llewellyn, Lisa Flowers, Angela Glaser and Daphne Joiner. Daphne is also a proper nanny who has raised about thirty children over the years and is a fount of wisdom.

Linda Frost deserves a special mention for coming up with the sub-title for this edition – thanks Linda.

My husband Edward has been my strongest supporter and a loving and kind father to our sons, Charles and James, on whom we have practised being parents. We think they are the world's best kids, but you will have to ask them how they think we did in a few more years.

Finally, many thanks to my editors at Hodder, Rowena Webb and Dawn Bates. They are a writer's best friend – humorous, accessible and full of good ideas.

Contents

Introduction

Amy was bouncing around the garden having a great time. Her mother Nicola and I were talking. Nicola was worried about her daughter.

'I don't want her to become too precocious,' she said.

'But she's a lovely kid,' I protested. Amy was one of the most secure, happy children I knew. I always looked forward to my children playing with her. 'Are there some problems with Amy?' I asked.

'Oh, no, she's a wonderful kid – everyone loves her,' replied Nicola.

'Then why change what you are doing?'

'Because someone told me that too much praise might spoil her.'

Isn't it amazing that we parents are so quick to listen to what others tell us about our children, even if our own instincts tell us that everything is OK?

What Nicola was doing was starting to doubt her own good common sense. Amy is a delightful child, full of self-confidence. Nicola is not praising Amy's bad behaviour, she is reinforcing her good behaviour. She is doing the right thing, and all she needed was for someone to tell her she was doing a great job and to keep up the good work. I only wish we had more children like Amy.

The real problem for Nicola was that she didn't have anyone to share her worries with – like a favourite aunt who had raised four children, perhaps. When we were concerned about raising children in times past, we would pop next door and talk to a neighbour or phone family members. Now we don't have the time to talk. I remember my grandmother having endless conversations over the back fence or on the telephone with her grown-up children about their growing-up children. Now it seems we are all bringing our kids up alone and feeling unsure. We also believe that the problems we run into are only happening to us. Not so. The same problems face every parent, but we just don't know it because we are so busy and live so far apart from each other and from our extended families.

This book is for busy parents. (Are there any other kind?) You can dip into it for ideas when you are stuck, or read a chapter when you have five minutes peace from the demands of parenthood, work, chores, etc. As a mother who works both inside and outside the home, I know only too well how difficult it is to juggle every-thing and remain relatively sane. Many who know me would say I haven't succeeded! I hope you find some comfort knowing that none of us gets it right all the time – I've owned up to some of my mistakes (my kids will tell you if I haven't), as well as to things which have gone well. I have injected some humour because it is one of the only ways, in my opinion, to survive parenthood.

However, if there is one underlying theme of this book it is that children need their parents to be parents first and friends second. No harm in being friends with our children, but our primary role is as parents. Children will push and shove and test the boundaries, and we have to hold firm. Caving in for the sake of an easy life when children are young just creates problems for them, and for us, when they get older.

I hope you enjoy the book and wish you well from those frantic younger years to those preteen and teenage years, when your lovely, fun-loving and charming children begin turning into grunt-ing, non-communicative hormonally-driven creatures who blame you for everything. But don't despair, they eventually come out of it and discover that you weren't so bad, after all. There is no point in holding you up in a long introduction. Good luck being a parent. We all need it! I got a bit carried away, so you'll find that there are more than 501 suggestions about how to be a good parent. There is always room for even more, and I'd love to hear from you if you have any ideas you think would be good for the next edition. Perhaps it could be entitled *1001 Ways to Be a Good Parent*? Contact me at the KIDSCAPE Charity address:

Michele Elliott
Kidscape
152 Buckingham Palace Road
London SW1W 9TR

PS Don't be misguided by the address of our charity. One woman wrote to say she was shocked that a charity could have such a 'posh address'. Well, Buckingham Palace Road has two ends – the Queen lives at one and we live at the other, next to Victoria Coach Station in a decidedly 'unposh' building, sponsored by the Grosvenor Estate.

PART I

Getting Through The Day

1

HE HIT ME BACK FIRST!

Ways to Stop Your Children Fighting Each Other

If it often seems that your children do nothing but fight, take heart. We all had a vision of happy, laughing children – and then we became parents . . .

You hear the scream from two rooms away, and you know it's serious: 'I HATE YOU!' You know from experience that your children are standing nose to nose, toe to toe, fists raised.

'I hate you a thousand times more than you hate me,' says the other one.

Blows are struck and both run in to you. The older one shouts, 'She hit me first.' 'But he hit me back first,' yells the little one.

Your own anger starts to match theirs as you attempt to untangle fingers from hair, right from wrong.

Why?

Why, you ask yourself, are they always fighting?

From observations of my own two, I'd say children fight for the same reasons adults do:

- It's exciting.
- It gets attention from 'grown-ups'.
- They like it.

- Because one of them feels less loved than the other.
- Because they haven't yet learned, or have forgotten how to share.
- Because one of them is angry at the general unfairness of life.
- To prove that they are 'in charge' – if only for a moment, if only with a brother or sister – in a world where children, and people, often feel they have little power.
- Because they see others fighting – in the family, at school, on television.

The problem for parents is deciding when, and whether, to live with the fighting or fight back.

Is Fighting Normal?

There is a great debate among 'experts' about whether fighting is normal and healthy, or whether it occurs so regularly it just seems normal. One book says that fighting is not good and can be avoided, while another says that a fight a day keeps the psychiatrist away. Some time I would like to put all the experts together with tired, fractious children *on a daily basis* and see what they actually do about it. I would also say never trust a 'friend' who says her children don't fight. She's lying.

Kate, nine, and Paul, five, were sitting next to each other. Kate was doing her homework while Paul was building a boat out of Lego. Mum was out of the room. Paul moved over next to Kate. She ignored him and moved over herself. Paul pushed his boat on to her paper. 'Get off,' said Kate, annoyed but still doing her homework. Paul poked Kate in the face and giggled. She shoved him away. He stuck his finger into her lip, at which Kate grabbed his hand and bit it . . . Paul screamed. Mum rushed in. Seeing Paul's hand, she yelled at Kate, and comforted Paul, saying to Kate: 'You know you shouldn't pick on him, he's much younger than you.'

Speaking as a working mother who often doesn't get it right, I think that a certain amount of fighting is normal, and even healthy.

Everyone has to learn to settle differences – and what you learn sorting out the everyday perils of growing up may help you stay on your feet on the front line of work and in relationships as an adult.

Here, Paul had engineered the fight and Kate has got the blame. She shouldn't have bitten him, but Paul clearly needs to know what's likely to happen if he continues bugging someone. Sometimes the rough justice of children works better than anything we can do. The mother might have done better to comfort Paul (after all, he had suffered in order to learn), and had a quiet word with Kate later – but none of us is perfect. This leads us automatically to a 'let them sort it out for themselves' philosophy, which is fine as long as the odds are fair and it works. When they aren't fair, and it doesn't work, we need to know that although fighting is normal it is never simple – there are always undercurrents, only some of which we can fathom out.

Strategies

Parents need strategies to avoid things getting out of hand – when nerves are at full stretch, for example, or when damage is about to be inflicted on children or home. In such cases, when you can't just let the fight run its course, try:

1. Being Specific

Give very specific instructions such as: 'Do *not* touch his car'; 'Do *not* hit'; 'Leave the room'. Children do not respond to 'Be nice'. Nice is for wimps.

2. Arranging Territory

Find a place for each child's toys and games which is their own. Ideally, give each a lockable box to keep special things in. This makes it clear that some things are their own and helps if you have to sort out a dispute.

3. Giving Them Ideas

Give children their own strategies. Ten-year-old Sam went berserk every time his sister said 'Sam is a sissy.' She loved winding him up. Sam's mum helped him work out things to say which made him feel less tense so his sister couldn't 'get to him'. He came up with 'Buzz off, elephant breath.' His mum got him to try: 'I love you, too,' and 'Yes . . . all great men are sissies,' or 'Twinkle, twinkle little star . . . what you say is what you are.'

4. Staying Out of It

Keep out of the 'everyday' fights as much as possible. If you only seem to give them attention when they fight, try giving them attention only when they *don't* fight.

5. Cooling Things Down

Make it less awful. When one of them says, 'I hate her,' say: 'Yes, you hate her right now. You don't have to like everyone all the time.' If you tell them, 'You don't mean that really; you love your sister,' you'll just create more anger.

6. Preventing Real Harm

Prise them apart. When things look nasty, try 'time out' in different rooms (if you can separate them), or threaten withdrawal of pocket money for both unless they cool down.

7. Discovering the Problem

Take the children aside separately and find out if there is a basic reason for their continual fighting – something that just keeps niggling away at them.

Karen and Anna's constant niggling and fighting was driving their mum nuts. She had tried everything, and finally sat down for a long talk with each. Karen thought that Anna got more attention and she was angry. Anna felt that Karen got away with too much and she felt cheated. Their mum asked them to come straight to her with their grievances next time and to ask straight out for some extra attention or privileges. Once the girls knew that what they wanted was on offer, they needed it less.

8. Finding Out When They Fight

See if there's a fighting time: it may be bedtime, bathtime, or when visitors come.

James, eight, was always picking fights at bedtime because he didn't like his older sister staying up later than him. His parents told him that age had its privileges, but they decided to give James an especially nice bedtime with his sister off the scene and his father reading him a story.

I noticed that my boys fight more after watching TV for over an hour. The funny thing is that it doesn't really seem to matter what the programme is about, they just get nasty and their best solution seems to be to bother each other. I think they need to move around instead of sitting there, so I ration their television viewing and make them go out. It works. (See Chapter 9 on video and television watching, page 89.)

9. Avoiding Self-fulfilling Prophecies

Don't tell your children they always fight or say it in front of others when the children are listening. It becomes a self-fulfilling prophecy. 'That's what we do best – fight!' they think. And they do.

10. Allowing Anger

Allow children to be angry, but safely. I invite them to draw awful pictures of each other, then they know you understand that they are angry. And they learn that drawing is a better way to vent their anger than hitting.

11. Using Humour

I think humour is a great weapon that parents should use as often as possible. A flippant remark can work better than a long analysis: 'I'll trade you in for a teapot'; 'I'll give you a million pounds to stop fighting' or some such gem might defuse the situation. The problem is trying to be humorous when you want to kill them!

12. Noticing Good Behaviour

If you can, catch your children being peaceful. Some days it may not seem possible, but there will be times when they are little angels.

Julie noticed one evening that Tom and Katherine were actually discussing something WITHOUT killing each other. Instead of saying anything, she wrote them each a little note: 'I like the way you talked to each other at teatime. Love Mum.'

It might sound soppy, but it can work wonders. Julie's other kids kept trying to do things so they could win a note, as well.

13. Undoing Bad Deals

Life is all about giving and getting a good-enough deal. Kids learn this from an early age and practise it relentlessly. Needless to say, as they're so important, deals cause horrendous fights.

Tony, six, is hysterical. 'I want it back,' he sobs repeatedly. 'It isn't fair.'

Lucy, his eight-year-old sister, walks in, steps over his sobbing form, and asks: 'What's for tea?'

'Give it back,' yells Tony.

'No,' says Lucy, very calmly and decisively. 'We made a deal'.

'What deal?' you ask, deeply suspicious of the transaction.

'He swapped his car with me and now he wants it back. I gave him three stickers that glow in the dark. It was a deal and we shook hands on it. Now he wants his car back and that's not fair.' Lucy is confident her case is airtight.

'The stickers definitely aren't as good as my car.' Tony is furious.
'But we shook on it and you can't go back on a deal.'

They look at you expectantly. The car is worth £5; the stickers
50p. Lucy knows this; Tony doesn't but feels he's been wronged.
While you don't want to undermine the initiative of a future busi-
nesswoman, you don't want her to throw her weight about, either.

The better child-rearing books say you should talk with the children individually and get all the facts. Then, democratically, you
should ask them to help you sort it out. I find that this approach
can often cause a burnt dinner and an exhausted mother.

'Sorry Lucy, it isn't fair,' you pronounce, rushing back to the
cooker to rescue the potatoes. 'The deal's off.' This is usually followed by howls of rage and delight, and provides the basis for a
comeback fight at a later date.

Power struggles are the basis of so many fights, for kids and
adults. At some stage, when the potatoes aren't boiling over
and tempers are cooler, we need to teach children to exercise
power and fairness at the same time. I feel we need to talk with our
children about the subject of power. It's a subject they take very
personally:

- Ask them to understand that everyone has power – even a little
  baby (if only to burst your eardrums). We have power over children; an employer has power over you; and children have
  power over brothers, sisters, other children, pets.
- Play 'what if' games relating to power, such as:

  a) What would you do if you knew someone in the play-
     ground was picking on a much younger child?
  b) What would you do if I made a deal with you that wasn't
     fair?
  c) What would you do if someone swapped £100 for a toy of
     yours and then wanted it back?
     Would it matter how much the toy was worth? It could be
     worth £4, £100, or £200.
  d) What would you do if you made a deal with your best
     friend and she changed her mind?
  e) Would it make a difference how long it took before she

changed her mind? Two minutes after the deal? Ten minutes after the deal? A week later?

From this, agree ground rules for future 'deals', which include a cooling-off time during which either party can back out.

What we want children to learn is that there is a way to use power so that people are not taken advantage of or left feeling angry. Misusing power causes unhappiness.

What to Do if They Won't Stop Fighting

Try putting them on a desert island and letting them exhaust themselves. Better still, put yourself on the island and leave them at home. Alternatively, try some last resorts, such as:

1. Making Them Laugh

Again, use humour to divert them – make a funny face, stick out your tongue, juggle, dance, stand on your head (carefully!) and just generally make a fool of yourself. Invite them to join in. It's hard to keep fighting when you're laughing.

2. Confiscating the Goods

Take away whatever it is that they are fighting over. If it is a television programme, turn off the television.

3. Restraining

Physically restrain them, if necessary, but don't hit them. Hitting only proves to them that it is valid to use force to end arguments.

4. Chilling Out

Put them into different rooms to cool off, make yourself a cup of tea and think pleasant thoughts, such as where you are going to go on your summer holidays *alone*.

5. Diplomacy

Find out both sides of the story then make a final judgement, telling them that is *it* – finished and over. No more discussion.

6. Giving a Time Limit

Set the timer and tell them to sort it out before the timer rings or you will. This works especially well if you say that they probably won't like your solution much.

7. Offering Alternative Pursuits

Give them a more constructive way to get rid of their anger, such as punching bags, making plasticine models, a three mile run . . .

8. Helping Them Find Their Own Solution

At a quiet time, involve them in finding a long-term solution to recurrent arguments. For example, if the fighting is always about who got the bigger share, do what my aunt who had six children did: make the children divide the portions themselves. Whoever divides gets last pick. Take turns dividing and picking. I watched my cousins take incredible care to fill the glasses exactly or cut the cake with medical precision. My sister and I were made to do the same – it kept us interested and quiet while we measured to the very last drop.

9. Loss of Privileges

Take away a privilege if the fighting continues. Try to agree which privileges might have to go in advance, so they can weigh up whether the fighting is worth it!

10. Toning Down the Language

Teach children that they can use words to sort out disagreements. Starting sentences with 'I don't agree with you' is better than 'You're so dumb', or worse. If you find your children are repeating your words when you fight with your spouse or partner, you might have to tone down or change your own way of arguing – and that's not easy! If possible, take them along to listen to a debate so they can see how issues can be argued out without fisticuffs or name calling.

Above all, don't despair. Most relationships do improve with age. When my sister and I were teenagers, I drew a line down the centre of our bedroom. She wasn't allowed into my side, and I wasn't allowed into hers. We argued about everything. I thought *she* was wrong all of the time, and she thought *I* was wrong all of the time. Today, she is my best friend in the whole world (even though she is *still* wrong about lots of things!).

Summary

If I had to choose five ways which seem successful most of the time, they would be to:

- *Make them laugh by doing something completely absurd. It is so embarrassing to have your parent do something like cluck around the kitchen imitating a chicken that they band together out of desperation.*
- *Teach them to be effective with words instead of fists. Give them specific, clever things they can say when a sibling (or another child – see the chapter on bullying, p. 275) taunts them. For example, if Gary can always get a rise from James by calling*

him 'stupid', James could be taught to say 'thank you' and walk away. Of course, Gary needs to be told off, as well!

- *Help them get their anger out.* It's all right to be angry at someone if there is cause. It's how you deal with that anger that gets you into difficulty. Teach children to state why they are angry and what they want to happen. Then give them strategies for coping with anger so it doesn't eat them up inside, or spill out into bickering, or worse. Writing letters, drawing angry pictures about the other person, thumping away on the piano or pounding nails into a board might help.
- *Stay out of the fights as much as possible,* but intervene if one child is really getting the short end of the stick. After all, that's why kids have parents.
- *Praise them when they're being good.* This is hard to remember to do, but it works wonders.

In any case, children don't always fight. Sometimes they sleep.

2

MODERN MANNERS

After the dust has settled from your ten-year-old's birthday, you ask him to write to his granny to tell her he liked the book she sent.

He is looking sullenly at a blank piece of writing paper: 'I didn't like it.'

'Well, thank her anyway. It will make her feel good.' There's a slight edge to your voice.

'I can't think of anything to say.'

'I just told you!' Exasperation sets in.

'Why can't I just ring? I hate writing soppy notes.'

'Because it's polite to write and ...' You stop. Why can't he just ring and not go through all this hassle? The answer is probably that, like most of us, you're not sure why not. This immediately threatens to undermine your insistence that the blank page gets filled.

Good manners are becoming harder to define. In our not-too-distant past we knew exactly what was expected manners-wise: if you got a parcel, then you wrote a thank-you note, however much it hurt.

I remember, when I was about seven, agonising over how to thank my Aunt Pat for the excruciatingly awful jumper she'd sent me for my birthday. It was three sizes too big and a horrible mixture of brightly coloured wools. Needless to say I wasn't very happy about wearing it. Nevertheless, I was obliged to put pen to paper and be thankful in writing. But my parents had taught me not to lie and I was totally honest about what I was going to do with the present:

Dear Aunt Pat

Thank you very much for the jumper. it is very big. there are many cold children in the world who do not get presents I will donate it to the Oxfam shop
love
  Michele

My parents' philosophy of manners didn't extend to being that honest, so the note was altered before being posted:

Dear Aunt Pat

Thank you for the jumper it is really nice of you to knit it for me. It must have taken a very long time thank you.
love
  Michele

But where do we stand on an old-fashioned concept like thank-you letters, when we live in a world of e-mail, fax machines, cordless phones and motorways that take us to Granny's and back in a day?

In any era there should be good, solid reasons for asking our children to do things. And, for me, that's the hard bit – working out the reasons and explaining them.

Some 'traditions' make sense to me, like saying 'please' and 'thank you' because it makes other people feel good, or giving up your seat on the bus to someone who is less able because it's kind. Others don't make sense – like children not speaking until they're spoken to. It seems to me that we need to work things out as we go along.

So, what about those thank-you notes? In fact, I do usually make my boys write them when presents come by post. One reason is that receiving a thank-you letter makes the recipient feel special; and because grandparents, especially, like to re-read notes and show them to friends.

There's another reason, too, which is hard to define. I think it's that sitting down to write focuses your thoughts and the result is a little part of yourself that's unique (provided you didn't copy it from your sister).

Remembering my own struggles, I do try to make it easier on my children, so here are a few tips.

1. Postcards and Pictures

It's hard to think kind thoughts when faced with a big sheet of blank paper. So picture postcards make good thank-you notes. You can let the child choose one from some you've bought – and even address and stamp it for them. Older children can write a few lines; younger ones can just write 'Thank you' and sign their name. Little ones can draw a picture of themselves playing with the gift, or perhaps donate one of those crackly paintings which you may now be using to decorate your fridge door (can you spare one?).

2. Telephone

We don't live in a perfect world, and sometimes I do let the children phone their thanks, keeping my fingers crossed that they will include words in the 'thrilled' and 'wonderful' category.

3. E-mail and Faxes

If you are lucky enough to have access to such facilities, well, why not? In our house we haven't so it isn't an issue. I still confess to a nostalgic love of receiving a handwritten note, but my kids quite rightly point out that I was 'practically born before the invention of the aeroplane'. (They do exaggerate so – I remember the Wright Brothers quite well . . .)

4. Be Realistic

Whatever method you use, common sense should prevail. When my youngest son was seven, he took a gift to a party attended by twenty children. Two days later, he received a thank-you note from the birthday boy. The child's mother had made her son write twenty thank-you notes the day after the party to people who'd been there to receive thanks in person. In our house we're lucky to find all the gifts at the end of a party, let alone know who gave what. You must be realistic about your expectations where good manners are concerned.

But it's realistic to expect basic table manners, isn't it?

Are Table Manners Important?

This is a subject of great debate. When we were kids you stayed at the table for the entire meal, even if you were bored witless. Should we continue to be ruled by the expectations of the previous generation? In our house, the answer is yes . . . and no. It is, of course, down to you to decide, but here are my guidelines:

- *Yes*: children should keep their mouths shut when they chew, should say 'please' and 'thank you', should wash their hands before sitting down, should not touch every piece of bread before choosing the best one.
- *No*: children should not be made to wait at the table while grown-ups discuss the state of the world. Family meals with conversations which include the children are a joy, and sometimes the only time in a day for exchanging news. When the children have finished eating and talking, why can't they say 'Thank you' and 'Please may I leave the table?' Seems fair to me.

But You Can't Win 'Em All

You're in the middle of a meal when your thirteen-year-old slouches through the door. He says nothing, pulls up a chair, does a boarding-house reach for the bread and grunts when you ask questions. Your eight-year-old smiles and asks you to please pass the potatoes and you think at least you've got it right with one of them. Believe me, in five years time your baby may be just as bad.

When children reach adolescence and start working out their own codes of living, they often start by rejecting most of the things they've been taught. So manners lose out – temporarily. My only advice is to keep up your own standards – you have rights, too!

It's worth remembering that quite mannerly adults have their lapses, as well, if only at certain times of the day. Hysteria in our house reaches a high point around evening dinner time. A few nights ago I heard myself inviting the boys to 'Sit down, shut up, and eat'.

By contrast, friends Anne and Tom took their two children to a restaurant for the first time. The waitress handed them their menus and then said to five-year-old Andrew: 'What would you like to eat, young sir?' He couldn't believe his ears: 'Did you hear that, Dad? She treated me like a real person.' Manners take time to learn, and we all learn best when we're praised rather than criticised. If we try to teach them with a barrage of instructions and criticism children soon stop feeling good about themselves. Respect and praise makes them feel 'real'.

Should They Be Made to Clear Their Plate?

Once, I stayed with an aunt who served me cooked carrots, a huge helping of them. They were overcooked, yellow and disgusting. I tasted them and said no thank you. In that house, though, manners dictated that you ate what was on your plate, even if you hadn't served yourself with it. There were, after all, starving children in the world.

Believe it or not, I had to sit at the table until bedtime. The next morning, the carrots reappeared on my breakfast plate. I was a stubborn little creature and never did eat them or stay with the aunt again. And I will not eat cooked carrots to this day. Children shouldn't be abused in the name of manners.

Since we want meal times to be a pleasure, I reckon the best way, if possible, is to put the food in serving dishes and let children help themselves. Have 'rules' about manners that you all agree to but, above all, make meal times fun. If you're too strict, too critical, meals become tense.

If you are thinking how on earth do we get them to at least try different vegetables or other foods, suggest that they have one spoonful and make it a little one. Bribe them with an extra helping of something they like! Or, if you are clever like my friend Linda, make the vegetable into interesting shapes and try to serve them raw. Vegetables really do taste better raw and they are supposed to be better for you. Get the children to help you prepare things, because they enjoy it and quite often nibble along the way. They are also more inclined to eat something they've helped to get ready because they are proud of their efforts.

Greetings – Beware the 'Hairy-chinned Aunt'!

Sometimes, being polite is just too hard, especially during school holidays and when the house is jam-packed with visitors.

Four-year-old Joseph hadn't quite mastered good manners when his grandparents turned up for Easter. 'Where's my Easter egg?' he demanded. 'What's the magic word?' asked his mother, trying to make the best of a bad job. 'Abracadabra,' he yelled.

He could at least have said 'Hello' first, although he could have got that wrong, too. The way you greet people depends on your manners policy, although you may not have been aware of making one. Greeting rules vary between families, nationalities and cultures. In some, everyone, including men, hug each other; in very 'British' households, contact is avoided. Hugging is great, but I think it is wrong to insist a child kisses or hugs someone if they don't want to.

Jennifer, forty-three, had a great aunt who engulfed every young visitor in a big bosomy hug. 'My aunt always wore a big brooch. I dreaded seeing her because she'd seize me and crush my cheek for what seemed an eternity to this terribly sharp, lumpy brooch. I loved her, she was a dear woman, but this dread of her hugs is a vivid memory.'

Beware of teaching children that good manners must mean unquestioning obedience or you could be storing up trouble. One day, they may need to be rude to adults in order to protect themselves, so it's important to teach children that their bodies belong to them. I will expand on this in the chapter about keeping children safe (p. 42).

Talk About Manners

The good thing about social conventions is that that's all they are – conventions. As such, they're subject to change, and thank goodness some of them have changed. But, all in all, we still need good manners – it shows we care about other people and that there are limits to the way we can behave towards others. In any event, children are on our side. They want to be spoken to nicely, they don't want to eat with slobs, and they like to be thanked if they send Granny a present. If you can talk about why you insist on certain things (admitting if you're not always sure of your motives) and work out adaptations to rules together for the good of everyone, then manners and kindness will become part of your children's way of life. When sorting out what to do about manners, try:

1. Working out your own policy and values.
2. Discussing with your children why manners are important.
3. Basing manners on common sense and kindness.
4. Teaching by example and lots of praise.
5. Noticing when they do things right.
6. Helping them send off thank-you notes, if necessary.
7. Insisting on everyone, adults included, using 'please' and 'thank you'.
8. Letting them leave the table if you have long, boring conversations which don't include them.
9. Not forcing a child to eat everything – that's not manners, it's child abuse!
10. Making sure they know that their safety is more important than being polite – they can break any rule in the book if it means staying safe.

3

BEDTIME

Five-year-old Marie comes out of her bedroom at least a dozen times a night asking for food, drink, a story or for assistance in getting the monster out from under her bed. Her exhausted parents cannot remember having a full night's sleep since she was born.

Eleven-month-old Peter cries constantly whenever he is put to bed, so that his mother has slept in his bedroom with him every night for the past three months. Whenever she tries to sneak out, he wakes and screams the place down.

Ten-year-old Bethan and her four-year-old sister have never had a problem about sleeping, except for the nightly request for an extra story or the occasional nightmare.

Are some children purposely trying to drive us to distraction at bedtime? Is there a 'I'm not going to bed quietly' gene we can blame? Most importantly, what are Bethan's parents doing right?

There are some tried and true tips which do help with getting children to bed, but you may have others which work just as well.

1. Give Sufficient Warning

a) One hour before you want them in their bedrooms
As the clock rolls round or digitally clicks towards the agreed bedtime, give your children an hour's notice that it's coming. I know they should be able to figure this out for themselves, but they do

seem to run on a different time scale and certainly have better things to do than go to bed, anyway.

Look at it from their viewpoint, they are having a good time and don't want to stop. It's your idea that they need sleep; they are convinced that they don't. Besides, they might miss something if they have to go to bed. Nevertheless, to sleep they must go, so the battle lines are drawn. Kids pull out lots of weapons, such as: hunger, thirst, need to use the toilet, monsters, 'not tired' and 'haven't finished my homework'. The sixty-minute warning helps them to start winding down and getting into the right frame of mind for bed.

b) Forty-five Minutes
Tell them they have fifteen minutes until they have to start washing, brushing teeth and getting ready for bed.

c) Thirty Minutes
That's it – time to get ready. Don't wait until the last minute. The faster they get ready, the more time they will have to themselves before going into their bedrooms.

d) Five Minutes
Countdown. Time to bring in snacks and drinks and to get ready for the story, or reading, or listening to music or all three.

e) Seconds Out
No excuses. Time to go to their rooms, get into bed and settle down for stories, hugs and kisses. I now give my children half an hour to read and listen to music before lights-out, but they are not to get out of bed.

So the entire ritual takes about an hour, plus whatever time you give them before finally turning off the lights. It isn't as complicated as it seems, it just means someone has to keep an eye on the time or set a timer or alarm clock to remind them.

I once babysat for a friend's little girl, Alison, who hated going to bed. She was three. This method worked a treat and continued to work for her parents, who were thrilled. What Alison liked best was coming to look at the clock to see how much longer she had. When the bell went off, she scampered into her bedroom, had a story and asked to keep the timer to see when I was going to come back to turn off the light.

2. Allow Staggered Bedtimes

As children grow older they expect to have later bedtimes than their younger brothers and sisters. This makes your life more complicated, but it is only fair. When my older son asked for a later bedtime, we allowed him to go to bed half an hour after his little brother. It meant two sets of time keeping, but it was worth it. Also, it gave me more individual time to spend with each child before bed.

There are problems sorting it all out, especially if your children share a room, as mine did. In order not to disturb the younger child, both children got ready at the same time – teeth brushed and into pyjamas. The older one then spent time either in the sitting-room or kitchen and the going-to-bed activities had to be adapted. We went into the room to tuck him in and, after a short while, his younger brother stayed sleeping.

The other main problem is convincing the younger child that it is fair. We set up a schedule by age, and told both children that when they reached a certain age, it would correspond with a certain, pre-determined bed time. You have to ignore protestations from your child that he is the 'only one in the entire school/ world/universe' who goes to bed that early. Check with other parents and then reply, 'If you don't go to bed you will be the only child in the school without a head,' or some other suitable comment. Say it with a demonic smile.

3. Have Bedtime Rituals

Children find it comforting to have the same thing happen before going to sleep at night. In our house, the boys still ask for nightly hugs and some sort of fruit, like an apple, even though they are both teenagers (only just). When they were little, there was always a story and a song. Now they read themselves to sleep listening to their own music, which is quite awful in my humble parental opinion.

If your children have a special blanket or toy or bit of rag that they need to help them sleep, be sure to have that to hand. Don't worry, they won't still sleep with a stuffed animal when they're forty. Anyway, if it's a comfort to them, it's a comfort for you, too.

If you are a 'split' family, as so many are today, and your children go back and forth between two parents and households, try to ensure that both parents are being consistent. It doesn't matter if the rituals are slightly different so long as they are fairly consistent in that parent's household. What does matter is if the children are unsettled, or behaviour is allowed which is not in the best interests of the children.

4. Try Using Night Lights

If children don't like to sleep in the dark, why not have a night light? The soft light can be quite comforting, though for some children the shadows thrown up by the light are more frightening than the dark. Other children prefer torches. I used to hide under the covers and read with mine, never thinking that my parents could see the glow through the bedspread.

Another possibility is to give the children those high intensity lights that only direct a small beam on a book. If your children share a room give those that don't like the light a night shade to cover their eyes.

5. Tackle the Monster Problem

'But Mummy, there *is* a monster under my bed. I see him!' Sigh! There are some wonderful books – *There's a Monster in My Wardrobe, Alexander and the Dragon* and others – which deal with children's fears of strange beings in their rooms. Try reading them the stories and asking them to make up their own. If they are still concerned, look under the bed and in the wardrobe, but be sure to say that you *don't* believe in monsters and there aren't any here.

One mother wrote to me to say that, when she was little, her parents made a big deal of 'looking for the monster' which convinced her even more that there was one!

There is a more sinister aspect to the monster story which, fortunately, doesn't affect most children. Several years ago I met a group of teenagers who had all been sexually abused and were now in care in a children's home. Of the nine young people, seven still had a fear of monsters and looked under the bed and in the wardrobe every night, even though they were fifteen and sixteen years old. For them, the abuse that happened in their bedrooms continued to produce monsters that many are still being counselled for today.

6. Use Humour and Laughter

Laughter relaxes children and grown-ups alike. Remember jokes you hear or take out a book from the library – something like 'Three Hundred Corny Jokes'. The humour might be very low-level, such as 'What's green and bounces?' 'I don't know, what's green and bounces?' 'Spring Cabbage.' But all I know is that it can add tremendously to the fun of going to bed if there is some sort of laughter every night. Ask your children to find a joke, too. Not a sick one, please . . .

7. Beware Wild Activities and Distractions

Years ago, I think it was easier to get children to bed quietly. Yes, there were the noisy fathers (at least in my house) or the chasing-around-the-house games, but there weren't all the possible distractions our children have to deal with today. For better or worse, we didn't try to stimulate our children into becoming mini-geniuses by making sure their cots were festooned with mobiles, mirrors, horns, drums and all sorts of colourful paraphernalia. Don't get me wrong, my children had all those things and more, but I sometimes wonder if the theory that beds are meant only for sleeping has some merit. Funny that I managed to do alright in school without all that kind of stimulation as a baby, but I didn't want to take a chance that my kids would miss out, so I bought it all.

Anyway, putting aside the stimulating toys that talk and teach, and things like the television, loud stereos, dishwashers and dryers which are part of modern life, try to avoid games and activities which wind the children up to a frenzied pitch. I remember the parents of three who came to see me because their children never seemed to settle down. The father was a great character and practical joker. It turned out that he loved to put the kids to bed with wild horseback rides, games that involved running around and lots of competition to see who would win, and he also liked to surprise the children by jumping out from behind doors. I was hyper just listening to his antics. Imagine how excited the children were – hearts racing, minds excited, sleep out of the question.

Bedtime isn't the time to horse around and get keyed up. Better to do that in the morning if you want to chivvy them along. Try cosy, low-key, gentle activities such as singing, relaxing exercises, rubbing backs, listening to story tapes or thinking of what Teddy might wear tomorrow. All of this should be done in a soothing voice bordering on monotony and, softly, softly, off they go to sleep. Using that voice continues to work right up through the teenage years.

8. Use Praise

So often we comment on how badly the children are behaving at bedtime. Try catching them doing something good and praise how clever they are:

'You're such a clever girl for brushing your teeth and being in bed on time. Well done!'

'I'm so pleased you managed to get all your homework done and go to bed without a fuss.'

'You're ready ten minutes early so you have ten minutes to do something you like before going to your room. That shows you are growing up. You're wonderful!'

Reward them with an extra story or five minutes longer staying up – it's worth it and much more relaxing than having to scold them or hurry them.

9. Give Them Extra Attention

There will be times when your children do need a little extra attention. In that case, go to them rather than letting them get up, and rub their backs or pat them. But be careful not to let this extra time become part of the nightly ritual.

If they begin to use hunger or thirst as an attention grabber, then leave a thermos of water by the bed or an extra apple so they can't use those old excuses.

For Marie's parents, this cut down their trips to her room by half. They combined that with looking for the monster *before* they left the room, and a firm nightly ritual which included one trip back to Marie's room and no more. Marie did throw a fit, but I advised them to go into the other room, shut their door and turn up the music. After about two weeks of hell, Marie now goes to bed like a lamb.

Peter's parents, too, have broken his habit of having to have mum or dad to sleep in his room. Peter didn't like it either, but they held on and he soon learned that they weren't going to come. 'Listening to him cry himself to sleep was horrible,' said his mother, 'but we are all happier now and he really likes his bedtime stories and cuddles. I do, too. Before, I used to dread bedtime and I was in a bad mood most of the day because of lack of sleep. Now, after the story and cuddles, I put on a tape and out I go. He knows that when the tape starts that is my goodnight.' At least Peter's parents won't have to go through the traumas that Marie's parents had for all those years.

10. Recognise True Distress

Of course, there will be times when our children's needs will mean we have to break the bedtime routine. They may be truly distressed about something that's happened, or sick, or having night terrors. The answer is common sense – go to them. It may be that you will have to take them into your own bed for a while. Sometimes, taking them into your bed is simply for your own convenience.

When our sons were babies and still needed nursing, that long walk down the cold hallway in winter (I had both children in the autumn – silly me) got to be a bit much. One night, when my first child was about three weeks old, I told my husband to leave him with us in bed because if I had to get up next time (we took turns), then my milk and I would surely freeze and we didn't have any baby bottles.

All the experts thought it wasn't a good idea for children to get used to staying in their parents' bed, or they might still be there five years later. I agree that kids permanently ensconced in their parents' beds is not a good idea. In our case, this didn't happen, because we made sure the boys' room was a more fun place to be. But I can't see there's anything wrong with occasionally allowing a distressed or sick child into your bed. Of course we don't want them moving in and taking over, but there are times when extra warmth and human contact is a much needed tonic.

Take, for example, the night after my youngest son's hamster died. He was inconsolable and felt guilty that he hadn't taken better care of the nasty, biting little rodent.

After I put him to bed, I could hear my son gulping down big sobs, and I just couldn't stand the thought that he was in another room when he needed to be hugged and comforted. My husband carried him in, which wasn't easy considering he was a strapping eight-year-old, and we both talked to him and cuddled him to sleep. The next night everything was back to normal.

I remember a father who came to see me soon after his wife had unexpectedly died. He expressed some concern that his twelve-year-old son wanted to sleep in bed with him. 'I really want him to, but what would people say?' Personally, I thought that it was more important for the child to have comfort and love than for the father to worry about other opinions. The man was simply a caring father who most likely needed the comfort of his son, as well, at a very difficult time.

Later, the son told me that just being in the same bed his mother used to sleep in and having Dad put his arm around him helped enormously when coming to terms with his mother's death. After all, we have to remember that the son was more than a little afraid his dad might die, too, so it was easier to sleep knowing he was there to look after him.

As with all these issues, parents have to use their own common sense, which is usually ten times better than so-called expert advice.

11. Prepare for Guests

'I was mortified. Here we were in the middle of an important dinner party which we had planned and worked hard to prepare, and suddenly there was my eight-year-old putting on a tap-dance show. The guests clapped politely, I smiled, and thought of how to get away with murder. My daughter had never done that before, but we rarely have guests so I hadn't thought about how to deal with her bedtime. After that exhibition, I don't think we'll have many more guests anyway!' Ellen was in despair.

If guests are around and your child suddenly decides that he or she is a budding actor, musician, magician or dancer, it may be because you aren't around to read the ritual story or give the obligatory snack. Or it may be that your stage-struck child has finally found a captive audience. If your guests are good friends or relatives, you might arrange in advance for a short show, which they may love, especially if they know it is going to end. I was once stuck at a dinner party which was constantly interrupted by the host's children, and after a while I began to smile through gritted teeth as I thought what little show-offs and creeps they were. The third time you hear 'I'm a little tea pot' sung out of tune with 'cute' antics is enough to make you want to run screaming from the house. I managed to stay seated, but only just. I was dying for the parents to pick up the precocious brats and sling them into their bedrooms. Instead they looked on with parental pride and indulgence. As Lucy would say in Peanuts *Aghhhhhhh!!!*

One way round the problem of what to do when you have guests is to farm your children out to friends or to bring in a babysitter. If your children are old enough and it is a weekend, why not allow them to have guests of their own? Get their food ready in advance, arrange to play a video or have games set up, and let them be the host or hostess. This worked quite well with my own children when we ordered take-away pizza and let them choose the videos they wanted. At one point I thought they had disappeared, it was so quiet.

If you want to stop your children bothering your guests, you can also tell the guests you are trying to stop the children's bad behaviour, and would they please help by paying no attention to whatever your children try to do. Don't do this on the night you are entertaining the boss, however!

One way to handle the entertaining-guests-versus-children's-bedtime dilemma is to warn your children the night before that you won't be able to spend time with them the next night. Then promise you will make up for it the night after that. Alternatively, you might be able to make time earlier in the evening, or record a special story on a tape, which the children can listen to once the guests have arrived. If you do this, try to make it a big deal so that the children look forward to it. If they ask you to do it other nights when you would normally read to them, don't! (Anyway, the ungrateful little monsters shouldn't prefer a tape to the real thing, but then kids will be kids.)

If you have guests and cannot give the fifteen-minute warning, use a timer or alarm clock so that they know when to start. Of course, that doesn't mean they will, but if you tell them you are counting on them and that you know they are grown-up enough to do this, their reaction might surprise you. Be sure to praise them like mad and tell them how proud you are of the fact that they can behave this way.

One thing I know for certain about bedtime, after years of parenting and helping other parents, is that the rosy picture portrayed in the film *The Sound of Music*, of the Von Trapp children singing their way to bed while the guests smile and applaud, just ain't how it is in real life. But then I'm sure you already know that.

4

HELPING YOUR CHILD TO MAKE FRIENDS

'But, dad, I don't want to go to school. No one likes me. I don't have any friends.'

Carol's father was nearly in tears when he came to see me. 'She is so miserable that I don't know what to do. I can't manufacture friends for her, and I don't want to do the wrong thing and make matters worse.'

Your heart goes out to Carol and her father. It is such a lonely feeling when you have no one to sit with at lunch or play with in the playground or go to visit after school. Yet other children never seem to lack friends. They appear to have a natural ability to attract people and are full of confidence. Are there some things we can teach children about finding friends and being a friend to others? You bet there are, and some are very simple. The earlier we start, the better. But there is one caution – some children will be very happy having one or two friends or a small group, while others like being friends with everyone.

Even in the same family, children will differ in how they perceive friendship. Harry, aged eight, loves being in the midst of a shouting, rowdy, tumbling group of children. As far as he is concerned, the more the merrier, and he isn't happy unless there is action most of the time. His brother Thomas, aged ten, has always had a few close friends and likes to play games with them or go to the cinema or for walks in the woods. Their mother can't understand how they could be so different, but they are both content so there is no need to try to change things. If it isn't broken, don't fix it.

But if you do need to 'fix it', here are some pointers about making friends which you can try with your children:

1. Identify the Problem

Did Carol have friends at one time or has she always been a loner? Has there been a 'growing apart' from a group of kids, leaving her out in the cold? It turned out that Carol was a bright eight-year-old who had usually had one or two friends, but who had always related better to adults. One of her friends had moved away during the summer and the other, Susan, seemed to be moving on to form new friendships – something Carol felt unable or unwilling to do. Carol was a slightly introverted child, and her previous friendships had come largely through the efforts the other children made to get to know her. She didn't approach them, but was delighted to be approached and included in things. She had no family, behaviour or academic problems; she was just unhappy about her lack of friends.

A discussion with Carol brought out some of her anxieties. Because she had never thought about making friends or felt the need to, the very idea of approaching a new person or group terrified her. She simply did not know how to begin, or even who she might like to be friends with now. She also felt rejected by Susan, who was spending less and less time with her because of the new friends she was making.

Some children will have other problems. Another child may be bullying them or deliberately excluding them (see Chapter 29, p.275, on bullying). Or they may irritate other children by doing something like wiping their nose on their sleeve, or burping all the time. Or they may live a long way from the rest of the class and miss out on socialising with the others after school or on weekends. Or they may, of course, be picking on other children themselves. It always pays to find out as much information as possible about the problem before you begin to try to solve it.

2. Form a Plan

I asked Carol if I could help her make a list of children she might like to know. The list included Susan and three other girls. We figured out a plan that Carol felt she could achieve. One of the girls on her list, Jasmine, seemed quite nice, but also a bit shy. This was an ideal person for Carol to try to approach, because Jasmine would probably welcome someone attempting to get to know her. The plan was:

- For Carol and her dad to sit down together and figure out what Carol likes in a friend and what friends might like from her.
- For her dad to talk with the teacher to ensure that everything possible was being done to include Carol with the other children, and to find out if there were any problems we didn't know about.
- For Carol to role-play with me to give her the confidence she felt she needed to seek out friends. I will explain how to do this later in the chapter.
- To invite Jasmine over.

If you are forming a plan with your child, it might not include all these steps, depending upon the circumstances. It may be that your child is new to a school and doesn't know anyone yet, but feels uncomfortable about making new friends. In that case you might just help by letting your child practise on you what to say, or by getting advice from the teacher. Inviting children over to your house might be all that is required.

3. Enlist the Teacher's Help

Most friendships are formed in school, so it is vital to get the teacher's help. Perhaps the seating arrangements could be changed to encourage more friendships to form. In Carol's class, the teacher had allowed the children to choose who they sat next to every day. After being alerted by Carol's father, she decided to assign seats and change the seating plan every three weeks. This gave children a chance to get to know more people, and it helped develop new friendships. It certainly helped Carol, as the teacher made sure she sat at a table with Jasmine, which gave the girls an opportunity to get to know each other.

You can also ask that the lunchroom and playground be discreetly monitored so that conflicts or hurtful incidents can be stopped before they get out of hand. It is best if this is all done with the knowledge of your child, but if this is not possible, you should contact the teacher in confidence for the good of your child. Most teachers are only too pleased to help.

If you get no co-operation, or feel that the teacher might make it worse, which unfortunately does sometimes happen, then see if there is someone else at the school with whom you could have a quiet word to enlist their help. Often the playground supervisors or lunchroom staff (called 'dinner ladies' in my day!) are people from your neighbourhood and they might be able to let you know how they feel your child is getting on with the other children. Also, they might be able to intervene in less obvious ways, because they know all the kids and their parents.

4. Figure Out What Makes a Good Friend

Very recently, I conducted a survey of 200 seven to eleven-year-olds and asked them what they looked for in a friend. I also asked teachers to set out their observations about why they thought some children were more 'popular' than others. Here's what both groups said:

- When children are seeking friendship they are drawn to someone who:

    a) smiles and is happy most of the time
    b) likes to join in and play with them
    c) isn't bossy
    d) helps them with their school work
    e) shares things
    f) makes them laugh and is fun to be with
    g) listens when they want to talk
    h) is kind

  i) sticks up for them
  j) doesn't change – they aren't nice one day and mean the next

- Teachers observed that children who were 'popular' with both students and teachers:

  a) were self-confident
  b) good at organising games and activities
  c) could shrug off disappointments and setbacks
  d) were good listeners
  e) had a good sense of humour
  f) had parents who were supportive
  g) had good communication skills, including being able to find something to talk about with other children and adults
  h) were healthy and often good at sports
  i) were able to sort out conflicts between children
  j) complimented others and were not critical

It might be a good idea either to duplicate this list and discuss it with your children, or make up a list of your own with them. Better yet, let them make one up themselves and then discuss it with them. It is an excellent exercise that sets children thinking not only about what they want in a friend, but how they are acting with other children. You might suggest to your child's teacher that, if time can be found, they try a similar exercise with the class. When I was teaching, I found it very useful to get the children talking about friendship, because it prevented problems forming. It was much more positive for the children to say to someone, 'You're not being very kind' instead of 'I hate you, go away'. At least the child knows where she might be going wrong instead of wondering exactly why she has suddenly become hated. (The word 'hate' was banned from my classroom and the children learned to be more constructive with their conversation. That isn't to say they were all friends, all the time. It wasn't Utopia, but it was fairly amicable.)

Carol and her father came up with a list that looked like this:

- What Carol wanted in a friend was someone who would:

  a) like her
  b) enjoy drawing, talking, reading, playing

c) be with her at lunch and playtime
d) come to her flat and sleep over sometimes
e) be nice

- Carol thought a friend might like her in order to:

    a) be liked
    b) share activities
    c) eat and play together
    d) talk about things
    e) think of things to do

When we met, Carol thought she could be kind (in fact, she was a very kind child, but a bit too sensitive) and that she could start thinking of things she and friends could do, like roller skating or going to the park. Her father, a single parent, was more than willing to provide opportunities for Carol and her friends to do some fun things, as long as they didn't cost much money.

Carol also thought she had to work on a way to go up to Jasmine and start a conversation. She tended to get tongue-tied, so we decided to practise – just the two of us, so she wouldn't be embarrassed.

5. Role-play

Initiating a conversation with someone or going up to a group to talk can be daunting. Adults I know who find it difficult say that every intelligent thought they've ever had vanishes, and they become blithering idiots. That sounds a bit harsh and self-critical, but if that's how they feel it's no wonder they hold back. What children need is a practised phrase or two they can use that slips out easily and gets them over that first hurdle. Carol and I came up with the following ideas for opening sentences:

- 'Did you see the programme last night about . . . ? What did you think of it?' Since many children watch television, this could be a common starting point.
- 'What did you think about the story we had in reading this morning (or yesterday or whenever)?'

- 'I liked your drawing in class. What kind of things do you like to draw?'
- 'What did you do over the weekend?'
- 'Would you like to go over there and play that game or do you have any other suggestions?'
- 'Would you mind if I sat here next to you?'

We practised with Carol being herself and me being the various children, such as Susan and Jasmine. I know Carol felt silly at first, but her confidence increased tremendously and she was soon able to try it out with the children. She was thrilled to tell me at our next meeting that it worked, and children actually talked to her and sat with her at lunch.

If children are old enough, explain the difference between a 'closed' question and an 'open' question. A closed question is more likely to elicit a plain yes or no response. 'Do you like milk?' 'Yes.' These kinds of questions usually start with words like 'do', 'did', 'is', 'are', and 'was'.

Open questions are more likely to elicit a longer response with more opportunities for conversation. 'What sort of things did you do when you were on holiday?' 'Oh, we went swimming and out in a boat. We played tennis a little bit, but I'm not very good at it.'

There is no guarantee that the person you are talking to will give you a better answer with an open question, but at least you are setting up the odds more in your favour.

6. Invite Children Over

In order to cement friendships and foster new ones, it often helps to have your children play at your home with others. This not only gives them the chance to get to know each other away from school, but gives you a chance to observe how your children are interacting and what their friends are like.

Try to make sure that a good time is had by the children. Help your child to think of fun things to do, such as arranging a trip to the cinema or going to the park with a picnic. Maybe there is a swimming baths near you, or an ice rink. It is also fun to do things the children might not do at home. I remember teaching a group of my son's friends how to play monopoly and some card games. They had never done that before, which amazed me. I guess computer games took over the world when I wasn't looking!

Carol invited Jasmine over and they made home-made pizza, watched a video, played with Carol's cat, had a water-pistol fight and generally enjoyed themselves. Carol now plans to include Susan and the other girls in a party she and her father are planning for her birthday.

7. Observe Your Child

If you can unobtrusively observe your children when they are with friends or trying to make friends, you can find out lots that might help. Obviously you can't be in the room the whole time, but you can be 'reading' next door or rearranging pictures in the hallway nearby or weeding the garden while they are outside. Leave the door ajar so you can overhear what's happening, or set up a game or tea in the kitchen and busy yourself in the background. Observe if your child is being friendly, judgemental, bossy, shy, too sensitive, tactful, humorous, aggressive or complaining. Then, try to encourage the traits mentioned previously that enhance friendships, and gently suggest ways to change the other traits (one at a time, please).

If your child is being too sensitive, you might suggest that sometimes people misunderstand what others are saying because they take things too seriously. Explain that reacting by crying or going into a shell doesn't help, because it makes others withdraw. Help your child to see that the other person did not mean to hurt her feelings and that she should not take things to heart so much.

If your child is too bossy, tell her not to be! It's likely she got it from you . . . Seriously, bossiness puts kids right off and we need to help our children to share and not to feel that they can make all the decisions.

Carol's father reported that she was very friendly and solicitous of her friends. She shared things and was good at taking turns and complimenting others, but was inclined to be hurt too easily.

'She seemed to take everything to heart, even silly little

comments. Luckily, the other girls didn't seem to notice too much, except when Carol got her feelings hurt because Susan was talking too much to Jasmine or Soon-Yi. Susan just turned to her and told her not to be so stupid. I could see Carol trying to control her emotions, which she did very well, but I thought she was too thin-skinned. I'm sure it's because she still feels rejected after her mother left, but we'll work on it. She knows she has to try to laugh things off more – actually we both do, so I guess it's partly my fault, as well.'

Good for Carol's father for admitting that he might be too sensitive, as well. It is a help to children to know that we have to struggle with the same problems as they do. It gives them hope.

I honestly think that if I could tell parents of newborn babies one thing to do with their children after loving them, it would be to laugh a lot and help them develop a sense of humour.

8. Change Undesirable Behaviour

In Carol's case there was no undesirable behaviour to change, unless you count her sensitivity. I wouldn't call that bad behaviour – more a sense of perspective. However, there are some children who don't have friends because they put people off.

If children are aggressive, have a quick temper, are bossy or refuse to share, other children will not want to play with them. If they have nasty habits like farting, burping, picking their noses or spitting, they will find everyone taking a wide berth. If they have poor personal hygiene, such as body odour or greasy hair, then it is not surprising they lack friends.

It is possible to change children's behaviour or personal hygiene if they, and their parents, are willing to try. I remember one boy who was so smelly that no one could bear to be around him. When I gently and, I thought, tactfully tried to talk with his mother about it, I was told it was none of my business and the family, which seemed normal in other respects, didn't believe in washing much because it was harmful to the body. Oh dear. The trouble is the boy knew he smelled and hated it.

I'm afraid I circumvented the mother on this one. We arranged for him to shower at school and put on fresh clothes we kept for him. So, everyday he would arrive in the clothes from home, wash, change, spend the day in his 'school clothes', and then change back into his 'home clothes' to go home. Mother never did find out, and the boy went on to become a very clean carpenter.

If children are acting in a way which clearly needs to be changed for their own good and for the good of others, don't hesitate to wade in. Practise alternative ways to behave until they become second nature to them. Arrange a time-out place for them to go when they are feeling aggressive, so they won't bother someone else. Tell them if they are bossy and explain how to approach people in a nice way – role-play with them *asking* kids to do things instead of *telling* them what to do. Don't look the other way if a child is picking his or her nose. Confront yucky habits, tell the child this is unacceptable in polite society and reward him when he doesn't do it. It isn't cute to be obnoxious.

9. Some Friendships Just Don't Work Out

Friendships won't always go according to plan. A child may try to be friends with someone, but it just doesn't work out for reasons beyond your or their control. It could be that they simply can't find anything in common. It might be that they were friends but now enjoy doing completely different things. Or a friend may have personal problems and just wants to be left alone for a while. Friends may also decide to do something which your child cannot or will not do, like steal or joyride. At least we all hope our children would draw the line at that kind of destructive friendship.

The message to get across to your children is that friendships do come and go. Some will last a lifetime, others only a day. If they have tried their best, perhaps it just wasn't meant to be, as my grandmother used to say. Talk with them about friendships that fail, if they want to talk, and assure them that there are lots of people out there to become friends with so don't despair. It does help if you can talk about a time when you lost a friend and what it meant to you. After all, your children can see that you've survived it, and that is a good role-model for them.

10. Enhance Your Child's Talents, Interests or Activities

Finally, help your children increase the number of people they can be friends with by encouraging them to develop their skills and interests. If a child is good at sports, find out about Saturday sports clubs or after-school lessons. Look into swimming, dance, tennis and gymnastics classes. Check out the local Scout troops, Brownie packs, acting or martial arts classes. See if you can arrange group music lessons. Not only will these things increase your children's self-confidence, they will give them a whole new group of people from which to find friends.

And, whatever you do, please encourage your children not to discard old friends as they make new ones. I don't know the rest of it, but I remember this song from my childhood:

> *Make new friends*
> *But keep the old;*
> *One is silver*
> *And the other's gold.*

5

THINGS THEY NEED TO KNOW TO KEEP SAFE

A child out playing can be snatched off a bike, bundled into a car or dragged out of sight in seconds. News of child abusers seems to surface weekly in the papers. Parents today face a difficult dilemma: how to give children the freedom to develop their independence, yet stay safe.

Things were so different when I was a kid. Remember leaving early in the morning with a packet of jam sandwiches and a drink? Mum would give a wave, absently tell us to be careful and not to get into trouble. 'Be back before dark' was the only definite rule. We got back on time, but then even after dark we played out with our friends, hiding behind neighbourhood trees and in dark alleys without a thought that we might be at risk. In the summer we were out until past ten pm.

Of course, we were warned not to go off with strangers, but you also said 'hello' politely if any grown-up talked to you. We were not aware of child abuse, or that danger might come from someone you knew.

I look back with rose-tinted glasses to those days of my childhood with a yearning for what appeared to be a safer and kinder time. It may not have been like that for everyone, but sometimes I worry about how on earth we can bring children up now so that they are safe in today's very different world, but still have some of that lovely innocence and sense of wonder we had.

It's no good asking our own mothers for advice. When they were bringing us up, they didn't seem to be hit by shocking news of yet another child murder. Nowadays, it's not just frightening to let our children go out to the park on their own for an hour or two, we wonder if it's safe to ask them to run a quick errand to the corner shop. As parents of this generation, we have to keep things in perspective and we have to work out new rules – and it's hard being a pioneer. The vast majority of children go through life without serious harm, but we still must warn all children that the harm is there. How can we go about this?

Accept That Children Will Lose Some Innocence

While we are busy being pioneers there is a danger that our children will lose their innocence as they are no longer shielded from adult worries and responsibilities. No one can blame us for wanting to keep our children safe, but there is a cost. Children are, of necessity, more vigilant and aware of dangers. For example, in the past no one warned kids about people they knew who might try to abuse them. So when children were abused, they didn't tell or weren't believed. Now they are told to tell if anyone tries to secretly touch or kiss them, but the price is they learn earlier about things we would rather they didn't ever have to deal with. But I think we have no choice, unless we never let our kids out of our sight, that is. And we must let them out.

Judging When to Let Them Out Alone

I vividly remember when I finally relented to my eldest son's burning desire to go, on his own, to the paper shop.

He was eight, I was thirtysomething. We lived in a block of flats on the sixth floor. Charles waved goodbye and got into the lift. I waited until the doors closed on his little freckled face, then rushed down the stairs. He went out of the front door, looked left and right about ten times and crossed the road before heading to the corner shop. Peering out from behind the door, I took deep breaths until I saw him return. I then charged up six flights of stairs to arrive back in the flat just ahead of him. When he came in bursting with pride and announced, 'I did it, Mum,' I could only gasp with assumed nonchalance, 'Clever boy.'

Allowing your kids out is exhausting! And, it would seem to us, dangerous. There's no denying children are vulnerable. Every parent's nightmare is that a psychopath will take them away, horrifically abuse them and murder them. But the reality is that the vast majority of children are quite safe, and most who are not are harmed by someone they know.

Sometimes, however, children go missing and stay missing. Some go missing and are found dead. No use then telling us that psychopaths are few and the chances are one in a million that a child will be in the wrong place at the wrong time. That won't stop us being terrified of letting our kids out.

Seeing those lovely young faces staring at us from newspapers, hearing their parents' anguished pleas on the news, knowing that 'there but for the grace of God goes my child' brings a chill of dread to any mum or dad. You know it will never be possible to protect all children from harm or horrid people, but you must try your best. The irony that they are far more likely to be harmed by someone they know than by a stranger doesn't quell the dread most parents feel.

Beware Being Over-protective

One mum I talked to, Jackie, thought she had solved the problem by shelving it. 'Whenever my children ask me if they can go out on their own, I tell them "next year". The difficulty is that when next year comes, it's always too soon.' Her son will probably still be asking if he can go to the shop when he's forty!

We all know parents who never let their children out of their sight. Sometimes it's understandable – for a short while. As one mum, Susan, told me: 'After a man attempted to snatch a girl from the playground at my daughter's school, I followed her everywhere.

But soon I realised the shadow behind the tree wasn't a wicked stranger – it was me, worrying all the time.'

We cannot teach our children to mistrust everyone, even if we feel that way. Most people like (or at least tolerate!) children and would never hurt them. We have to curb our natural tendencies to protect children, or they will choke on the cotton-wool we wrap them in and never learn to stand on their own feet.

Preparing Them for the Outside World

But what do you do when your children want more freedom than you think they can handle? Every parent's heart will sink when they hear these accusations:

- 'You always treat me like a baby.'
- 'My friends stay out till midnight.'
- 'No other parents want to know where their children are.'

It's natural when children try to gain that extra bit of independence, but we can't give in when we know they shouldn't be roaming the streets at an unearthly hour. We should resist, stoutly (even though we're pleased that they've the guts to try it on with us).

We must, however, let them spread their wings. We owe it to kids to teach them to cope in the world. We *must* show them how to develop strategies to use – just in case they come into contact with someone who tries to harm them.

And talking about it isn't enough. Don't just tell a child to look both ways before crossing the road – take them by the hand and practise crossing the road with them. The same applies when teaching children about yelling, kicking and running away from dangerous situations – don't just say it, get them to do it until you are satisfied they could summon up a really convincing yell at anyone who tries to molest them.

The following are some typical situations when children may be vulnerable, and some tips on preparing them how to act.

Using Public Transport

Andrew, aged twelve, was on his way back from a soccer match. He caught the train home and somehow ended up in a carriage on his own. A gang of youths got on at the next stop and started taunting him. Though Andrew ignored them, they shoved and pushed him around. Finally, they beat him and kicked him in the groin. They left the train and Andrew staggered home without reporting the attack.

His mother, horrified, sought medical help and rang the police. When the officer pointed out he could have pulled the emergency cord, Andrew said he'd considered it, but thought he would have to pay a fine as the sign said 'only use in an emergency'. The poor boy hadn't realised this was an emergency!

We need to ensure that children, particularly ones brought up to have good manners, understand they have a right to protect themselves. Talk about basic rules for travel on public transport with your children. Tell them to:

1. Always travel in carriages where there are other people.
2. Choose a carriage near the guard.
3. Find the emergency lever or cord, read the instructions, and use it if necessary.
4. Stay on the bus, tube or train if they think they are being followed, tell the guard or driver and ask to ring home from the manager's office.
5. Use only licensed taxis, if possible, or a mini-cab firm that the family knows.
6. Turn around if someone follows them from the stop or station, and go back to where there are other people.

Using Public Toilets

Frances told me that when her son, Martin, was nine, they were at a fast-food restaurant and he went to the loo. He came out looking pale and agitated. A man, attracted by the number of children known to go there, had located himself just inside the door. When Martin came in, the man pounced, fondled him and left. Martin had been too frightened to run, let alone cry for help. There were many people around who would have heard him and helped, but he didn't know how to react – fast and at once.

Many's the time when I have stood outside the men's loo shouting to my boys, 'Everything OK?' The Gents is one of the first places mums get excluded from, but is also one of the most likely places where a pervert might try to grope a child. Fathers out alone with daughters can't go into the Ladies, but thankfully this kind of offence is rare in female loos. However, girls have also been assaulted in isolated toilets, so they should be warned as well.

Talk to your children about what they should do if they find themselves alone in a public lavatory and in trouble. Suggest they should:

1. Leave immediately if someone tries to touch them or chat them up.
2. Tell an attendant, if there is one.
3. Never go into a cubicle with anyone, no matter what they say.
4. Never be afraid to make a fuss, if there's a chance someone will hear.
5. Never go into isolated public loos if they are by themselves.

Using Lifts and Stairwells

Paula, aged ten, had lived in the same block of flats all her life. Her mother says she is fairly streetwise, but recently a terrible thing happened. Paula's mum found her daughter crying at their front door. Between sobs, she blurted out her story. Her mum said it was all she could do to keep from screaming as she listened.

Paula had got into the lift and noticed a man she instantly felt uncomfortable about. But it didn't occur to her to get out again, and in a moment the doors had closed. Suddenly, the man reached over, stopped the lift between floors and turned off the light. He told Paula he'd kill her if she yelled or made a fuss. He then stripped her and indecently assaulted her. The child did as she was told because there was no chance of escaping. She told her mum she'd wanted to get out when she saw the man, but hadn't wanted to appear rude.

Little Paula did the right thing by not fighting back when the man said he'd kill her. But if only she'd been prepared to follow her instincts and get out of the lift in the first place, it might have prevented the traumatic assault.

Discuss the dangers with your children. Tell them to:

1. Be prepared to go back out of a lift immediately if they feel uncomfortable for any reason about another person.
2. Wait until the next lift – an empty one or one with lots of people in it.
3. Use the stairs instead, if they are safer.
4. Be wary of dark stairwells – best to wait and walk up with other people.
5. Get away as quickly as possible if someone threatens them on a stairwell – run in the opposite direction or run up to the door of a flat and knock loudly. (If you live in a block, you could talk with neighbours and arrange flats for kids to go to in case of emergency.)
6. Yell, if there's a chance of being heard.

Going Out and About

Twelve-year-old Melissa was waiting for a bus when a man joined the queue. He moved close to Melissa and whispered something to her. She froze when she heard the stream of filth. Although there were at least ten people in the queue, Melissa was too frightened to move away and the obscenities went on for what seemed like for ever before the man calmly walked off.

Melissa told no one until three months later when she approached me after I'd been giving a talk to her class. She repeated what the man had said and then spilled it all out. She'd been having nightmares and, each time she waited for a bus, was scared that the man would reappear. It had never occurred to her to leave the queue and walk into the shop nearby or to ask for adult help.

Explain to your children that if someone talks obscenely, or exposes himself, they should:

1. Ignore them – put their fingers in their ears, turn or look away.

2. Always walk towards shops or houses or, if on public transport, move purposefully elsewhere.
3. Tell their parents, teacher, or police.

Coming Into Contact With an Abuser

Children may be at risk from someone they know who might try to abuse them. What children need to know are strategies they can use to either get away or tell should something happen. One of my other books, *Keeping Safe**, deals with this in depth, but here are some suggestions for talking with children about this difficult subject:

1. Not Everyone Can Touch

Explain to children that their bodies belong to them. No one should touch them in a way that makes them uncomfortable or confused and touching, kisses and hugs should *never* be kept secret.

2. Tell All

Tell children to tell you if anyone asks them to keep touches, kisses or hugs secret, even if it feels good. Sometimes abuse is not physically painful and it can feel good. This confuses the child even more.

3. Some People Have Problems

Explain that most people love children and would never harm them, but that some people have problems which might lead them to touch children where they should not. It is OK for children to touch their own bodies, of course.

4. Don't Say Too Much to The Abuser

Tell your children that they should never threaten an abuser that they will tell. It might be that they have to go along with what is asked and then tell you. (If they threaten an abuser, he or she could turn nasty and hurt the child. Better that the child should get away and tell you.)

5. Role-play

To reinforce the idea of safety, play 'What if?' games with your children. Ask things like, 'What would you do if someone you knew asked you to keep a kiss a secret?'

Be low-key when talking about all of these things. You will find that children take it in their stride. Be sure to work out with them who they would tell if something did happen. Help them make a list of people they know and trust.

When Do You Allow Them Out?

When I was setting up KIDSCAPE (the charity which teaches children how to keep safe), I asked over 4,000 parents what they did about giving their children freedom in safety.

The only thing they all agreed on was that the maturity of the child and where you lived were important in determining when to allow children out to play. How do you judge maturity? Each parent has to decide, but the consensus was that they allowed:

- children aged nine to go to local shops and cross small roads
- children aged eleven to use public transport in daylight
- children aged twelve to go shopping or to the cinema with a friend in daylight
- young people aged fifteen or sixteen to go out at night, with a curfew of eleven pm or later for special events.

There are hundred of safety tips I have worked out in my job and the great reward for me is when a child tells me, 'It works!'

Tom, aged ten, told me he'd been on his way to school when a man drove his car up on to the pavement, right in Tom's path. The man leaned out of the car and tried to grab him. Tom backed away, yelled a deep, loud yell and ran all the rest of the way to school, where he collapsed like a heap of jelly. He'd been taught in one of my classes just the previous week the lesson of yelling, running and getting away. He had practised it and it may have saved his life.

The positive way to look at this problem is to realise we can instil confidence in children by teaching them practical things they can do if they come under attack. It's something we can work on a little bit at a time, as soon as they are old enough to understand about learning to fight for themselves.

It isn't a cosy, safe world, and bringing up kids seems more difficult these days. But then, even riding a bike has become a major safety issue. When my eldest son's bike was stolen, we replaced it at our local bike shop, along with a new cycling helmet, knee pads and gloves. Recalling our carefree bike-riding youth with none of these accoutrements, I remarked to the old gentleman who runs the shop that it was amazing that any of us ever grew up, lacking as we were in safety measures. 'Times were different then,' he said, shaking his head. I think he's right.

'Can I go out to play?' 'Yes, my love, but remember to run away quickly if anyone tries to grab you, don't talk to anyone you don't know and scream your head off if you feel in danger. Have a good time and be home by dark.'

Safety Practice

Here are two exercises every parent should do with their children when they are old enough to go out on their own:

1. The Yell

Yell 'No' from deep in the stomach. Do this plenty of times, then repeat in front of a mirror until the child is not shy about doing it. Polite children are most at risk of being unable to yell at an attacker.

2. The Yell and Run

Practise yelling while running away at the same time.

General Tips to Make Children More 'Streetwise'

Teach your children:

1. *Never to take short cuts.*
2. *Not to wear a personal stereo on the street – it makes them an easy target.*
3. *To keep enough money to make a phone call.*
4. *Not to carry large sums of money.*
5. *To stay in a group if possible.*
6. *To always tell you where they are going and with whom.*
7. *How to make an emergency telephone call.*
8. *That if someone they don't know talks to them, pretend not to hear – the other person may be looking for a fight. Look confident and walk quickly away.*
9. *That they don't always have to be polite – they can scream, kick or ignore an adult if their safety is at risk.*
10. *That their safety is more important than anything and they can break any rule to keep safe.*

* *Keeping Safe* is published by Hodder Headline and available in bookshops.

6

BOOSTING YOUR CHILD'S LEARNING POWER

Alarm bells are ringing. No, not the fire engine type, the 'Monday morning and it's time to get the family ready for school' alarm clock type. Your children, tired out from their strenuous weekend playing with friends, are ignoring the alarm. Somehow, Mondays are always like this. In you go.

'Good morning. Time to get up.' No response.

Five minutes later. 'Time for school.' Groan.

Another five minutes and your friendly, 'I'm a positive parent' line is wearing thin. 'Come on, get going. You only have thirty minutes.'

Three minutes later. Overhead lights on, cold water in glass and raised voice shouting, 'If you don't get out of that bed immediately, I am going to throw this entire glass of water over you.'

Finally they are out of the door, on the bus and now it's completely up to the teachers. Or is it?

Twenty minutes later, as you are going out of the door to your second job – you know, the one that pays the rent – you reflect on your first job, being the parent of school-aged children. When you get home tonight there will be homework to supervise, helping Sam with his maths, Natalie with her spelling. Not for the first time you wonder how we can help kids to do well, to like school, to love reading and writing? (Perhaps to become rich and famous novelists who will keep you in your old age so you can give up your job? Dream on . . .)

Teaching children is too important to leave it all up to the schools. Unless we're in this together, it won't work as well as it should. There are some basic things we parents can do with our children which will encourage their learning power:

Teach Them to Love Reading

We can instill a love of reading in our children, which will help them in anything they do in school and in life. It is probably the most important skill they need to learn. You might try some strategies such as:

1. Keeping Books Around

The most obvious way to start is by having lots of books, magazines and newspapers around your home that appeal to you and to your children, and to spend time reading them – without the television blasting away in the corner. It is hardly surprising that children who grow up in homes like this learn early that reading is a valued activity. Magazines like *National Geographic* and *Reader's Digest* are great to have around. I remember not being able to read all the words in *National Geographic*, but pouncing on it for the wonderful and exotic pictures. Even with the advent of television, I think the fascination of absorbing the photographs and stories at your own pace still holds true for both adults and children. *Reader's Digest*, with its bite-size stories, points to ponder, and humour is ideal to draw children into the joy of reading and to hold their interest. There are other publications and books specifically for children – if you can't afford to buy them new, look in markets or go to the library.

2. Using the Library

You don't have to be a millionaire to have books – remember your local libraries. Take your children and help them select books they are interested in. By all means suggest books, but don't impose your own tastes on them. Give them time to browse and discover things for themselves.

3. Reading to Your Children

From the time they are small right up until they are turning into teenagers, most children love to have a story read to them. In fact, I was speaking at a conference recently about children's books and one of the other speakers late in the day announced that she was going to read us a story. You should have seen the reaction in that audience of 200 adults when she began to read. People who were starting to leave stood transfixed at the doors, those sitting down relaxed back into their seats and everyone had a smile on their faces. We sat listening for twenty minutes to this wonderful story-teller, and there was a collective sigh when she finished before thunderous applause. There is, I firmly believe, something magical about being read to, especially when you are a young child sitting on a parent's or grandparent's lap.

Besides the benefit of learning to associate reading with warm and loving feelings, children who are read to develop a solid vocabulary base and an ear for pronunciation which will stand them in good stead in school. If you read books about things which interest them and leave other books about these same subjects lying around, they will pick up the books and start reading on their own.

4. Getting a Good Dictionary

Reading dictionaries can be fun, especially the illustrated children's dictionaries. If grandparents are trying to decide on a gift, why not suggest a dictionary instead of a toy. I know, I know – kids love toys as well, but the dictionary will last for several years and I suspect the toy might not make it through the holidays. As your children get older, ensure that you have dictionaries that will be useful to their age group.

5. Buying Them a Torch – Put the Lights Out

One mother, Liz, approached me because her son Andrew found reading boring. He also had a hard time falling asleep and, because of this, had trouble in the mornings being alert at school. She had done everything she could think of, but to no avail. He was having problems at school and she and her husband were in despair that their bright child was not succeeding.

We established that Andrew was allowed to watch television after dinner and homework, right up until bedtime, as a way of relaxing. It was fairly easy to come up with a solution to Andrew's difficulties and it had nothing to do with my years of experience as a child psychologist and everything to do with my grandmother.

When I was a child, the lights went out at a certain time and that was that. The problem was that my sister and I were usually in the middle of reading something and complained bitterly about how unfair it all was. My grandmother bought us each a torch and said we weren't to use it for reading at night. She was a sly old fox – we spent many a happy night under the covers finishing that crucial chapter.

So, for Andrew, it was decided that he would go to bed at the normal time and the lights would go out fifteen minutes later, but only if he was reading something of his own choosing. Otherwise the lights went out when he got into bed. Well, give a kid that kind of choice and guess what he opts for?

Andrew was also given a torch (a low-light kind that goes out automatically when laid down, to prevent any danger of burning) with the same admonishment that my grandmother gave. I also suggested curbing his television viewing gradually so that he wouldn't see it as punishment. He was turning into a couch potato and this had to be addressed. His parents also enrolled him in an after-school sports activity to get him more exercise.

Within one month Andrew graduated from reading comics to reading short stories, started sleeping better and improved at school. The only thing his parents had to do was to make sure the torch was out of his bed before they went to bed. Who needs experts when you have such a wise grandmother?

6. Giving Book Tokens

It is fun going to the book store to choose your own book. Put a book token in your child's Christmas stocking or give it as a present for whatever holidays you celebrate.

7. Listening to Your Child Read Aloud

Reading aloud is a skill which helps children to pronounce words properly and to develop confidence in speaking. It also helps you to assess your child's understanding of what is being read. Little and often can be the key to enjoyment. Try having your child read for just a few minutes at first, and do it often. This will depend upon age and concentration level. The object is to enjoy it, not turn it into an onerous task.

Let's say you are doing this with your seven-year-old daughter. If she is struggling, help her out by reading it with her. Give masses of praise and emphasise what she does right, not what she does wrong. Ask *specific* questions to see if she understood what she read. Take, for example, the Grimm Brothers fairy tale Hansel and Gretel:

> 'Why do you think that Hansel and Gretel were taken into the forest?'

> 'What plan did Hansel think of to help them find their way back?'

> 'How do you think that Hansel and Gretel felt when they were lost in the forest?'

> 'Why do you think the witch was so mean?'

> 'How did the children defeat the witch?'

> 'Do you think the children were angry at their father for being left in the forest?'

You can, of course, ask general questions about how she liked the story and if she has any ideas for ending it differently. This is good for fostering ideas and creativity. You may even give her an opportunity to write her own story, as we turn now to helping children to write.

Teach Your Child to Enjoy Writing

Fourteen-year-old Nick has just completed his first novel. It isn't going to set the world on fire and probably won't be published, but Nick has loved writing it. He began writing stories at the kitchen table when he was about four. His parents praised his stories and always displayed them on the front of the refrigerator. They stapled them together in a little cover, on which Nick drew a picture. They proudly showed them, in front of Nick, to their friends and relations, who also gave Nick lots of encouragement. Someday Nick will be published, but he likes writing so much that he doesn't care. How can we get our children to be as enthusiastic about writing even if they aren't destined to be the Dickens of their generation? Most of us would even settle for a child willing to write a brief thank-you note! Try the following:

1. Show an Interest Yourself

It is no accident that parents who are writers produce children who write. If Mum or Dad have a place where they regularly write, whether it's letters or books or articles, children usually end up sharing that interest in writing. It is reinforced by the parents.

It is the same for reading, music, science and other subjects. It is very motivating for a child when he or she sees parents engaged in an activity they clearly enjoy. Let your child see you writing, talk about it at mealtimes, read aloud some of your own words and encourage your child to do the same.

2. Create a Place for Writing

It's easier to sit down to write if there is a place that doesn't have to be cleared especially. Arrange somewhere for each child to write, even if it is just a corner of a desk you managed to pick up at a used furniture market for next to nothing. In fact, a desk or table and a quiet place to work helps most children with whatever they are learning. I know that it isn't always possible, and that some kids *can* shut out the world and work, but most cannot.

3. Keep a Journal

Give your children a journal or diary and encourage them to write in it on a daily basis. It gets them into a lifelong habit of expressing themselves in writing for their own pleasure and use.

4. Get Your Child a Pen Pal

Pen pals are fun and children love to get mail. If your child's school does not have a pen pal scheme, find out from your local newspaper, library, information centre or council if they have a list. Another way to find one is to write to a local newspaper in a country or area your child is interested in, and ask for correspondence. The only caution here is to make sure that the person your child is writing to is another child and not someone who preys on children. It might help if you made contact with the child's parents.

5. Use Computers

In the world our children are growing up in, computers are essential for communication. Although I certainly want my children to be able to write legibly, it would be unrealistic to expect that they would laboriously write out everything by hand. I had a difference of opinion on this from another author, who says that his books are superior to those written on word processors because they are handwritten and that 'writing should be painful'. My reply was, 'Rubbish – writing is expressing yourself, the method you use is not as important as the words and messages you write.' I suppose the debate will go on, but I happily confess that this and all my other books are word-processed.

6. Don't Always Correct Their Work

If your children start writing for pleasure and show you their work, focus on the good things. Praise their choice of words, the way they describe the characters, the humour or drama. Don't immediately correct grammar or sentence structure as it might turn them off. There will be plenty of time for helping them with the nitty gritty of writing after they've caught the writing bug.

7. Writing at School

Check with your child's school to make sure they are giving children time and encouragement to write. I was horrified one year to find one of my sons had a teacher who *only* used workbooks where the children filled in the answers. In my humble opinion, these workbooks should be burned, because filling in blanks leads to blank minds and lack of creativity. Not that I'm prejudiced!

One way to handle a situation like this is first to have a word with the teacher, who may have a perfectly rational explanation for the workbook method. Say that you understand the use of workbooks (you may have to be diplomatic here), but that you feel children also need to practise writing letters, journals, essays, etc., to help them hone their skills and develop their creativity. It is possible that the teacher will take your point and change. If not, have a word with the headteacher to find out the philosophy of the school and how they teach writing under the National Curriculum. If you are still not happy, you can continue to make a fuss or start giving your child extra tuition at home, perhaps by introducing him or her to the joys of keeping a diary or journal. Better yet, encourage your children to write their own books and 'publish' them, complete with covers and pictures. Children love to see their books 'in print'. (All you need is a stapler, glue and steady hands to 'bind' the book.)

The final step would be to look for another school, but that might be a bit drastic if everything else is going well. You could offer to help the teacher by setting up a 'write and publish your own book' club with the children. Takes time, but it really is fun.

Teach Your Children to Spell

Winnie the Pooh said it best: 'My spelling is wobbly. It's good spelling but it wobbles and the letters get in the wrong place.' The spelling of the English language, with all of its irregularities and quirks, has got to be one of the most difficult things children have to learn. Just think about the different sounds which go with the same letters and how confusing it must be for children. For example, we teach children that 'g' is for girl, and then along comes 'g' for giant!

We had Spelling Bees when I was in school, and masses of helpful little quotes to get us through, but it was never easy.

1. Use Helpful Hints

If your child is having difficulty with a particular word or category of words, try teaching them some memory aids such as:

- 'i' before 'e' except after 'c', unless it sounds like 'a', as in neighbour or weigh
- knock off the 'e' when adding 'ing'
- to spell 'occasion' – remember: two 'c'uffs on one 's'hirt
- Egypt – say Egg Ypt (pronounced 'egg wiped') to remember where the 'y' goes

2. Teach Them a Word a Day

If your children have a list of words to learn for the week, try learning one or two a day. Put it up on the fridge. Put it up in the bathroom or in their rooms. Ask them to try to spell the word or words from the previous day at the end of the day, so by Friday they may be able to spell all the accumulated words from Monday onwards.

3. Listen to Their Spelling

Put some time aside for your children to spell their words aloud before they are tested at school. Be patient and don't criticise. It is a bore learning how to spell and you can acknowledge that, but it is important.

4. Reward Good Spelling Marks

If your child brings home a good spelling exam, make a big deal of it. Post it where everyone can see. Make a special treat or a star chart, if they are younger. Give them lots of praise and tell the rest of the family how well they've done. The problem is that there is nothing intrinsically rewarding about memorising spelling, so you have to make it as painless as possible.

5. Use the Dictionary

Make sure your children know how to use the dictionary and how to scan through if they only have half an idea how a word is spelled. If you are lucky enough to have a word processor with a spell check then by all means use that too. These are a godsend for children with learning difficulties such as dyslexia (see below).

Teach Your Child Maths

Now this is something I can only ask other people about. It's not that I am a maths illiterate, but I come close. Oh, I have no problem adding, subtracting, dividing and multiplying, but algebra and trigonometry utterly defeated me. However, I can beat my sons' calculators in adding columns of figures and I am assured by maths experts that there is no such thing as a maths illiterate and that everyone can learn maths. Perhaps my motivation wasn't strong enough. Certainly one of my sons seems to have overcome any genetic defect he may have inherited from me and is doing well in maths. So what can we do to foster good maths skills with our children?

1. Shopping

An obvious way in our family was to take the children shopping and let them figure out the products which were least and most expensive. Now, many supermarkets do this for you on the little signs under the products, but your children can still try it for themselves. They can also figure out approximately how much the shopping will cost by adding the products together and rounding up or down to get a ball-park total.

2. Pocket Money

Give your children their pocket money and help them work out a budget. They can use a piece of paper or a little book to record what they spend or save (save?!). Help them decide how to be more efficient with their money before they ask you for a raise.

3. Sort Things Into Categories

Ask your children to sort their toys into categories and count how many they have in each category. For example, your daughter may have four categories, such as soft furry toys, drawing materials, books, games. Ask her how many she has in each category. Point out how food stores put things on the shelf in the sections, such as vegetables, fruits, dairy products, bread, etc., and see if your children can come up with their own categories.

4. Counting

When your children are learning to count, think about all the things you can use to help them. Count the segments in oranges, the Smarties in a tube, the houses on the street as you walk by, the number of segments in a chocolate bar, the stairs you climb – anything. The only problem is that this can become an obsession. A woman who works with me, aged forty-nine, still counts everything in threes because of a game they played as children. She drives us bonkers!

5. Measure Things

My youngest son loved the tape measure left in his Christmas stocking one year. He measured everything in the place and we carefully recorded it in a book he carried around in his pocket.

6. Use Flash Cards

For some things in maths, like learning tables, there seems to be no way around memorising. Many a long night we spent in the kitchen with both children reciting their tables and us using flash cards. We couldn't afford the printed ones, so we made our own.

Teach Your Child Science Skills

Many of the questions children ask are in some way related to science. Why is the sky blue? Where does rain come from? What is snow? How does the clock work? Where did I come from? A child's natural curiosity can be used to help her develop skills needed in science.

1. Answer Questions

This isn't as easy as it sounds. One of my children asked me how nuclear power plants worked. Though I know a little about them, the question was beyond me. But the library had some brilliant books with illustrations, so we both now know how they work and my son won a first place at the local science fair with his project – he built a nuclear power plant from cardboard tubes, pipe cleaners and sugar cubes. Good old *Blue Peter*! The moral is: if you can answer, do; if you can't, find help.

2. Encourage Observation

Encourage your children to touch, smell and look carefully at things. By pointing out size, shape, texture, colour and other characteristics, we can start children on the road to analysing materials and objects they come into contact with in everyday life. As they get older, they can use tools to measure, weigh and generally to compare and observe their world. Scientists are keen observers, and this is probably one of the most important skills we can help children develop. Don't forget that game we all played as children – looking at ten or more objects on a tray for twenty seconds, then covering the tray and trying to remember what the objects were and describing what they looked like.

3. Notice How Things Work

If a child is interested in how clocks run, find an old clock, take it apart and explain it. If you don't know, ask someone who does. There are many mechanical building toys on the market which make good presents, but these are sometimes too expensive. Old toys or electrical equipment can be just as good. Why not take the motor out of the old hair dryer and tinker with it?

Hands-on science museums are marvellous places to take children, because they can push the buttons, turn the levers and pump the handles to see what happens. Some factories and plants have public tours, too, so you can go along and find out how cars are put together, how water is filtered, how steel is made or ceramics are fired.

4. Make Things, Do Experiments

If your children are interested in building something or setting up an experiment, get the tools together and help them. Draw a plan, forage for old pieces of wood or whatever, and have a go. If it doesn't work out, learn from it. Edison, when asked by his staff if they should give up on an experiment which had failed 900 times, was reported to have said, 'Give up? We now know 900 ways it doesn't work – carry on.' They eventually succeeded. There are some very good books which give step-by-step instructions for doing simple home experiments. Check with your library or with the school.

5. Enjoy Nature with Your Child

Go for walks, notice how the animals live, talk about why the leaves change colour and fall in the autumn, discuss how plants are necessary for life on earth, look at the stars and talk about navigation skills – the list is endless and exciting. The opportunities to enhance your child's interest in science are there for the taking.

Teach Your Child Test-taking Skills

I remember studying like mad for tests and dreading them. I wish someone had helped me with a few test-taking hints. Explain to children that there are some guidelines about taking tests:

1. Not Cramming

Studies have shown that cramming for tests the night before is not a good way to learn. No surprise there, but kids still try to cram everything in at the eleventh hour.

2. Organisation

Make sure your children have the necessary papers organised so that the information they need can be found without hassle. If they use a notebook, get dividers and help them label them so they can easily find their work. As they get older and have more subjects to study, buy, beg, or borrow a used two-drawer filing cabinet. Using files, they can instantly lay their hands on the materials they need.

3. Repeat Aloud

One very effective way to remember information is to repeat it aloud several times. Give your child time to practise saying the information aloud and then repeat it to you. It is also effective to write down the information and then to say it aloud.

4. Practise

If possible, give your child a mock test based on the information that is likely to be covered. It can increase confidence, but you must make sure your child understands that the test they are taking might be different. Check with the teacher if you are unsure.

5. A Full Stomach

Make sure your children have a good breakfast and plenty of time to get ready during the morning of the test. A relaxed, well nourished child has a better chance of doing well than a harried, hungry one.

6. Last-minute Review

Go over anything your child is unsure of on the morning of the test. Not too many things, but one or two crucial ones.

7. Praise

Send your children off feeling good about themselves. Tell them you know they'll do their best and that you'll be thinking of them.

Difficulties

Some children will have problems with some subjects because they aren't interested or talented in them, or they don't like the teacher. But some children may find it difficult to read or write or spell or do maths because they have some form of dyslexia, which scrambles things or makes them incomprehensible.

Dyslexia is an information processing difficulty. It is estimated that about ten per cent of children are affected by it. A friend of mine who is dyslexic said that I might understand what it is like if I tried reading the newspaper upside-down and backwards, and then tried writing the same way. 'You could do it eventually,' she explained, 'but think of all the extra time and effort it takes me to get the same information you get so easily.'

The irony is that, most often, children with dyslexia are just as bright, if not brighter, than other children in their class. So, not being able to learn in the same way as their peers can be very frustrating and discouraging.

If your child seems to be bright, but is having trouble keeping up with classmates, you may want to seek help. Ask the school to refer you to one of the organisations which specialise in teaching children who are dyslexic. One such organisation is the highly respected Dyslexia Institute, which gives individual tuition to children and helps the family to cope with the emotional overlays dyslexia often brings. The Dyslexia Institute (see p. 325, Where to Get Help) has kindly given permission to reproduce the following from one of their leaflets to help parents know what to look for:

Recognising Dyslexia

If the answer is 'yes' to most of the following questions, you would be wise to seek advice.

From the ages of 7–11, is your child:

- *bright in some ways, but seems to have a 'block' in others?*
- *having particular difficulty with reading and spelling?*
- *putting figures or letters the wrong way round, such as 15 for 51, or b for d?*
- *reading a word and then failing to recognise it further down the page?*
- *spelling a word several different ways without recognising the correct version?*
- *exhibiting poor concentration when reading or writing?*
- *having difficulty understanding time and tense?*
- *confusing right and left?*
- *answering questions orally, but having difficulty writing them down?*
- *unusually clumsy?*

There may be other explanations for any of these problems, but if your child seems to have several of them, it is worth checking to see if dyslexia might be the case. One other important clue is that this does run in families, so if great uncle George was the same way, it might well mean you need help.

Don't despair, lots of extremely creative, intelligent and successful people are dyslexic. One even became one of the best-known authors of children's stories – Hans Christian Andersen. What it does mean is that your child will need specialist teaching and advice to make learning easier or, in some cases, possible.

Study Habits

No matter what subjects your children are learning, there are a few vital points about study habits which will help them:

1. Set aside a quiet, well-lit place to work.
2. Have a set time for doing homework, with no telephone calls or distractions allowed.
3. Establish a routine for studying – when, where and how.
4. Take short breaks. Studies have shown that we learn best in twenty to thirty minute segments, with five or ten minute breaks in-between.
5. Organise school work. Use a small notebook to write down assignments, and a monthly or yearly planner to plot out long-term work, such as term papers or revisions.
6. Ask for help if they don't understand something.
7. Practise. Languages, music, art, physical education and other subjects may all require practising in order to master specific skills.
8. Take good notes in class.
9. Keep up with assignments – a little work every day prevents last-minute panics.

Parents should set aside some time to look at homework, if it is appropriate (some teachers say that parents should not be involved in homework at all). If your child claims 'there is no homework' and you don't buy it, check with the teacher. Whatever the philosophy of the school, children benefit when parents are interested in the work they are doing. Ask about what your child is studying and offer to help with any difficulties.

The Five Most Important Things to Do

My husband is a history teacher who is going to be very annoyed that there isn't a separate section on history! But by the time he realises it, the book will be in print. The problem is that there are too many areas to go into detail about here, unless we want to turn this into an academic exercise. Many of the skills and suggestions in the sections above will be useful in history, music, art and languages. I am not forgetting that physical education is a vital part of children's learning, as well, and that practice and persistence is an essential ingredient of learning power.

However, if there were only five important things to remember about helping children to learn, I reckon they would be:

1. *For parents to set an example of loving to learn.*
2. *To be an 'approachable' parent – one who encourages a child to find out the answers and helps if they can't.*
3. *To keep in contact with and co-operate with your child's teachers, so you can work together to create the right environment for kids to enjoy learning.*
4. *Not to dwell on failures. Nothing so undermines a person as having failures brought up again and again. If a kid doesn't do well with something when he should have, then discuss it and drop it. No one's perfect . . .*
5. *To say something positive to your children about their achievements or their attempts to achieve. It's that word again – Praise, praise, praise.*

7

MONEY MADNESS

How to Help Kids Deal with Money

'How on earth are we going to manage this month? Back-to-school clothes, new trainers, music lessons, food, mortgage, MOT – what can I sell?'

'The children?' said my spouse, hopefully.

'Well, I'm not sure how much they would fetch.' The idea was tempting. 'But why would anyone buy kids with hollow legs who can devour half the refrigerator in a night-time raid and think that life's necessities include computers, televisions, mobile phones, roller blades and a weekly allowance? By the way, they've asked for an increase in their pocket money.'

'*What?* When I was their age, I . . .'

I interrupted him. When he was their age you could go to the cinema for fivepence. 'Yes, I know, dear.'

'Can't you teach them to manage money better?'

'Yes, I think perhaps *we* can.'

Children, just like us, need to learn how to budget, save, and spend money. Unfortunately they are not born with a money sense – unless it's the feeling that parents have an endless supply of it!

One of the more difficult things we have to teach children is how to manage their (and our) money. Granted, I think it is more difficult today because children see and want so many things that cost money – lots of it. An average child will be subjected to hundreds of thousands of adverts before he reaches the age of sixteen. It seems to me that most of those adverts are inviting my children to spend my money on things they don't really need, or won't use for longer than two weeks.

We can rail against this modern madness, but what we have to do is to develop a money sense in our kids. How?

1. Explain Family Finance

My children attended a school where most of the other children had lots more money than they did. Because my husband was a teacher there, we didn't have to pay for tuition, which was great. What wasn't great was that the kind of money many of their classmates had to spend was, in my opinion, crazy.

Once, when my eldest was six and going with a group to a birthday bowling party, he casually asked me for £10 to spend. His pocket money at that time was about fifty pence a week, so he was asking for the equivalent of twenty weeks' money at once. I couldn't believe it.

It turned out that some of the children were given that kind of money when they went out, and that they blew it on sweets, arcade video games, fizzy drinks and the like. Even more disturbing was that some of the children had unlimited pocket money, as well as being given nearly everything they asked for – such as remote-control cars which reached twenty-five miles an hour, costing as much as £200. In contrast, my son had saved pocket money, done little jobs around the house for pay, and asked for birthday money to buy a £15 remote-control car that chugged away just about as fast as you could walk. Poor deprived kid? I think not.

I sat down with him and explained in simple terms the kind of money his father and I earned, what we had to pay for food, rent, clothes and expenses, as well as what we were putting aside in case of emergency, or if he and his brother decided they wanted to go on to higher education. I think I used a tube of Smarties to show him the proportions. Then I explained that the parents of the other children might earn more, or have perks from their companies so that they had more money to spend.

After I explained all this briefly, and told my son that he had chosen the wrong parents and better luck next time, he very sweetly offered to take a cut in pocket money. I guess I overdid it!

Seriously, it is important that children know what you can and can't do, and why. Obviously, you will want to tell them that this is private business (or you will get them bragging about how poor you are) and that it is just between members of your immediate family. Also, you don't want them to worry that you cannot provide the next meal, so don't go into great detail or paint a gloomy picture that will keep them awake at night. Some parents just say they can't afford certain things and leave it at that. I would opt to include the children as much as possible, because it gives them a sense of responsibility in the family (and it may spur them on to become millionaires – who knows?)

2. Be Fair and Consistent with Pocket Money

When children are given pocket money on a weekly or monthly basis, they quickly learn that no money means no treats and that money spent is money gone. The worse thing you can do is to agree pocket money and then bail your children out when they spend it all in the first ten minutes. It won't kill them to wait until next week for more sweets or comics, even though they will claim it is a fate worse than death. Stand firm and you will teach them the value of budgeting and saving in the kindest possible way.

What Does It Cover?

One decision you have to make is what the pocket money should cover. Some parents arrange it to include transportation, school lunches and treats. Others reserve pocket money only for treats. Some don't give pocket money at all, and just respond to requests for money, which I personally think is a big mistake (unless they cannot afford any pocket money at all on a regular basis). The problem with this last approach is that you are constantly bombarded with 'I want' and 'I need' for every little thing.

Age

It seems a good idea to start giving regular pocket money from about the age of five, when children start school. Try to give about the same amount that other children are given (within reason, of course). Check with other parents and talk with your children about what they think is fair.

If you have children of different ages, I think it is fair to give them different amounts of money. For example, my children are three years apart in age, and the older one gets more money than the younger because he goes out more with his friends. As my younger child becomes more independent, his allowance will go up, too. Of course, the younger one never thinks it's fair and the older one never thinks he has enough, but I always tell them they can trade us in for new parents as soon as they save enough money. So far, we're safe!

Budget

Sit down with your children and help them to work out a budget for their pocket money. Explain that, if they spend it all every week, then they won't have anything saved in case they want to buy something special or go somewhere with friends.

3. Discuss Advertising

Because we are all subjected to advertising, it helps to talk about how the advertisers try to tempt you to part with your money for their goods. There is no point in attacking the advertisers, they are doing their job. What we need to do is instill a bit of realism and cynicism so that your children are not easily taken in by every new product that comes on the market.

One way to do this is to sit with your children and watch advertisements on the television. Point out that those toys zooming through space are being 'zoomed' by children's hands, which can't be seen on the screen. Children may think they look like more fun than they turn out to be. Also, point out the price subtly shown in the bottom corner of the screen, usually in small print. Discuss how much these things cost, what percentage of their pocket money it would take to buy them and whether they really want them or are being manipulated into wanting them because of the superb advertising spiel.

4. Teach Them Comparative Shopping

When children go shopping with you, either for groceries or for something they need or want, always try to do some comparison between prices and products. Then, when children are spending their own money on something, they will get into the habit of making sure they are getting the best deal. Take them to sales and show them why it is often best to wait to buy something until the price drops. That way, they save money which enables them to buy something else.

Look at the ads in the newspapers and magazines and point out the differences in prices for the same or similar objects. If you are shopping for a big family purchase like a car or refrigerator, include your children in your deliberations. Ask what they would do if it was their money.

If you are having some decorating done and receive two or three different quotes for the same job, use this as an opportunity to explain why you finally decide to go with one firm instead of another, or whether you decide to do the job yourself, if you can. There will be times when you do not choose the cheapest option because you don't think the quality is good, and children need to know that, as well.

Another way to educate them is to go to markets, where it is usually possible to bargain. Initially, this tends to embarrass children. I remember taking my sons to Portobello Market and having them tug me away when I offered less money than the trader asked. 'Mum, give him the money,' hissed my youngest. 'Whose side are you on?' I hissed back. I guess I should have prepared them better before we went, but now they are old hands at bargaining and I think it's great.

5. Let Them Have Their Own Savings Account

As soon as your child has saved a little money, or perhaps gets some birthday or holiday money from relatives, consider opening up a savings account. When they are about seven, they can sign for some accounts themselves, which is a big thrill for children. When they turn thirteen they can open up an account with a cash card, which also gives them practise in managing their money.

It might be an idea initially to include a small amount in their pocket money which you agree they will save, just to get them into the habit. When they are older, you may want to put their pocket money into their account and let them try to manage their own finances for a month. It is a safe way to learn before they are turned loose in the big wide world. It may save them from getting into debt – a trap many young people fall into when they leave school or try to manage on a grant while completing higher education. Beware penalising them for doing well, however. One sixteen-year-old boy managed to save more than he ever had when he was given full control of his money. His parents then decided that he could live on less and cut his monthly allowance. The lesson they were teaching him was spend, spend, spend or you'll be sorry! If kids do manage to save some extra, for heaven's sake don't take it away. Give them a bonus!

6. Encourage Part-time Jobs

Doing a part-time job is an excellent way to enable kids to become more self-confident and to learn first-hand about discipline, business and finance in the real world. You do a job, you get paid and you feel good about yourself. You can also spend and save more, and eventually buy things you need or want.

My sister and I opened up a lemonade stand on the corner outside our house one summer when we were about six and seven years old. We squeezed the lemons, added sugar and water and sold the concoction for a penny. We made a fortune and immediately spent it on comics. The next day we were ready to do it again, when my grandmother informed us that if this was to be a regular business then we needed to buy our lemons and sugar. What a rude awakening – until then we hadn't realised that business incurred expenses. Most likely now our little stand would be closed down for not following some bureaucratic ruling!

My first job was as a waitress when I was sixteen. I remember going for the interview and the thrill of being hired. Getting there on time, being neatly dressed, getting my first meagre pay packet – it was wonderful. Even spilling a whole glass of water on my first customer, which reduced me to tears, had its rewards – he left me a tip because he felt so sorry for me! I have always been grateful that my father encouraged me to work part-time, because it gave me a solid sense about money and also convinced me that continuing my education was the best option for me.

Caution

There are opportunities for kids to get part-time jobs babysitting, delivering papers, washing cars, mowing lawns or weeding, but there are two notes of caution. The first is to make sure it doesn't interfere with their school work and cut off future education options. The second is to thoroughly check out the situation. Don't, for example, allow your child to go for an interview with a private individual you don't know, or to a strange place. One thirteen-year-old girl saw a card in a newsagent's advertising for a babysitter. There was no number to ring – the instructions were for her to leave her number with the newsagent and the person would ring her. The 'father' rang, arranged to meet her at what turned out to be a deserted house, and then sexually assaulted her. If someone wants your child to do any kind of work, they should never object to meeting with you. You should insist on it.

Let Them Handle It

Finally, if your children do get jobs, give as much advice as is needed and then let them handle it. If they don't show up on time or fail to do what is asked, then they may lose the job. If that happens, it will teach them about the responsibility of keeping a job and what it takes to get along in the world of work. Help them learn from the experience and try again. This, I know, from unfortunate first-hand experience.

That wonderful first job I had as a waitress ended abruptly. Six weeks after I was hired, I left some money on the till, intending to ring it up after I cleared the table. When the supervisor saw it, I was summoned and dismissed for not following the rules. I was crushed. I eventually landed another waitressing job which I kept for two years, so I guess I learned my lesson.

7. Explain Credit

Explain to children what it means to buy something on credit. If you have a mortgage, explain about the monthly payments and how long it takes for the house or flat to belong to you. (Forever is the right answer, I think.) You might show them a statement from a credit card, and explain that if the balance is not paid off on time then interest charges are incurred.

One of our sons wanted to buy a particular CD player and had saved quite a bit towards it. One afternoon he saw the CD in a sale at a considerable saving, but he still did not have enough. We agreed to lend him the money if he paid it back to us (interest free, aren't we nice?) on a monthly basis. The first two months were fine, but on the third, he begged off saying he had 'heavy expenses'. We postponed the payment, but the next month the excuse was the same. This time we said absolutely not, and made him come up with the money. I felt like an ogre, but there was no other way to get him to realise that he had committed himself and we had trusted him. He paid it off, grumbling but wiser. We told him the banks and credit card companies would never be so kind!

8. Be Realistic

Having said all this, there may be times when you either have to come to your child's rescue and give a little extra money, or negotiate a new deal. One Saturday, all of my eldest son's friends decided to go to the cinema because they had all recently turned twelve and there was a '12' rated film they could finally all see together. Although he had the money for getting into the cinema, he didn't have enough for popcorn and a drink. I really didn't think it was an unreasonable request, so he got his popcorn.

There may be something your children find while on a school journey or on holiday that is not budgeted for, and they ask you to buy it. Or they find they cannot manage on the money they are being given and/or are earning, and are really struggling. After going through their budgets with them, you may agree and help them out. If it happens every week, you'd better look into what's going wrong. But, on an occasional basis, I think it's absolutely fine to save them – after all, we are parents first (and loan sharks second!).

8

TEACHING CHILDREN TO DO CHORES WITHOUT TEARS

If there is one thing which seems certain to cause families to fight, it is getting children to do work around the house. Not only do children resist, body and soul, to avoid moving one dish from the table to the sink, parents fight with each other because they disagree on what, how many, how often, and when chores should be done. I remember vividly a fight with my sister about washing the dishes and setting the table. My father always said we could have done the work and walked to China and back in the time we were arguing. 'It *is* your turn, I did it yesterday.' 'No, you didn't.' 'Yes, I did.' 'Didn't!!' 'DID!!!!' As the noise and indignation rose, one or the other parent would fly into the kitchen and demand that we got on with it 'or else'. Usually that did it. We were never quite sure what 'or else' meant, but neither of us was prepared to be the first to find out.

I suspect it is even harder today for parents than it was when I was growing up as, most of the time, both parents or a single parent work outside the home. Help from the children becomes vital if the household is to run with any semblance of order.

So what are the tricks to get children to share in the work at home without having to resort to threats and murder? Try some of the following and see what happens:

1. Let Them Do It

Children will always allow you to do their work for them. Wouldn't we all if we could get away with it? There is very little which is intrinsically rewarding about taking out the garbage or washing dishes, so it isn't surprising that they quickly figure out how to get out of things. Look on the bright side, it means they are clever.

A favourite ploy of children is to do the chore slowly or badly so that we become frustrated and step in. I once bit my tongue and dug my fingernails into my hand to stop myself leaping in and making my son's bed. It had taken him forty-five minutes to put on the sheets and the duvet. Must be a world record.

Sometimes, your child really is trying to get it right and needs lots of encouragement from you. Say how pleased you are they stuck with the task and got it done. Offer suggestions or minimal help if they are just learning. Tell them they are doing a good job and that it sometimes takes a while to learn to do something new.

If you jump in and do the chore for the child, she or he will quickly learn the skill of 'getting mum or dad to do it'. Yes, it is easier to do it yourself, but in the long run your children will learn how to be responsible if you let them get on with it, no matter how long it takes. Be sure that you haven't asked them to do something that is impossible for their age and maturity. I was horrified when a friend of mine complained that her nine-year-old was so irresponsible because the child had run a bath for his sister and the water was too hot. Oh no – that kind of responsibility belongs with the parent, not with the child.

2. Don't Expect Them to Enjoy It!

Children will not be thrilled that they have to do chores. Don't expect them to whistle while they work and be cheerful because they are being allowed to help. When my sons were about two or three, they loved helping Mummy. Now that they are teenagers, help seems to be a four-letter word. So, ignore them if they are glum, but do insist that they get on with it anyway.

You might try saying, 'What do you think I'm going to say?' instead of 'This is the tenth time I've asked you to clean your room?' or 'What should you be doing now?' Keep your voice calm and just keep repeating your request or question.

Having agreed with them earlier that they are not to do anything else until they finish the chore, turn off the television, if your child has diverted to it. Or give him or her notice that they can hang up the telephone in one minute, if that's what's preventing the chore getting done. If after the warning they don't hang up, do it for them. Ignore their howls of protest. It will give them something to talk with their friends about – being a misunderstood teenager.

When they finally do the chore, give them lots of praise and point out that next time they could do it in half the time, if time is important to them. Be sure to notice and comment whenever they do act responsibly – praise works wonders for all of us.

3. Organising the Chores Beforehand

It helps if there is a list of chores which need to be done and children are allowed to choose in turn which they prefer. You can alternate who goes first every week. It also helps if you can estimate the time, so that children get equal measure as far as possible. It may seem a pain to do at first, but it does work. The following is a list we worked out, which might serve as an example:

TO DO LIST	TIME	WHO WILL DO WHEN
Set the table	5 mins	_____
Clear the table	5 mins	_____
Sweep the floor	5 mins	_____
Clean the toilet	5 mins	_____
Vacuum sitting-room	10 mins	_____
Vacuum hall	10 mins	_____
Clean balcony	10 mins	_____
Dust sitting-room	10 mins	_____
Mop bathroom floor	10 mins	_____
Shake out rugs	10 mins	_____
Water plants	10 mins	_____

TO DO LIST	TIME	WHO WILL DO WHEN
Rake leaves	15 mins	_____
Sweep path/pavement	15 mins	_____
Wash the dishes	20 mins	_____
Dry/put the dishes away	20 mins	_____
Make cake	20 mins	_____
Make packed lunches	20 mins	_____
Prepare dinner	30 mins	_____
Do one load laundry	30 mins	_____

Notice that ironing and tidying-up bedrooms are not included on the list, because these are personal chores, not chores for the entire household. Obviously the list of chores has to be adapted for your own family and for the ages of your children and the 'breakability' of your dishes. With the list above, your child might be doing between an hour and two hours housework a week, but you will need to take into account the amount of homework demanded of your children and that they do need time to relax and enjoy being children. The idea is not to turn your house from a battlefield into a labour camp, but to eliminate the 'it's not fair' or 'I did it last time' argument.

If you have a pet that the children begged you for and promised to help with (promises, promises), then devise a separate list. In our house, one boy is responsible for walking the dog each day after school, and it is recorded. They swap, as long as someone walks him. The real hassle is getting them to clean up the mess, but we have gloves and bags specially designed for the purpose.

4. Show Them How to Do The Task

Children are not born with the ability to know how to do chores, more's the pity. We have to show them how to get things done in the easiest and most efficient way. If they then go on to do it in their own way, fine, as long as it gets done to a certain standard. When I was showing my six-year-old how to wash dishes, I:

a) Made sure my 'good' dishes were not being used. There was no sense setting up an impossible situation where I would explode as my dishes did the same on the floor. Actually, my son was an excellent dishwasher, but seems to have completely lost the skill now that he is a teenager. Strange!

b) Helped him to get out the detergent and put a *small* amount into the sink with warm water. I also explained that we use washing-up liquid, not the soap powder designed for clothes. My poor father once came home and found that my sister and I had very helpfully waxed his car. No one had pointed out to us that floor wax was only for floors. As far as we were concerned, wax was wax. Not so, I'm afraid. The car had to be refinished and we learned the hard way that there were different substances for different jobs. Luckily, my father had a sense of humour and we survived to tell the tale.

c) Gave him the washing-up cloth, and a stool to stand on. I showed him how to wash the first plate and then let him get on with it. As he progressed, I explained that we wash the glasses and cups first, then the plates, etc. Families do it their own way, but that's what happens in our household. We also rinse all the dishes, which he learned to do. All in all it was a great success, and he was quite proud of his achievement.

Most chores will need to be demonstrated and explained. Remember: patience is a virtue.

5. Motivate Them to Work

Now comes the crunch. They've chosen their chores, learned how to do them, you have the expectation level about right and you are willing to let them get on with it. And you wait ... and wait ...

Help them get into the mood by asking what they are going to do first. 'Which task do you want to get out of the way first?' is a good question to kick off. It usually helps if you can be doing something in the same room. Children sometimes like the company, and chatting together makes the time go faster. 'You can get started on the dishes while I clean the front of the cupboard' might work, or

'Let's listen to the radio or a tape while we're working.'

You can also link the chore to something they want to do: 'We'll go swimming as soon as you finish clearing the table,' or 'I'll get out the storybook so I can read it to you as soon as you sweep the floor.' You can also say, as I do now with my sons, 'You can go out with your friends as soon as you wash the dishes.' Getting away is a big motivator at times! 'No television until you water the plants,' or 'You can watch for an extra half hour if you water the plants now,' are ways to motivate the procrastinating kid. Bribery also works (see Chapter 23, p 219, Ways to Bribe Your Child). The problem there is that you might run out of bribes, or patience, or both after a while.

Another idea is to set up a chart and offer points to those who finish their chores. Points can lead to a special treat, like staying up later or being allowed to go for an ice-cream. If your children are young enough, one way that motivates them is to play 'Beat the Clock' – set the timer and see who can get their chore done first, but the job *has* to be done properly.

6. Don't Spring Chores on the Children

Most people appreciate knowing what they are going to have to do at work during the day. We might be aware that certain chores need doing, and expect our children to remember that if it is Tuesday they should be setting the table. OK, we've set up the chart, but it helps if we remind the children of the chore they are doing that day, perhaps at breakfast, so that by the time they get home to do it they are mentally prepared. There will be times, though, when everyone just has to pitch in and help, regardless of the chart and your best intentions. So, prepare your children for that eventuality with reminders that, sometimes, unexpected visitors arrive or an emergency occurs and it's 'All hands on deck'. Plans go flying out the window and you will count on them to help.

Whatever happens, remember to continue to give praise even though you expect their help. Children, like all living creatures, love to be recognised for the good they do.

7. Allow Them to Exchange Chores

If your children sign up for or agree to do a task, but arrange an exchange between them, that's great. If the exchange works to everyone's satisfaction, then you don't have to get involved. But sometimes an older child takes advantage of a younger one and tries it on. Intervene if there is a dispute which is obviously unfair – you can undo deals (see Chapter 1, p. 8 about fighting) and that, too, is a learning experience.

You can also exchange chores with your child. Peggy, mother of six, hates to vacuum. Her son doesn't mind because he does it while listening to his personal stereo. He hates tidying up his room, so they have an agreement to swap. The only fly in the ointment is that Peggy's husband has a thing about kids cleaning up their rooms and thinks Peggy is molly-coddling their son. Personally, I think the father is wrong, but I leave that to Peggy to sort out. She can handle it, believe me.

Please note one special time when no one should have to do chores: on birthdays – and this includes parents!

8. Agree Consequences for Not Doing Chores

You may not need this step, but if your children are not doing the chores in spite of your best efforts, gather the clan together and decide on consequences. Then, no one will be surprised when they end up having to pay for their lack of action.

Tony and Gill and their children have worked out the following consequences if someone doesn't complete chores:

a) Someone else does the chore and the culprit (for want of a better word) must pay back the time spent by doing an equivalent task, which the person who has done the chore can choose. The person can also choose when and where the task is done and the culprit has no choice in the matter. It can't be something horrible and nasty – it has to be another chore, not an invented, slave-labour job.

b) The culprit loses privileges, such as going out or watching a programme, for the equivalent amount of time, plus penalty time (say an extra 30 minutes).

c) The culprit gets up an hour early and does the chore. My sons have had to do this to complete homework they 'forgot' until bedtime. It's a great ploy to say that you can't go to bed, having read, played a game and watched television, because you suddenly remembered your maths isn't finished. Nice try!

You will most likely be able to come up with consequences of your own, but it does help if everyone knows that there are penalties, and they will be enforced.

9. Label Your Children as Good Workers

Brag about how helpful your children are, and make sure they hear you. I know it goes against the grain of some people to brag about their kids, but do it anyway. Too often we say things like, 'Justine is the messiest kid I know – her room is a pigsty.' It may be true, but it is also true that Justine is getting the message that she is messy and may even start saying, 'I'm just messy.' It all becomes a self-fulfilling prophecy and Justine becomes 'the messy one'.

On the other hand, if Justine hears her parents complimenting her neatness and her helpfulness, that is a much better label. 'I'm helpful and neat' is a good message, not a negative one. If Justine's parents also say that her work was good or that she really tried hard, that will reinforce the idea that Justine is a good worker. It wouldn't hurt to ask Justine to tell you how she thinks her work is, so she starts to develop her own sense of pride.

The only note of caution here is not to turn your child into a perfectionist by demanding military-style standards. Not only is it unrealistic, but some studies have shown a link between eating disorders and *extreme* perfectionism. This doesn't apply to most of our children, even if they like to keep their things very tidy, but beware of overdoing the 'perfect worker' bit. Stick with 'you really stuck to that job', 'good', 'well done', 'great effort' and 'nice try' type comments.

10. Withdraw Your Labour!

If you have tried everything and the children still don't follow through, try withdrawing your labour. If one of your responsibilities is to drive the children to football or some other activity they enjoy, but they haven't completed their chores, go on strike. If you are supposed to make dinner and no one sets the table, make yourself a cheese sandwich and retire to read or watch television. When people complain they are hungry or that 'You have to drive me to football right now', say sorry, but why should you be the only one fulfilling your responsibilities when you haven't got any co-operation? Better yet, ask your children if they have any idea about why you are doing this. Then ask them if they have a solution. It is amazing how the shock of it all can bring about a new attitude towards chores.

If it gives you any hope, I have been told by many friends with grown children how neat and tidy their children became when they got their own place. But you can't set up your ten-year-old in a flat, so we just have to keep working at getting them to be good workers. When I was growing up, my sister was incredibly messy, while I was very neat, and we shared a room. She drove me nuts when clothes, both clean and dirty, tumbled out every time I opened anything. Her half of the room was horrible. As I mentioned earlier, one day while she was out, I drew a white chalk mark down the centre of the room and thereafter refused to let her into my half. I was a real creep about it, and she became messier and messier. But there is justice – my sister, now a solicitor, turned out to be quite house-proud, but her children drive her crazy. She rang me to complain that, 'They are so messy I can't even get into their rooms.' Who says there isn't a God?

9

WATCH WHAT THEY'RE WATCHING

Videos and Television

It's the year 2084 and Douglas Quaid (Arnold Schwarzenegger) is escaping from the henchmen of a treacherous tyrant. As Quaid runs up an escalator, shoving and pushing bystanders out of the way, the enemy opens fire, killing an innocent man. Quaid grabs the man's body, using it as a shield. The man's body is shot several times more, in close-up gory detail, then is discarded as the fight goes on, people diving for cover as automatic weapons rip in every direction.

No-one spares a thought for the human shield. He was disposable and unimportant to the plot of *Total Recall* (classification 18). Definitely not my kind of film. So why did I watch it?

In fact, my twelve-year-old son borrowed it from a friend, also aged twelve. The friend got it from his local video shop with the help of his older brother.

Until then, I'd thought I had the video and television business licked. The rule in our house is supervised viewing after nine o'clock on the television, and no 18-rated videos. Any other videos are judged on their merits. But I'd forgotten about what happens when children get together. I'd managed to catch *Total Recall* and felt I could at least influence my son's reaction to it. I knew, though, that he'd be exposed to others at overnight stays and birthday party 'treats'. I spoke to my son and he just said: 'Don't take a hyper-spaz, Mum. It's no big deal. Anyway, it's just like watching a film on television.'

Wrong! At least with television viewing I felt fairly safe if the kids were watching before the nine o'clock watershed, which is supposed to ensure that nothing untoward is shown that will harm children. But with a video there is no 'safe' time. They can get a copy of a film you consider totally inappropriate and watch it over and over.

Are Violence and Sex Scenes Harmful?

Should we accept that our kids will see violent videos and ones with degrading sex scenes sooner or later? Should we save our 'hyper-spaz' for something we can really hope to cut out?

As usual, the experts are divided. One recent study said that children were not affected by violence shown on video or TV, especially if it was in fantasy or cartoon style. (Personally, I think there's a world of difference between a flattened cartoon tomcat which is easy to accept as fantasy, and the realistic portrayal of people being violently murdered.)

Another study showed that children *are* affected by what they watch, and their behaviour *does* become more violent. This is countered by another study which suggests that it's not the content of the video that matters, but the amount of movement and action. Their conclusion is that children become just as aggressive watching a fast-moving football match as they do when seeing a violent, 18-rated, blood-and-guts film.

I dislike, and shield my children from unnecessary and graphic violence. I don't mind my children seeing loving and appropriate sex scenes (depending upon the ages of the children) but I will not allow anything that portrays sex in a degrading fashion.

The Evidence

Are children affected by television and video viewing? Well, in Tyne and Wear, the real experts – the children themselves – conducted their own survey. Pupils at Astley High School looked at the power of TV and videos. They asked a group of eleven and twelve-year-olds which specified media influenced them the most. The results would not surprise parents, though it might surprise the researchers.

- **What influences you most?**

Videos	63%
TV	37%
Magazines, cinema, books	0%

- **Would you switch off a programme because of:**

Boredom	93%
Violence	0%
Don't know	7%

- **Do you watch videos supposed to be for older people?**

Yes	90%
No	10%

The pupils went on to question some eight and nine-year-olds and found that the majority said that they had seen videos such as *A Nightmare On Elm Street* (18). A small minority had seen sexually explicit videos.

It's clear from this that many children *do* have access to videos which most parents would prefer they did not see. It's also clear that young children are seeing quite violent and sexually explicit videos, if not at home, then at the homes of their friends – and they're not switching off unless they find them boring.

The most telling statement of all is that children themselves say that videos influence them more than TV, books or any other media. My common sense tells me that they will be influenced by good *or* bad videos, because children learn from what they see and hear. (Anyone who has ever sworn in front of their young child, and then had the embarrassment of hearing him repeat it in the middle of a crowded supermarket, will agree that children *do* pick up on adult behaviour!)

It seems clear to me that, whatever the experts say, we live in the video age and need to make decisions *now* about what our kids might be watching tonight.

In spite of legal safeguards which have cleaned up videos since the early days, the message of many, readily available films is that violence, physical and sexual, is all right. The way to solve problems is to torture someone and then 'blow them away'. If the job is done in as bloody and violent a way as possible, so much the better. These messages can be especially influential in homes where such issues are rarely talked about.

Careful parents can have trouble, too. Eight-year-old Colette began having persistent nightmares, waking up sobbing in terror. Her mother couldn't work out what was wrong at first. Gentle questioning revealed that Colette and a friend had watched *A Nightmare On Elm Street*, hired for the friend's older brother's birthday party. Colette's mother was shocked and upset – she had been so careful about what her children watched and had even restricted TV to an hour a day. She had heard horror stories about children seeing harmful videos but, like me, she never expected it to happen to *her* kids.

What Should We Do?

Sixty per cent of homes in Britain now have video recorders, so it is becoming almost impossible to ensure your children never see inappropriate films.

One young mother was shocked when she arrived early to collect her three-year-old from the childminder's and walked in to find the children watching *The Punisher* (18).

Horrified, she watched for a few minutes and counted twenty-four violent and bloody deaths, including a mother and two young children being blown up in a car. The childminder said they were 'too young to be bothered by it'.

If You Want to Protect Your Children

1. Tell People

Ensure that whoever is minding your children does not show them videos you do not approve of. Say something like: 'Jenny has terrible nightmares and I don't want her to see these videos.'

2. Use Reputable Shops

Deal only with reputable video shops that cater for a family audience. They should be members of the Video Standards Council and/or the British Video Association, both of which promote a Code of Practice along with the British Board of Film Classification to protect young people. (See the Video Classification Guide at the end of this chapter, p. 99.)

Age
Make sure that your video shop knows the ages of your children and will not give them videos for an older age group. If they do, the shops are breaking the law. Our local shop, a member of the Video Standards Council, records children's birth dates.

Sexual Violence
Ask your local video shop not to stock videos which are sexually violent or degrading. If they won't co-operate, then ask for these to be on the top shelves, or in another room, or for the cover pictures to be removed so that only the titles show.

3. Check What They Are Watching Elsewhere

Check what your older children are watching at their friends' houses. Make sure your older child is not 'treating' your younger children to inappropriate videos.

4. Talk to Other Parents

If you can, agree with other parents not to hire certain videos. This eliminates the 'everyone does it' argument.

5. Make a Decision and Stick to It

Ensure that you and your husband/partner agree that the children shouldn't see certain types of videos and stick to your agreement, even if the kids argue like mad. Your decision is what counts; never mind about another kid's parents or if you disagree with the classification rating.

6. Explain Your Reasoning to Your Child

Talk to your children about why you dislike these and other videos you object to. Explain that sex should not be degrading or violent and that you object to the images and the way people are shown being particularly nasty to each other. Explain why you dislike violence or bad language and how you think it affects people.

7. Tell Them It's Fiction

If they have seen a bad video or late-night television fictional programme that you object to, explain that it isn't real life – that is not how people should behave towards each other. You can also tell them that the people in it were only acting, if they are upset by what they saw and are having nightmares or other reactions.

8. Help Them Avoid Peer Pressure

Help your children decide what to do and say if they are at a friend's house where a shocking video is shown. If they feel very brave, they can walk out of the room and say why. If they can't do that, they can pretend to be ill, go to the loo, say they're bored or sleepy.

9. Have a Code

Work out a code, so that your child can ring you if they wish to get out of a situation. One child I know rings and asks: 'Has Aunt Jill arrived yet?' This is her parents' cue to ring back in a few minutes to say a relative has arrived and they need to collect her.

10. Watch the Video Beforehand

Try to watch videos, especially before younger children see them. Some parents think 'PG' means 'nice for children to watch with their parents'. It doesn't! (See the Video Classification Guide, p. 99.)

11. Don't Be Afraid to Turn It Off

If the door is closed and there is a lot of giggling or too much silence, drop in on the kids and offer them popcorn – anything actually, as it's only an excuse. Never underestimate the power of surprise as a parent. If the video is unsuitable, stop the show and explain why. They know why, but it doesn't hurt to tell them again.

12. Use Caution

Ensure that you don't leave any videos around that you don't want them to see. Children like nothing better than to sample forbidden fruit. Don't we all?

When I was growing up we had a player piano. My father made a point of telling us that some of the rolls were not meant for children. What did my sister and I do the minute my parents left the house? You guessed it, we found the piano rolls and played them. I think one was called 'Lulu', about a rather loose woman who was the life of every party. Another was 'Refrigerator MaMa' with words to the effect that PaPa was going to make her hot. We didn't understand it all, but we thought it was great! We gathered all our friends together, sang the words with gusto and pretended to know exactly what we were singing about. How innocent it all seems now.

I can't imagine that I will ever look back on some of the violent videos and think how innocent they were. Maybe I'm wrong, but I feel that some of these videos, with their explicit images and messages, are and will remain totally unacceptable for children.

Decisions, Decisions

Of course, sometimes you don't mind your child seeing certain television programmes or videos. You may disagree with the rating or the time it is being screened or be just too tired to argue. At home, in spite of our 'no 18s' rule, I wanted my children to see *Mississippi Burning* (18) because it was based on a true-life incident and dealt with racial prejudice. We watched it together, discussed what happened and learned how harmful and stupid prejudice is.

Another time, I made the mistake of letting my young son, then five, see *Jaws* (PG on video) on TV. He was terrified and I spent ensuing days explaining about special effects and how they built the shark, and anything else I could think of to assuage his fear and my guilt. Although that was years ago, he still tells me it's my fault he doesn't like horror films because I let him see *Jaws*. One of my many mistakes as a parent, I'm afraid.

The Positive Effects of Television and Videos

In spite of the dire warnings and the bad effect that television and videos can have, I think we have to remember that it can be a brilliant way to open up new possibilities for children. Think of all the wonderful and creative things that children learn from programmes such as *Blue Peter* or *Tomorrow's World*. My children know so much about the world from documentaries and the news, and they ask searching questions about important issues such as ecology, poverty, wars, etc., that have come from their exposure to television. It wouldn't be fair to leave out the good points, so here are some ways we can help television and videos benefit our children:

1. Pick Out the Best

There are so many interesting and, dare I say it, educational programmes on the television that it is worth going through the week's offerings and marking the best. It is also worth getting out a good video if it portrays something that you feel is important for your children to see. My feeling is that we should use the television as a friend and mentor, or we should get rid of it entirely. I think it is fairly unrealistic to expect our children to live in a television-free environment, so I've opted to make the best of it.

2. Allow Some Junk

Have I gone mad? No, there are some programmes which I think are a waste of time, but are not particularly harmful. They are just rather mindless, in my adult opinion. But all the other children watch them and not letting my children see them would deprive them of a 'social tool'.

Also, I think everyone needs to vegetate occasionally, and it won't kill them to watch one or two 'mindless' things a week. The other reason, I rationalise, is that if you make everything off limits then the forbidden fruit syndrome sets in, and the programme becomes an icon. Cop out? Maybe, but we all have our foibles.

3. Use Television to Inspire

When I was a child I was taken to see *Peter and the Wolf*, which inspired me to learn to play musical instruments. I only ever saw it once. My children have been lucky enough to see *Peter and the Wolf* in the theatre, and on television and video. They both play instruments – yes, through example, but also through the inspiration of the television.

Television can also inspire good deeds. The plight of starving children or earthquake victims or refugees brought into our home on the 'box' has inspired some quite selfless acts, and made my children more sensitive to the needs of others. I only heard about children in need when I was a child; they *see* the children, and the picture in this case really is worth a thousand words.

4. Tie the Programmes to Books and Activities

Little House on the Prairie was one of my favourite books as a child, along with *20,000 Leagues Under the Sea* and *The Time Machine*. If kids are going to watch programmes, then give them the books first and reinforce the book with the video or television programme.

Follow-up a programme on space or electricity or the human body with a visit to a local science museum. Or use a programme about history to spark off a visit to an exhibition of artefacts from that period. For example, a programme about finding the tomb of Tutenkhamun combined with a visit to see an Egyptian mummy can fire a child's imagination for life.

5. Create a Fun Atmosphere

If you are going to use the television and videos for 'family times', then make it an occasion. Get an especially good video or choose a programme, order a pizza or pop some popcorn, turn off the lights and have an evening together. It really is great fun.

The Value of Books

Whatever we do, we won't always get it right. Parents never do. But at least we can keep learning, and I've learned something extremely important from the Tyne and Wear survey. When the eight-year-olds were questioned, it was found that not a single one had a parent who read to them.

Yes, it's true most of them can read quite well on their own by that age. But sitting close to someone and reading with them or to them from the same book, beats everything else for a cosy time – even the family television evening. It can also lead straight into important discussions about life, death, love, brutality, tenderness, the universe and everything. It would be tragic if the video age robbed us of this way of conveying our values to our kids. And think of the electricity we'd save!

Video Classification Guide

Uc Universal. Particularly suitable for children – probably made just for them.
U Universal. Nothing unsuitable for children. The whole family might well enjoy it.
PG Parental Guidance. For general viewing, but some scenes may be unsuitable for young children. Parents should check it first. If it's an action film, it might have some violence. If it's romantic, it might have some sexy scenes and very brief nudity. Also may contain 'mild' swear-words.
12 Suitable for persons of twelve years and over. There may be stronger moments of violence or references to teenage experiences, but nothing gratuitous. There may also be swear-words that you wouldn't hear in a PG video.
15 Suitable only for persons of fifteen years and over. Not to be supplied to any person below that age. There may be a fairly adult theme, or scenes of sex, violence or drugs which, while not particularly graphic, are unsuitable for younger teenagers. There may also be some sexual swear-words.
18 Suitable only for persons of eighteen years and over. Not to be supplied to any person below that age. It might contain vivid scenes of sex or violence, explicit language, and very explicit language which will frequently mean sexual swear-words.

The Video Recordings Act 1984 outlaws the most obscene and sexually violent videos; requires other material to be classified; makes it illegal to supply an age-rated video to a child under that age (regardless of what the child says, or even if he had legitimately been sent for the video 'by my Dad/Mum'); makes supplying unclassified material (unless informative, educational or instructive, or concerned with sport, religion or music, or which constitutes a video game) illegal.

If you believe a video shop is acting illegally, contact the Trading Standards Office at your Local Authority, or the Video Standards Council.

Additional Guidance

Many video sleeves now contain additional information which can help you decide about 12, 15 and 18 videos and their suitability for your children. This is in the form of a box which has comments in more detail about the video. An example might look like:

Theme/Content: *Drugs, Gangs, Political Corruption*
Language: *Very Frequent, Coarse*
Sex/Nudity: *Occasional, Strong*
Violence: *Strong, Sexual Assault*

I think I'll pass on this video, thank you!

The initiative to give this additional information came from the video industry, which has also put out a very helpful leaflet for parents, entitled 'Mum, Can I Watch A Video?' Copies can be obtained through KIDSCAPE, address at the front of this book.

10

WHAT ABOUT THOSE BLASTED COMPUTER GAMES?

Does it worry you that when it's a glorious sunny day outside, your child is glued to his computer game indoors?

Does this sound familiar: 'Mother to son: Over.' Silence. 'Come in Son: Over.' Silence. That's more or less the extent of conversations in our house these days. For there are aliens in my home – small, spaced-out creatures sitting with hunched shoulders, hands fused to small square boxes of controls, eyes glued to a fast-moving homicidal maniac on a screen.

That's the bad news. The good news is that these aliens make few demands and almost no mess. They've learned enough English to say 'I'm hungry', they can shout 'Nooooo!' or 'Yesssss!' according to the antics of their maniac, and '*Pleeease* don't turn it off!' when the object of their obsession is threatened with disconnection. Yes, I allow my children to play computer games. You may as well know this from the start. I swore it would never come to this, but I have succumbed to the inevitable. I may as well confess the rest, too – both of my children have also had a go at Virtual Reality.

Virtual What?

If you saw *Lawnmower Man*, or *Terminator 2*, or watched some television game shows like *Cyberzone*, you will know what Virtual

Reality (VR) is in principle. It gives the illusion of being inside and part of a life-size computer game (see Virtual Reality Explained later in this chapter, p. 110).

But to experience VR properly, you have to go to an amusement arcade which features this new technology. It's fairly expensive, and if you are lucky, there won't be one near you. That said, I am sure there must have been a similar reaction to the introduction of electricity, telephones, radio and television, and would you want to be without any of those? And I'm conscious of family history repeating itself – I remember my grandmother lamenting the fact that I refused to go out to play when *The Lone Ranger* came on TV. 'Your brain will turn to mush,' she prophesied (correctly, some will say).

It's Unreal

I guess though that, like me, many parents feel uneasy about computer games and VR. Aren't they removing kids too far from the real world? Well, watching television and talking on the telephone to distant countries, or to an answering machine, has already removed all of us from everyday reality known in previous centuries. On a very rushed day, I deliberately try to time my telephone calls so I can talk to other people's answering machines, thereby avoiding lengthy person-to-person conversations.

So, before we condemn computer games out of hand, let's try to acknowledge their good points:

a) There's no mess when children are playing with them – they aren't dropping paint or Plasticine on the carpet.

b) They are relatively quiet – only a few grunts and shouts and occasional unprintable phrases punctuate the air, interspersed with sighs of despair.

c) Studies claim computer games improve hand to eye coordination as well as stimulate a child's imagination and creativity. They are also claimed to develop their powers of logic, memory, problem-solving and intuitive skills, and get a child used to being challenged.

It's a pretty impressive list, isn't it? But, personally, I suspect that these studies were paid for by computer game manufacturers. I do have to add another bonus point to the list, however – playing these games helps research skills. My children carefully researched several studies to convince me of the games' benefits!

And here are the good points to acknowledge about Virtual Reality:

a) VR, say its supporters, makes us all active participants in technology, unlike television which is passive.

b) The technology is being used to advance knowledge. For instance, I'm glad it may soon be possible to dissect a frog without harming it (see Virtual Reality Explained, p 110). My biology teacher was a sadist who would come around the class to check on our progress with a dissection while munching on a tuna sandwich. 'Great frog-leg sandwich,' he used to joke. A man of sophisticated humour.

c) I'm also delighted that a VR game is being developed which will allow you to 'ski' while curled up on a sofa in your sitting room. No broken bones, no frozen fingers or kamikaze snowboarders . . . I could get into this. Last year I tried to learn how to ski down some real nursery slopes: no poles, bending my arms and body, repeating 'I am a bird'. As I slid, screaming, down the hill on my back, dressed in yellow, I did resemble a bird – a canary in its death throes.

So Why Worry?

To be honest, part of the reason I worry is because I don't understand the games. They are part of the new world of technology which children pick up with enormous speed and which, even when I try my hardest, I can only manage slowly.

I thought when we had children that they would grow up like my husband and me and that we could teach them the ways of the world. Hah! The other day I couldn't get the video recorder to work, so in despair I called for my youngest son. He fixed it in seconds – something he and his brother have been able to do almost from the time they could walk! In the old days you'd call for the man from the repair shop, not your child.

Let's face it, they're teaching *us* the ways of the world. Maybe our children really are aliens – super intelligent aliens sent to help us!

But there are serious concerns about computer and video games. The Professional Association of Teachers asked the government to investigate how the games influence children. Are children relating more to games than to other children? One *World In Action* television programme concluded that children who were addicted to playing the games showed more anti-social and aggressive behaviour towards others. Granted, this wasn't a 'scientific study'. But it seems to make sense that, if children have a steady diet of winning points for aggression in the games, then they will learn that being aggressive is OK.

Beware of Physical Harm to Your Child

As well as the preceding worries, don't forget that children might also suffer physical harm from the games. As parents, we need to be aware that there is a slight risk of epileptic seizures, even in children with no family history of the problem (see Precautionary Measures below). The number of cases is tiny compared with the overall number who play the games, but manufacturers have now added health warnings to labels. Japan has launched an investigation into reported cases of deaths induced by computer games.

What About Books?

One objection I have to the games is that they make it harder to get kids to read. When a child's mind is reeling from the fierce battle that has just taken place on the screen, it's hard to switch to the gentle activity of reading a book. But I *want* my kids to read and here's why:

a) Reading improves their vocabulary, spelling and grammar.
b) It expands their imagination.

c) It increases their knowledge of the world and allows them to experience things beyond their own lives.

d) It helps them to learn about other cultures and customs.

e) It increases their attention span, which in turn helps them to concentrate better on school work.

f) It gives them a chance to try out different situations in their head, to work out what they might do.

g) It gives them ideas to talk – and think – about. Good old-fashioned moral dilemmas, such as whether the hero should do a bad thing for a good reason.

h) Reading is not accompanied by annoying little beeping sounds.

i) It's a lot cheaper – I calculated that you could buy five or six books for the price of each game.

Take an Interest

A further problem for me is the way that computer game fights have no moral themes – no justice, and nothing to give us insight into ourselves. You just zap as many people as you can. The ethos is simply 'kill 'em and get to the next level'. My fear is it's possible that, in later life, some of these little aliens might become completely divorced from reality and zap other people just as they learned to zap their on-screen enemies.

The bottom line is, I think, that these games deliver self-absorption, but not self-enlightenment. If our children insist on playing them, it's up to us as parents to provide some sort of balance, by plugging away at them to read, to discuss, to think. And if we are worried about the continual zapping and killing, then we'd better sit down and talk about that with them.

Parents shouldn't pretend the games aren't there – we need to find out more about them:

1. Ask what happens in the games.
2. Sit down with your children and see them (the games, not the children) in action.
3. Discuss any violence and ask the children what they feel about

it. Ask if they think it might make children who play the games be violent towards real people.
4. Praise anything worth praising so you are not seen as totally anti-games.
5. Should you disapprove of a game, don't be afraid to show it.
6. Watch out that you don't get addicted yourself!

I talked with my kids about the violence, but they seemed to be quite clear that this was a silly, if fun, game and that of course they knew it wasn't real life. 'It's like the *Tom and Jerry* cartoons you said you liked as a kid,' exclaimed my youngest with a certain amount of pity and embarrassment that his mother could have liked *Tom and Jerry*.

But I do worry a lot about kids who play constantly without parental input or discussion. It seems to me that getting points for shooting, decapitating or knocking down opponents cannot be good for impressionable, growing minds.

I'm not forgetting how we all watched *Tom and Jerry* and *Road Runner* cartoons as children – talk about violence for the sake of it! Still, none of my friends has grown into Hannibal Lecter, so I try to keep my worries in perspective. And I'm not quite as concerned about video games which have graphics, like *Tom and Jerry* does, as I am about Virtual Reality, in which you appear to become the person doing the killing. My kids think I'm over-reacting, but I don't agree. The problem is that Virtual Reality seems to be *the* birthday party thing to do, and kids love it. That means either banning them from parties, which I won't do, or lots of discussion to get things into perspective, which I can and will do.

Precautionary Measures

Because of the danger of computer-related epileptic seizures, you should seek medical advice if your child is already subject to fits. Do this *before* allowing him or her to play these games. In any case, encourage your child to:

1. Take lots of breaks – never let them play for more than an hour at a time.

2. Sit as far away from the screen as possible. If you think your child may be at risk of a seizure, make sure he or she sits at least eight feet away and covers one eye with a patch – for a seizure to occur, the flickering on the screen needs to register in both eyes simultaneously.
3. Keep hand-held games at arm's length.
4. Ensure that the room lights are on – the less contrast between room and screen, the better. So be careful about children using hand-held games in a dark car.
5. Never play when unwell or tired.

Perfect Play

You may not always manage to impose all these tips, but do make sure you:

1. Negotiate

We had a real tussle when it came to negotiating how long and when my children could play. We finally agreed on weekends and non-school days – with a time limit.

2. Plot

There is a new device which allows the screen to be used for a limited period and you can programme it for each child. (Admittedly it won't help if your children know how to hack in and reprogramme the device!)

3. Confiscate

If necessary, take away some vital part of the game – and simply ignore their squeals of protest.

4. Advertise the Rules

If your children are left in someone else's care, ensure that the guidelines are known. You cannot monitor them when they are out of sight, but you can at least try to influence the adult in charge. Don't make it so unpleasant, however, that no one ever invites your child over to play.

5. Encourage Other Interests

Take your children skating or bike riding, or sign them up for a pottery class or music lessons. Sometimes children play these games for lack of anything else to do. (See Chapter 6, p. 53 – Boosting Your Child's Learning Power.)

Good Health

As well as the danger of computer-related seizures, parents need to be aware of the other health risks, whether using a TV, monitor or hand-held game. These include:

a) Eye strain.
b) Lack of exercise during endless hours of play which can affect body development, particularly leg and shoulder muscles.
c) Headaches and neckaches.
d) Teeth-grinding – this can often be caused by tension.
e) Constipation or even piles from sitting down for too long.

To be fair, a lot of these could affect children who don't play video games, so keep things in perspective. I know an overweight, anti-social pain in the neck whose mother never allows her to do anything that is pure fun.

Let's face it, some kids will be affected and others will play the games with no ill effects. Then again, maybe this is just my way of justifying my lack of character in submitting to my sons' pleadings for their computer games in the first place . . .

Warning Signs

There are a few things we should look out for, just in case we suspect our children are turning into couch-potato television or video game addicts. Get tough and turn it off if your child seems to be:

a) Unwilling to walk anywhere and wants to be driven in the car even the shortest distances.
b) Overweight or non-energetic, yet still consuming large amounts of sweets and crisps.
c) Bored all the time.
d) Uninterested in going out, cycling, skating or playing any kind of sports with friends.
e) Completely out of shape, unable to walk up stairs without pausing for breath or being winded.
f) Only interested in watching television or playing video games.

Parent Power

For most of us beleaguered parents, there has to be a middle ground. What we must ensure is that we and our children carry a sense of morality into the future. You see, it was worth my Gran uttering those solemn warnings about watching TV – look how I've remembered them to this day.

This *is* a computer age and there's nothing we can do to change that. But we can be aware of the dangers and make sure the kids don't turn out to have mushed brains or soggy muscles. (I wish *we* could blame computer games for our lack of exercise and blurry eyes!)

One last thought: video games may improve hand to eye co-ordination, but give me a book any day. Think of all that hand to eye page-turning co-ordination you get.

Virtual Reality Explained

It started as a military system for simulating combat. Now it's one of the buzzwords of the decade. In the long term Virtual Reality could revolutionise work, education and play.

VR is computer-generated pictures with sounds and sensations so authentic that they seem real. With VR games machines, players wear a helmet fitted with two tiny TV screens which give 3D vision. In more advanced games, they also wear gloves which give the illusion of tactile sensation – you see an object and can pick it up and move it as though it were real.

As computing power advances, it will be possible to give biology students, for example, classes in dissection without real specimens. And, with new fibre-optic cables, it may be possible to create an illusion of being in the same room as people on the other side of the globe.

Something Nasty on the Computer

Parents should be up-to-date with the Internet. Jay walked into his twelve-year-old son's room and found him engrossed in a 'very nasty pornographic image on his computer'. Jay pulled the plug. His son was actually relieved because he had gotten in over his head and didn't quite know how to extract himself.

Pornographic pictures in full colour: sadomasochism; women bound, gagged and being tortured; group sex; bondage; children having sex with animals – everything from bestiality to child porn is available. And much of it can be pulled up by our children, if they have access to the computer Internet.

'Surfing the Net' (looking at the various things that are available) has become a favourite occupation of children and young people. Of course you can click on to lots of wonderful information through the Internet – current news, the latest scores in sports matches, new book publications and even bird watching and beekeeping guides. But many parents are not aware that our children can also gain access to horrendous and degrading pornography, as well as put themselves at risk from paedophiles who 'surf the Net' to try to contact potential victims.

This isn't pie in the sky. In a recent case in the United States, two children were lured away from home by people they'd been corresponding with on the Internet and police are prosecuting individuals who have downloaded pornographic images of children. Children have also joined 'Chat Rooms' which are party lines that can have all kinds of participants from other children to paedophiles posing as innocent 'pen-pals' to get children's names, addresses, telephone numbers and photographs.

The good news is that you need to know certain codes or have a clued-up friend to access the pornography. The bad news is that many teenagers do know the codes and, having pulled up the material, can load it on to disks which can be used by younger children on their own computers, even if they are not connected to the Internet.

What's to Be Done?

We can't forbid our children to use computers – they are an essential tool. Children have to be computer-literate or they will not be able to cope in the world, but we have to protect them at the same time. Here are a few suggestions:

1. *Explain to your children that there are some things to beware of when using the Internet:*

   - *Remember that anyone can use the Net and pretend to be someone else. The person they think is another child or teenager may be a 'dirty old man' (or woman).*
   - *Never give their full name, address, telephone number or other personal details to someone down the line.*
   - *Never arrange to meet anyone without checking with you first.*
   - *Never send anyone a photo without checking with you first.*

2. *Find out about how to restrict access to these 'services'. There are some software packages which can block access. Check with computer stores and on line service providers about how to do this.*

3. *Put the computer in a room that everyone has access to, if possible.*
4. *Drop into the room if your children are using the computer and take an interest in what they are doing. Get them to explain to you how to use the Internet.*
5. *Monitor the amount of time your children are spending on line. If they are using lots of on line time, especially late at night, they may be in danger.*

We may not be able to shield children completely from the harmful bits of the Internet and its millions of channels. Children will experiment and forbidden fruit has a strong lure, but we need to be aware, to monitor and to talk with children so they can make good safe choices while 'surfing the Net'.

11

FAMILY MEALS

Ways to Survive When Eating Out

The family meal is losing out to TV, take-aways and teenage schedules. Why should we reinstate the tradition?

My husband had rung at four pm. 'Looks like I won't get away for ages. Go ahead with dinner without me.' When I got home from the office, my elder son Charles was rushing out, a sandwich in one hand and a drink in the other. 'Rehearsal night, Mum, see you later.' Exit.

'Well, it's you and me for dinner, dynamite,' I said hopefully to James. The look on his face informed me what was coming – a request to watch TV. So much for a family dinner.

Why did it worry me so much? What were we missing? My mind went back to my earliest meals, when our family was living at grandmother's. At once I could smell the aroma of her homemade stews or casseroles that simmered on the stove all day.

We children would eagerly hang around the kitchen, hoping for a taste. Six o'clock sharp we sat around the table to eat, often with friends or visiting relatives. Dinner-time was noisy, interesting, delicious and could go on for hours.

This meal was the focus of our day and we all vied with each other, children and adults alike, to tell the most interesting thing that had happened to us that day. At the centre of it all was Gran, dishing out the food, telling us not to talk with our mouths full and ensuring that this nightly ritual was more than a simple refuelling of stomachs. Dinner, and what happened around it, gave us a sense of belonging and it confirmed us as a family.

Why Family Meals Are Important

I began to look at my own family. Yes, we did do quite a bit together – weekend outings, holidays, that sort of thing – but we did not have the same sense of togetherness I remember from sharing those daily family meals when I was a child. I was left feeling that there are many mums who, like me, are breaking with a tradition we would prefer to keep. Were we having the same opportunity to develop family unity? Did it matter if I wasn't that old-style pillar of the family; if we had thrown-together meals so often, or take-away pizza eaten from the box? What else were we missing?

Good for Communication

We find out all sorts of things when we can sit down to family supper. While reviewing the events of the day just past, it's also a good time to pick up on the beginning of problems.

Is Sara being bullied? Is Paul in over his head with that new girl-friend? Do the kids understand the various issues being talked about, like AIDS and drugs?

It's also a good time for parents to air their views. I remember when my sister, aged eight, had been picked on by some local children and we were discussing it at dinner. 'She deserved it,' I said from my superior, year older position.

'Did you help her?' asked my father.

'No, why should I?'

'Because you stand by your family,' said my mother. 'You can disagree all you like at home, but outside you stick together.' This conversation took place over a chicken stew and I can recall it as if it were yesterday.

Time to Show You Care

One generation back, the mother was the pillar of the family. I do know that part of me still likes and hankers after 'being a pillar' – organising, cooking, cementing my family together.

I also know that I don't want to go back to my mother's day. I don't have the desire to perform her role. I like my life, I enjoy lots about the fast, busy modern world, yet I also want to give my children that warm, cocoon-like environment which fostered all those old-fashioned values that my parents passed on to me. I want my children to experience the parental caring that the home-prepared, shared meal communicated.

And what a difference when parental care isn't there. One of my son's friends, Andrew, loves coming for meals at our house, because his parents are often out to dinner, and when they are in they like to eat separately, later. Andrew prefers even our hastily produced spaghetti and bread sticks eaten all together at the kitchen table to the food he and the au pair get at home. He once said when going home to dinner, even though he knew it was steak: 'I'd rather stay here – it's so empty at home.' He's right: although I loved the home cooking of my childhood, it isn't the quality of the food that matters most, it's the quality of the company.

Helpful Hints

Sharing the Chores

Many things are better now. I'm glad that one of the bad messages from my childhood no longer prevails – the idea that girls do housework and cooking while the boys can be free to play. In our house we all pitch in with the work to some degree – I refuse to raise boys who cannot take care of their personal needs themselves. Then, they can decide for themselves about upholding the tradition of family meals.

Making the Decision

We got together for a family chat. Did this tradition of eating together matter to us all? We decided that we:

- Liked the idea of sitting down together. The kids said they actually missed family meals, much to my delight.
- Would try to get up a little earlier in the morning so that we could have breakfast together. Controlled chaos is the best way to describe mornings in our house, with the children wanting an extra five minutes to sleep, the dog whimpering to go out, my husband ironing a clean shirt and me groping around for my contact lenses, but we'll try!
- Would arrange a dinner time each morning and be home by then, if at all possible.
- Would all help prepare breakfast and dinner and clear up afterwards.
- Would not watch TV while eating, so our attention could be focused on each other, making real communication possible.
- Would make every supper a family meal. Even if it is a last-minute-rush take-away pizza, we'd get out the check cloth for the table and stick a couple of household candles in empty wine bottles to make it a candlelit supper.

Accommodating Everyone's Tastes

One of the dilemmas we face now is that healthy eating and food allergies mean that not all family members can always eat the same things. When my mother put food on the table, the whole family ate whatever was on offer and no one even dared think about having their own special meal. Now, you might have to make a vegetarian or vegan meal for your animal loving thirteen-year-old, pudding with no additives for your E-allergic eight-year-old, and free-range roast chicken for the rest of them. Short-order cook was not an option you chose, but that's how things are. So, sitting down together doesn't necessarily mean that you will be harmoniously nibbling on the same dish, but that doesn't matter (except, of course, to the cooks) as much as the talking, debating and sharing that should go on in mealtimes.

If different folks need or like different foods, then accommodate as much as possible and enlist everyone's help to make it as pleasant and easy as you can.

Encouraging Your Child to Talk

Children are most inclined to interrupt and talk when adults are deep in a good conversation. Sometimes, unwelcome bits of half-chewed dinner accompany the interruption. Children aren't deliberately being rude – they are stimulated by what they hear and want to contribute.

Though manners are necessary and no one wants children who are unappetising to be around, let's not quash enthusiasm. What we *don't* want are children who are so worried about being polite that they're nervously silent. To me, it's better to excuse a bit of food accidentally spilling out of a mouth because a child is so excited to tell you something than to reprimand him or her for poor manners. This might be the only time everyone gets to talk together in a busy day.

Ten Things to Help Make Family Meals Happen

1. *Plan a time at least three times a week when you will all be together and can sit around the table. It can be breakfast, lunch or dinner.*
2. *Don't worry if your child doesn't want to eat at the meal, just being there is enough. Our sons sometimes stop for healthy chips or sweets on the way home and then say they aren't hungry. Fine, we want their company anyway, even if it's only for fifteen minutes.*
3. *Encourage your children to invite their friends over and always be welcoming. 'What's one more at the table?' my Gran said whenever someone was hanging around at dinner time.*
4. *If possible, go to a restaurant with your family. Without the normal distractions, it is amazing how much more talkative*

everyone is and (touch wood) children are usually polite and charming when you're out. Yes, I know there are horror stories about Johnny screaming the place down because they didn't serve chips, but they are mostly well behaved!

5. *Turn off the television. That favourite television programme can be taped, or dinner-time negotiated around it. Better still, unplug the damn thing.*

6. *Take the phone off the hook. Train everyone to answer the phone by saying: 'We're just sitting down to eat, I'll get him/her to ring you back after dinner,' or 'I'd love to talk but the pie is just coming out of the oven.'*

   Ask your children to tell their friends not to ring during supper. And when you ring anyone around dinner-time, start with, 'Are you eating? If so I'll ring back.' Chances are that the kids will pick up your style.

7. *Use any occasion for a special meal – good reports, sports awards, Fridays, shortest or longest day of the year, 'un-birthdays', pets' birthdays, first day of winter – anything for a change and a bit of unexpected fun.*

8. *Make it happy – if you've got a bone to pick with anyone, don't do it at the table. Making family meals into a battleground destroys the reason for doing it in the first place.*

9. *Give everyone a ten-minute warning before the meal is ready to eat. It drives cooks nuts when the meal is getting cold during last minute loo visits and 'the programme's just finishing – I'll be right there' comments. To avoid tension, plan the time to coincide with the end of the favourite programme or activity.*

10. *Don't do it all yourself – many hands do make light work. Mealtimes shouldn't make anyone the martyr of the family: the 'Look what I did for you' attitude is enough to put us all off eating together for life.*

Eating Out

At least when you eat at home you are (somewhat) the master of your own fate. Going to restaurants with young children, however, can be a disaster. Here are a few things you can do to make eating out more enjoyable, learned the hard way by Yours Truly:

1. Choose the Right Restaurant

It would be daft to take young children to a very expensive, posh restaurant. The other diners are most likely trying to get away from noisy, playful, chatty children and you wouldn't be very popular. Anyway, it would be impossible to relax and have a good time yourself. Choose a child-friendly place, especially for your first outings. Much as I dislike fast-food places, we practically lived in them when our children were small. No-one minded your kids being there and it was a great way to introduce children to the joys and rules of eating out.

2. Telephone Ahead

If you are going to a restaurant you are not familiar with, telephone ahead to see if they are geared up for children. Better that than arriving to find that you aren't welcome and they aren't prepared.

3. Go 'Off-peak'

If possible, take the kids to the restaurant early, before it gets crowded.

4. Take Toys and Entertainment

Keep your children occupied with games, toys, crayons and paper. Bring along any special equipment they need, such as cups with spouts, or bibs.

5. Ask for Small Portions

If the restaurant doesn't have a children's menu, ask for a smaller portion, or two plates and split the dinner between your children (*if* you can get them to agree on what they want to eat).

6. Avoid the Exotic

Most children are not terribly adventurous when it comes to food. Try to order food they know and like. If you want to let them try something unusual, order it yourself and let them taste a bit. Whatever you order, try to make sure it doesn't take hours to prepare – the rule is the quicker the better for young children.

7. Sit by a Window

My children always loved it when we could sit near a window, and so did I. We could play 'I Spy with My Little Eye', we could watch all the people and cars going by – it just made the whole experience more pleasant.

8. If All Else Fails, Leave!

If the children freak out, then cut your losses and go. You can always ask for a doggy bag. It isn't fair to spoil the meal for the other diners.

Our two boys are really quite a pleasure to go out with now. The only trouble is, they have a taste for those expensive restaurants I mentioned earlier. I can't wait until they are working and can afford to take *us* out! I always have been an optimist.

Enjoy Them Now and Plan For the Future

Family meals are not a feature of our lives for long. Children grow up so quickly and prefer to do their own thing. I will miss the hustle and bustle and hassle of it all, but I hope the tradition of our family suppers will carry on to my grandchildren. (Grandchildren – a few years to go yet, but I can wish.)

Still, I like planning ahead. Even though my children are only teenagers and definitely not ready to be parents yet (is anyone ready to be a parent?), I'm sure my grandchildren will love my chicken dinners!

12

QUIZ:
HOW DO YOU RATE AS A SCOLDER?

All parents need to scold their children – it's a part of our job description! But it can be done well and helpfully; so badly it's useless; or so scathingly that it's woundingly worse than useless. Should we review ourselves as critics?

- 'That's the last time I let you go on your own to get your hair cut – you look terrible!'
- 'You spilled your milk all over the carpet, you stupid boy!'
- 'How could you get such low marks? I am so disappointed with you.'

Do these sound familiar? How well do you think they rate as constructive? Can we learn to do better – is there a *best* way to criticise?

Maureen, a friend of my grandmother, used to criticise her children in the most inventive way. She gave them points out of ten, like the judges for ice-skaters. So, if Barry came home with poor marks, she would take out her cards and silently give him one out of ten. Maureen only added a remark when Barry did something she thought was good. Then the cards would come out with eight or nine out of ten and a comment like: 'Well, Barry, that was really clever of you,' which was her highest praise.

Despite those low marks when he first went to school, Barry ended up going to university and now works as an engineer. He laughs about his mum's strange method, but admits that it worked – and that he uses the same cards with his own kids.

I'm not suggesting we all rush out and get a set of cards. In fact, children need definite rules and the totally silent system, the complete avoidance of criticism which Maureen used over the school marks, definitely wouldn't be right for all occasions.

Let's see which way you'd react and how you'd criticise – and then use the marks to rate how well you are doing. Granted, we all react differently depending on how energetic or how exhausted we are feeling. So give yourself the benefit of the doubt. When you are choosing your answers, pretend that you are in your *best* parenting mode!

QUIZ

1. 'My Child Is So Careless'

Robert, aged ten, is carelessness personified. He knocks things over and spills things, and generally drives you nuts. Today, he is working on a school project and you walk into the sitting-room just in time to see him tip over a glass of juice on to the carpet. Do you:

a) Put him up for adoption at once.
b) Lose your temper and call him a stupid fool.
c) Scream 'Watch out!', rush over and try to stem the flow of juice while saying: 'I told you not to bring drinks in here. Now get a cloth and help.'
d) Smack him and make him clean it up.
e) Calmly leave the room, asking him to deal with it himself.

Points

a) *Score one (for humour).*
b) *Take two points (for honesty).*
c) *Score five. This is a natural way to react. If Robert shouldn't have been drinking juice in the room then he should help to clean it up. You haven't called him names or belittled him.*
d) *No marks. Hitting a ten-year-old over a spilled drink only teaches him that making mistakes will lead to violence.*

e) *Minus five (for lying – it's impossible for anyone to be that saintly!).*

2. 'My Child Plays His/Her Music Too Loud'

Charles loves music, especially if it is loud, has a driving beat and no discernible tune. His younger brother has the room next to Charles and cannot concentrate. Charles claims he cannot do his homework without his music. You love music as well. You are constantly battling with him to 'turn that thing down'. It has come to a crisis. Do you:

a) Throw his sound system out when he's at school, denying all knowledge when he returns.
b) Sell his sound system while he is away. Then claim that there was a burglary and say that only his sound system was taken. Offer him your sincerest sympathy, but explain that the insurance money doesn't cover his loss.
c) Tell him firmly and calmly what volume you (and his brother) can stand. If he won't co-operate, impose a 'silence time' when no music can be played, so everyone can get work done.
d) Go in every night and turn it down and keep going in every time he turns it up. Don't back down.
e) Offer to help him find another family to live with until he starts showing an appreciation for Bach and Mozart.
f) Buy him a set of earphones for his birthday.

Points

a) *One point for trying, but no more because of lack of inventiveness.*
b) *Two points for imagination, but watch out when your child asks to see the police report.*
c) *Five points, if you manage to stay calm; three if you don't. This is one of those times you just have to be the firm parent for the sake of your other children and your neighbours, let alone yourself.*

d) *Three points for being tenacious. You may eventually win just because your child gets tired of you continually coming into the room.*

e) *No points, but two points if you can get your child to see the sense in recent studies which have shown that you learn more effectively and remember more when you listen to calming classical music such as Bach and Mozart, than when you listen to the Top 40.*

f) *Four points, but only if you ensure that he doesn't go deaf from playing the music in the earphones too loud. Researches are finding that kids who listen to music played too loudly are suffering long-term damage to their hearing.*

3. 'My Child Is So Untidy'

Theresa has left her room in a complete mess. She promised you it had been tidied up when you gave her permission to go out. When she returns, do you:

a) Tell her she didn't live up to her part of the bargain and keep her in for an agreed length of time. Then make her clean up her room immediately.

b) Yell at her.

c) Make her move out.

d) Tell her that you now know she is a liar and that you'll never trust her again.

e) Icily call her a sloppy pig and refuse to talk to her for a few hours.

Points

a) *Of course, this reaction gets five. We can all work out that this is the most logical and constructive thing to do. (That doesn't mean we do it, though.)*

b) *Well . . . two points. Maybe you think she deserves it, but it doesn't really solve anything.*

c) *One point. (Just joking.)*

d) *No points. Never call a child a liar or a thief – she may live up to these labels.*

e) *Score one. Shame can work, but not nearly as well as reason. She may well be a sloppy pig, but this method won't make her change her ways.*

4. 'My Child Was Rude'

Kathryn calls a neighbour a 'silly old woman'. The neighbour complains to you. When you call Kathryn, do you:

a) Smack her, march her to the neighbour and force a tearful apology.
b) Ask her what happened. If she has been rude, make her apologise in person and explain that even if your neighbour provoked her, calling people names will not be permitted in your family.
c) Tell your neighbour she *is* a 'silly old woman' and challenge her to a duel.
d) Call your daughter a nasty little creep and give her a suitable punishment.

Points

a) *No points. Your daughter will learn nothing about manners, but a great deal about fear.*
b) *Award yourself five. You have given your daughter a chance to explain her side of the story. If she has been rude, then you have also allowed her to learn from her mistake, take the logical consequences of her actions (apologising) and to understand that you value being kind and polite.*
c) *Minus one. She may be, but watch out for her left hook.*
d) *No points. All you are teaching her is that calling people names is acceptable.*

5. 'My Child Isn't Doing School Work Properly'

Tim's teacher reports that he is not trying and is getting poor marks. Do you and your husband/partner:

a) Express your disappointment, tell Tim you can't understand what the problem is and inform him he can't watch TV or go out until he improves.
b) Get really angry, tell him he is a stupid good-for-nothing who will never amount to anything in the future.
c) Trade him in for a gerbil – they don't have to study.
d) Ask him what he thinks the teacher said. Find out if there is any reason for his poor performance (other than sheer laziness) and see if you can spot some way to help. Work out how he can catch up or change his study habits, and tell him he can do better and that you'll help.
e) Sigh and look hurt and exasperated. Ask him how he could do this to you after all you've done for him.

Points

a) *Three points. This is such a normal reaction, and at least you admit to it. However, Tim doesn't get a word in and that may be part of his problem.*
b) *No points. If he's a good-for-nothing, why should he bother to try at all?*
c) *One point. Gerbils are good company.*
d) *Score five. Lucky Tim – someone really cares how he feels and is willing to help. He knows you are not happy with his performance, but there is hope.*
e) *Minus five. Loading a feeling of guilt on to a child without helping with the problem is clearly going to make things doubly hard for him.*

6. 'My Child Is So Quarrelsome'

Stephanie is constantly bullying her younger brother. You've just heard a thud and a piercing scream and here comes your son, crying, 'She hit me.' Do you:

a) Grab your daughter by the arm and say: 'I'm fed up to the back teeth with you – go to your room immediately.'
b) Say: 'Get out of my sight both of you. I am sick and tired of this constant bickering.'
c) Take a deep breath, comfort your son, then find out what has been happening. Has your son been bugging your daughter or is she picking on him because she is angry, annoyed or frustrated about something? Give appropriate punishment or counsel.
d) Wonder why the devil you ever had children – life *used* to be so peaceful.
e) Ring the travel agent and book a trip anywhere, as long as the plane leaves within the next ten minutes.

Points

a) *Score two. But only if you didn't grab her so hard that it hurt. Sometimes getting the child out of the way saves her from being murdered (by you?).*
b) *Three points for this one. It's fine to give yourself a break from children occasionally, until you can decide what to do. Don't feel you always have to come up with the right solution instantly. Sometimes a little 'time out' will cool things off until everyone feels more ready to talk about it reasonably.*
c) *Take five points. Finding out what the problems are might just save you a lot of future aggro. We all know that children's squabbles are not always what they seem. This will probably only be possible when you feel that* you *can cope.*
d) *Two for this. Join the crowd and don't trust anyone who says they have never thought of it. By the way, you only get the points if you didn't say it aloud in front of the children. If you did, score minus one.*

e) *One point for creativity. It would have been four, but I booked before you!*

How Did You Score as a Critic?

Have a look at this not-too-serious guide to your score totals.

- **25 to 30 points**   You're brilliant!
- **20 to 24 points**   You're normal, but could improve.
- **15 to 19 points**   You're tired and need a break.
- **10 to 14 points**   You've gone past the sell-by date. Get help.
- **Minus to 9 points**   You've got a good sense of humour, but you should have stuck to raising goldfish.

Kids can drive you up the wall, and no parent gets ten out of ten every time. But knowing how to criticise in a positive, helpful way is one of the most important skills we can learn. There are a very few basic rules I think we can all follow:

1. Taking a 'Time Out'

Sometimes we need to give ourselves time to calm down before we come down like a ton of bricks and do something we'll regret.

2. Remembering That We All Make Mistakes

Children need our guidance to help them learn not to repeat mistakes, but they will make lots of them growing up. That's what growing up is about, and if we expect our children to always get it right, we're in for a lot of aggravation.

3. Remaining in Control

We will need to scold and to discipline children at times; it's not good for children if they never learn that there are consequences to bad behaviour. But if we can scold in a fairly calm and reasoned manner, children will hear what we're saying instead of cowering in the corner because we're yelling like a demented banshee. (Who, me? Yell? Never!)

4. Admitting Mistakes

If we get it wrong we have to make amends and apologise. It's only fair.

5. Maintaining a Sense of Humour

That doesn't mean we laugh while we are talking to the kids. It just means we have to keep all of these transgressions in perspective and maybe have a little moment of humour between the adults after it's all over. Of course, this doesn't apply to the more serious problems (see Chapter 24, p. 229 – What to Do When Your Kids Screw Up). Personally, I don't know how people without a sense of humour survive parenthood. I certainly feel sorry for their children!

By the way, let me know if you've found a really effective way to get around the terrible haircut mentioned at the beginning of this book. I told my son either I went with him next time or he could pay for it himself. Nil points to me . . .

13

WAYS TO AVOID SPANKING YOUR CHILD

'Stop that this minute or I will smack you.'

WHACK!

'Owooooooooooo . . .'

Familiar? It should be, considering that one survey found that ninety per cent of parents in the UK think that smacking a child is an effective way to teach discipline.

I know that most parents reading this book hate the idea of smacking; no good parent could enjoy inflicting pain on their own children. But parents also want to make sure their children do not grow into horrible, obnoxious creatures, and smacking seems to be one of the answers.

So, I'm about to make myself unpopular: I don't think we ever have to use smacking to discipline children. I think most parents smack children because that's how they were brought up, and they think that 'sparing the rod spoils the child'. I declare here that I was never smacked as a child being brought up in the late forties and fifties, so I don't consider my opposition to smacking to be 'trendy'. In our and other families it just wasn't the norm to hit, and that was years ago. My children have never been smacked, and they have been great kids.

Regardless of your philosophy of raising children, the problem is that smacking is easy and, sometimes, parents just don't have the time to think of other more constructive things to do. I will resist the urge to go into the moral arguments, except to say that children can be brought up as responsible, happy and law-abiding citizens without resorting to hitting, and that several European countries have already banned the smacking of children.

If you want to try some alternatives to smacking, and I hope you do, then here are some suggestions:

1. Hold the Child Firmly

Many parents say that the only way to teach young children about dangers such as fire or cars, or to stop a temper tantrum, is to administer a quick smack. The theory is that the child then associates the danger with the pain of the smack. If your young child persists in getting into dangerous situations or throwing tantrums that place him or her in danger, then grab the child and hold him or her firmly to you, saying 'Stop' in a strong voice. Continue to hold the child until he or she calms down, then explain the danger and your displeasure that the child hasn't listened.

2. Ignore When Possible

Children have tantrums, but rarely do they have them without an audience. Shops seem to be a good place, and it can be incredibly embarrassing to have your child writhing around on the floor screaming his or her head off while self-righteous people stare at you and stage whisper, 'That child needs a good smack.' You may have to pick the child up and carry him or her out of the store, but the best way to stop tantrums is to walk away, completely ignore the tantrum and watch from a distance (where the child cannot see you) to ensure that he or she is safe.

3. Reward Them When They're Good

Children do want to please their parents, but they also want our attention. If we only pay attention to them when they are being naughty and we smack them, then they will act up until they are smacked, because any kind of attention is better than none.

Do your best to tell them how pleased you are when they are being good. Say how much you like the way they are playing together nicely, or how glad you are that they acted so grown-up while you were shopping. You will find they will tug your sleeve and say, 'Aren't I being good?' to get your attention, instead of doing something awful. (See Chapter 23, p. 219 – Ways to Bribe Your Child – for reward ideas.)

4. Tell Them What Bothers You

Explain to children that certain things drive you to distraction (if they don't already know!) and that you will be less likely to punish them if they avoid doing those things.

5. Tell Them the Consequences in Advance

Tell children what will happen if they continue in the behaviour which is wrong, and then follow through. Knowing in advance that they will not be allowed to see their favourite programme if they insist on fighting often stops the fight dead in its tracks. If it doesn't, don't let them see the programme, or you will be making a rod for your own back.

Possible consequences include:

- missing television
- being isolated with nothing to do – such as sitting facing a blank wall for five minutes (an hour is far too long)
- not being allowed to go on an outing
- taking away a toy for a period of time
- not allowing a treat, such as a sweet

None of these things actually helps the child to learn 'good behaviour' and it is better to use reward. However, there may be times when you feel you need some sanctions, because nothing else seems to be working and you are at your wits' end. Using ideas like this may help you to avoid smacking, but do work on positive rewards too.

6. Set Limits

All children need limits, and to know what the limits are. Tell your children the kind of behaviour you expect and what will happen if they transgress. But also tell them what will happen if they behave. They will test the limits – all kids do. I told one of my sons that he was not allowed to go out on a school night and that I always wanted to know if he was going to be late home from school. One night he didn't ring, and came waltzing in two hours late. I was hysterical, imagining all sorts of terrible things happening to him. First I hugged him, then I yelled, 'Where have you been? You know the rules of this house, etc. etc. etc.' It turned out that a group of kids had gone for a pizza after school and invited him. He didn't want to seem 'like a baby' who had to call home for permission.

Although I sympathised with his desire to be independent, as far as I was concerned he knew the limits, had chosen to break them and he lost some privileges as a result. We then set up new limits as, clearly, he was starting to need a bit more leeway after school. But I still insisted that he ring me, even if he did it in secret.

7. Don't Expect Too Much From a Young Child

Be sure that you are expecting the child to do something that is possible for his or her age and level of maturity. You would not expect a two-year-old to fully understand the dangers of cars, so supervision and constant explanations are in order. You would expect a nine-year-old to understand the dangers of playing with matches, so punishment would be in order if he or she persists in playing with them in a dangerous way.

The End Physical Punishment of Children campaign (EPOCH) was launched by Penelope Leach, the world-renowned childcare expert, and psychologist Peter Newell in 1989. It aims to change attitudes towards children, and to help people recognise that it is as wrong to hit a child as it is to hit an adult. It is an uphill struggle, but they have written some very clear guidelines for parents, some of which they have kindly given me permission to quote here.

If you would like more information from them, or copies of their leaflets, their address is at the back of this book.

EPOCH suggests:

1. Tell Often

With young children, it can take hundreds of tellings over months to get them to do something like put their toys away. Patience and lots of little tricks such as: 'I bet you can't put your toys away before the timer goes off,' work a treat. They will forget, but they aren't being naughty, just very busy getting on with all the things they have to do in their young lives.

2. Ration Don'ts

Your child will simply stop hearing them. 'Don't' works best for rules you want him to keep whatever the circumstances, like 'Don't climb trees, it's dangerous.' Try not to make rules that vary according to circumstance and which might have to be broken. 'Don't interrupt me,' for example, is a silly rule, because you may need to be interrupted in an emergency or if a child needs to go to the toilet.

3. Driven to Distraction

If your child will not listen to you and you've started to deliver a smack, divert the blow to the table or to your knee (ouch!). The sound will interrupt the behaviour and the child will hear what you say far better than if she or he was crying.

4. Cool Down

If you feel your temper going, make sure your child is safe and leave the room until you've cooled down. The child or baby may cry at being left, but that's better than crying for being hit.

5. Grab

Little hands that get into danger are better grabbed than smacked. Grabbing them is quicker and attracts just as much attention.

6. Superior Size

Use your superior size to lift a child who won't come or carry a child who won't walk.

7. Substitute

If you've started to say, 'Stop that this minute or I'll . . .' you may have time to substitute 'scream' for 'smack'. Do it, as loudly as you can. Your child will be surprised and impressed and your tension will vanish (or at least diminish).

8. Punishment Fits the 'Crime'

If you feel you must use punishment, make sure that it follows directly from the 'crime' so she or he has the chance to learn the lesson you mean to teach. If a child rides a bike on to a road you've forbidden, take the bike away for the afternoon or longer. As for spanking: nothing will make your child believe that you do it for his or her sake: 'I hurt you because I don't want you hurt' is too devious a message for any child or adult.

Working Against the Majority

I think smacking teaches children that it is all right to hit someone if you are bigger and stronger, and that hitting is a way to solve problems. I know most parents smack because they love their children and think they are doing their best to raise them right. I guess on this one I will, for the time being, be in the ten per cent minority of British parents who disagree with smacking. But I will be working hard to make the minority a majority.

PART II

Getting Through Life

14

TWENTY QUESTIONS – HOW WELL DO YOU KNOW YOUR CHILD?

Do you know what your children want to be when they grow up? What they like and dislike about themselves? Or what they would wish for if you gave them one wish?

Give a copy of this quiz to your child and fill one out yourself, then compare the results and see how you score. I reckon we don't know our kids as well as we think we do!

1. What is your child's favourite food?
2. What food does your child dislike the most?
3. What does your child most like about him/herself?
4. What does your child dislike most about him/herself?
5. What do you do that most embarrasses your child?
6. What would your child like to change about him/herself?
7. What would your child like to change about you?
8. What would your child change about his/her siblings?
9. What does your child want to be when s/he grows up?
10. What would your child do with a £100 gift?
11. What does your child most worry about?
12. What does your child like best about you?
13. What is the thing your child is most frightened of?
14. Who is your child's best friend (or boy/girlfriend?)
15. Who is your child's least favourite person and why?
16. What subject does your child like best at school?

17. What subject does your child like least at school?
18. What is your child's favourite activity away from school?
19. Who would your child like to talk to if s/he had a problem?
20. If your child was granted one wish, what would it be?

SCORE

Give yourself one point for every time you match your child's
answer. Before you score your answers it might help to know that
none of the parents I tried this out on scored higher than 15. The
parents who scored the highest had the youngest children. I think
that means the older they get, the less we know our kids – or the
more they don't tell us. But then that won't surprise parents of
older children, and perhaps we don't really want to know everything about them or what their favourite activity is!

- **15 to 20 points**   Amazing. You deserve a gold star and a
  holiday.
- **10 to 15 points**   Well Done. You must be a good com-
  municator and your child likes to talk to
  you.
- **5 to 10 points**   Not Bad. Try to find out more about
  what your child is thinking and be more
  observant.
- **0 to 5 points**   Not Good. Perhaps you should consider
  growing mushrooms instead of children?
  Sit down and talk with your child and
  take the quiz over again.

Of course this quiz is just a bit of fun, but it is a good way to start
finding out more about your kids. Ask your children to make up
their own quiz to give to you. I promise you it will be much more
difficult than this one!

15

GETTING KIDS TO TALK TO YOU

'What did you do in school today?'
  'Nothing.'
  'Did you have a good time at the party?'
  'Yea.'
  'How was the school journey?'
  'OK.'

In our house, getting kids to talk is sometimes like pulling teeth. In fact, I would like to pull their teeth when they answer in mono-syllables and I want to know every detail and what happened. Other times, like when I am ready to go out or rushing around like a mad thing trying to juggle telephone calls, dinner, writing and sanity, they saunter in and start chatting away like jay birds! So how on earth do we get our children to talk to us?

1. Ask Specific Questions

Children may talk more if the questions are phrased in a way that requires a longer reply. Frankly, I'd be happy with one sentence at times. Try opening up the conversation with questions like:

- 'What book are you reading at school?'
- 'What was the funniest (weirdest, worst, etc.) thing that happened in school today?'
- 'What problems are you doing in maths?'

- 'What did they give you for lunch at school? What did you like best?'
- 'What kinds of experiments are you doing in science?'
- 'What songs are you singing in music? Do you like them or think they aren't very good?'
- 'Who do you think had the best time at the party?'
- 'What kinds of food did they give you to eat? What did you think of it?'
- 'How would you rate school today on a scale of one to ten? Why?'
- 'You seem sort of thoughtful tonight, I wonder what you're thinking about? I'd like to know if you feel like talking about it.'

Don't fling all these questions at them at once or they will think you've gone mad, which will probably confirm what they suspected all along!

Notice that these questions are asking for more than a yes or no answer. There is no guarantee that children will be more forthcoming if you ask them specific questions, but low-key, information-seeking questions are more likely to elicit a response. If they don't carry on the conversation, let it drop and go on to talk with someone else, but at least you've given them a chance.

2. Swallow the Editorial Comment – Don't Judge

Julie: 'My teacher is stupid!'
Mother: 'Don't talk about your teacher that way – it's rude.'
Julie: 'But she is.'
Mother: 'I said don't talk like that.'

End of conversation. As parents we all have feelings and judgements about how children should behave and talk. Julie was trying to get her mother to talk about a problem with her teacher, but she didn't succeed. Her mother wasn't prepared to listen and take Julie's feelings into account. We've all done it. I remember my youngest telling me he was hungry and me saying 'No, you're not, you've just finished eating.' After all, he couldn't be hungry unless he had a hollow leg. I was wrong – he did have a hollow leg!

How could Julie's mother have encouraged Julie to talk?

Julie: 'My teacher is stupid!'
Mother: 'Oh?'
Julie: 'You won't believe what she did today.'
Mother: 'What?'

Notice that Mother isn't saying the teacher is stupid, but trying to get Julie to tell her more about what happened. Julie's mother is keeping her judgements to herself, even though she may think Julie's teacher is the best thing since sliced bread. As parents we often seem to deny our children's feelings, to jump to conclusions that somehow they are at fault, to give advice without finding out enough about the facts or to defend the other party if our children are complaining about someone. One little boy rang his mother at the office in tears because some children had picked on him. Before he could finish his first sentence, she interrupted with 'What have you done to them?'

Face it, we all make mistakes when our children try to communicate with us, but the bottom line is that if we listen and give children a chance, they'll be more inclined to tell us things. Granted, it will still be on their terms.

3. Allow Your Children Their Opinions

Children usually end up with the same values and many of the same opinions as their parents – when they are parents themselves. Until then, we can help communication by discussing issues, but not feeling threatened if our children do not agree with us. Even very young children have strong opinions about what they like to eat and wear, which may not suit us.

Lynn, a friend of mine, insists that her children are always colour co-ordinated. I'm not kidding! Whenever they go out together as a family, everyone wears red or blue or beige, or whatever. Her eldest son, aged eight, is beginning to rebel. In his opinion, this is a silly idea and he wants to wear what he wishes, regardless of what the rest of the family does. Lynn, an otherwise normal person in my opinion, is having to adjust her own views about this, or her son has stated he won't go out with them. At least he is talking to his mother about it, but if she doesn't allow him to form his own opinions about this relatively trivial matter, I predict problems in the future over other issues.

Encourage your children from a young age to tell you what they think, and praise them for telling you, even if you don't agree. That doesn't mean you have to change your opinions, however, and you may want to have non-acrimonious discussions about your differences. For example, if your ten-year-old comes home and declares that eating animals is disgusting and she is now going to be a vegetarian and you don't agree, then tell her you are glad she is thinking about these issues. Let it ride for a while, and then let her know in a non-judgemental way what you think. But, at the same time, do not force her to eat meat.

One of the most exciting aspects of raising children is watching them grow and develop into their own people. As the oft-quoted Prophet Kahlil Gibran said about children: 'You may strive to be like them, but not seek to make them like you.' I would humbly add that most of us secretly hope they will adopt our more enlightened opinions and values and somehow shrug off our own worst faults.

4. Compliment Them

When your kids talk, try to find a natural way to say something complimentary about what they've said or how they've said it. When one of my sons decided to talk with a bizarre accent, I thought he sounded like a moose with marbles in his mouth. But I told him that I was impressed with his talent to mimic. Very few people tire of hearing praise about themselves or about something they have done. In our parental role, it seems as though we spend a great deal of time talking to our children about what they've done wrong, and how to correct their faults. No wonder they can be wary of talking to us. They have learned that the less they say, the fewer things we can find to criticise. I'd be quiet, too, if the majority of my conversations ended up by someone saying 'What's wrong with Michele and how can we fix it?'

Here are a few ways to compliment children when they are talking to us:

- 'I admire the way you said that.'
- 'You've really thought this through, haven't you?'
- 'You're clever.'
- 'I like talking with you.'
- 'I can see that you feel strongly about this. Strong opinion can help to change things.'

Beware of complimenting without conviction or cause. Kids can see right through false compliments. Better not to say anything than to fake it.

Use compliments frequently, even if you are not having a discussion. Find a reason to tell your child that:

- you are glad he is persevering and learning his maths, even if it isn't his favourite subject
- you are delighted she has tidied up her room
- you are pleased he was responsible and came home on time
- you are proud she stood up for a friend
- you know he was disappointed he didn't get the part he hoped for in the school play, but you think he has been very mature in handling the situation.

All these little communications will encourage your children to talk more, because they will feel good about being with you and good about themselves.

5. Be Light-hearted

If we can maintain a sense of humour and stay fairly laid-back, kids will be more likely to talk. A father I know called Tony treats everything as a crisis. The minute a subject is raised he is yelling, tearing his hair out (what little is left) and going on and on about how terrible it all is. When one of his children got in trouble at school for a minor infringement, you would have thought the world was going to end. It makes you wonder what will happen if he has to deal with a real crisis. It is no surprise that the children in his family never bring anything up for discussion. Mealtimes are eerie – no one wants to venture an idea or bring up a problem for fear they will be hung, drawn and quartered.

Another father who is a friend of mine, Gary, says that in their family they have shouting matches. His children feel confident enough to state their views strongly and they all enjoy these discussions. Listening to these free-for-alls as an outsider, his children might seem rude and difficult. But if you listen carefully, you will hear peels of mutual laughter and respect for one another, as points are argued. Gary is very laid-back and funny and has clearly given his children permission over the years to talk. And talk they do. He says: 'Sarcasm was out. Facts were always corrected. Feelings were allowed. Humour was essential.' A good formula if ever I heard one.

6. Allow Them to Shine

We went to dinner with an elderly aunt recently. She is probably the most self-centred and talkative person I have ever met. She had not seen our children for several years. The gist of the conversation was:

Boys: 'How do you do?'
Aunt: 'Not very well. My arthritis is acting up. My children never come to see me. When I was your age I . . .'

We surfaced two hours later, shell-shocked and dying to get away as quickly as possible. She never asked a single question about the boys or us, or the outside world, for that matter. The only thing we knew for certain was that, whatever else might be bothering her, her lungs and tongue were fine.

I asked the boys what they thought of the afternoon. 'She wasn't very interested in anyone else, was she?' commented one. 'I can see why her children never come to visit,' said the other, 'I bet she never asks them anything about their lives.'

Kids, and the rest of us, I suspect, like to have the spotlight at least once in a while. If all conversations are about the adults and adult concerns, children will soon learn not to talk. Try asking children about areas you know they are good in or can talk about with some authority. With young children, it might be the drawings they have done or the song they have learned to sing. Let them sing it, and give lots of praise. Older children might have expertise in sports, music, academic subjects or a hobby. Asking anyone about something they like or do well will usually bring a good response, especially if you pay rapt attention when they are talking. Obviously we don't want little show-offs who pout if someone is not paying constant attention to them, but we need to remember to give kids that chance to shine, even if we have to engineer it.

7. Avoid Lecturing

If you ask kids what irritates them most about parents, the top answer I always get is: 'They're always lecturing.' True. Our job seems to incorporate teaching, and lecturing is part of teaching. If children think that talking with parents will usually result in some kind of lecture about either the good old days or the bad habits of the children, then they will clam up. We do need to get them to brush their teeth, to tidy up their rooms, to do their homework, be kind to others and turn off the television. And, sometimes, that means a lecture, but it doesn't have to always be like that. Try:

- Using fewer words. For example, if Marina keeps forgetting to brush her teeth say: 'Toothbrush,' instead of 'You've forgotten to brush your teeth again.' If Alex has neglected to take the dog out say: 'Dog,' instead of 'You're being irresponsible about the poor dog again – he has to go out now.'
- Describing the situation factually instead of directing your anger at your child. For example, if Charles should have emptied the dishwasher, say: 'I see the dishes are still waiting to be put away,' instead of 'You lazy boy, you haven't put the dishes away.' If, as at our house, the children are constantly using the telephone, say: 'Please, I need the telephone now,' instead of 'Get off that telephone this minute.'
- Writing notes. Darcy, mother of two, uses this method often

and swears by it. For example, if the children know they should not turn on the television until after a certain time, she puts a note on the television saying: 'Only turn me on at six pm, please. Thank you.' If Bethan has forgotten to clean her room, she puts a note on the door saying: 'Room – Tidy Please'.

I know some of this won't be possible in a bustling family with working parents. We might be tempted to put a note on Gareth's door saying: 'Room for Rent, Kid Leaving', having lectured him for an hour using a thousand words because he didn't get off the telephone immediately. However, it does work, especially if you give your children the choice between lectures and a few words. And it is such a relief to your vocal cords and frayed nerves!

8. Respect Their Silence

Sometimes kids just don't feel like talking. For that matter, neither do we. Give your children the space to think and reflect when they need it. One of the mistakes new counsellors and psychologists make is to try to keep people talking. When I listen to the tapes I made with my first clients in 1968, I shudder. Every time they were quiet for longer than about thirty seconds, you could hear me coming in with some inane remark. My supervisor kindly pointed out that silence was useful, and people need time to collect their thoughts and to decide what to say next, if anything. Talking is important, but silence can be a tonic, as well.

9. Share Your Feelings

When talking to your children, be sure to explain that you, too, sometimes find things difficult. We think that, as parents, we have to be perfect. It helps kids tremendously to know that we made mistakes growing up, and to find out if we talked with our parents or grandparents. My sons have heard all about the time, aged eleven, I decided to lead a school rebellion against our hated uniforms. I organised all the girls to come to school in strange outfits, or so I thought. On the day, only six of us turned up inappropriately dressed. Our parents were called and we were sent home in disgrace, though I suspect the teachers did see the funny side of it. My father had a chat with me that evening and I still recall that he asked me why, told me that he understood and said that peaceful protest was the democratic way of changing things we didn't like. He said he wasn't going to punish me, but asked how I was going to handle the situation. I wrote a note to the headmistress and ended up wearing the uniform everyday.

I learned that a better way might have been to ask for a meeting with the Head before going all out on strike. My other crimes, such as pelting cars with eggs, taking apples from a neighbour's tree, going to a friend's house without telling anyone thus sparking off a police search, and other things too numerous to mention, help when my boys do silly things they should have done differently. At least they know they have a misguided mother who also did silly things and somehow survived to become a more or less responsible adult.

10. Find the Best Time and Place to Talk

Whatever skills we use when talking with children, nothing will work when they are doing homework, or watching their favourite television programme, or getting ready to meet a friend. Attempts to converse will almost always end in failure. It is frustrating for both parent and child. I can sympathise, when someone rings me at the office and I'm in the middle of finishing something important, I'm afraid I don't listen at all well, nor am I much of a conversationalist. Kids are no different. They are moving at their own pace and have their own agendas, so we have to adjust if we want to get through.

Try, instead, talking to your children while they are in the bath (if they haven't reached the privacy stage) or at bedtime, when they welcome the extra time because they don't have to go to sleep immediately. Some of the best and more rewarding conversations I have had with my sons have been at night with the lights out. In fact, even my eldest teenager still likes talking then. Now that they are older I might rub their backs and ask them how things have gone or if they are having any problems I can help with. When they were little, I read to them and cuddled them and we talked. If they were worried about something, like starting school or the dark, I tried to find a book with those issues so we could talk some more.

All this has paid dividends, but don't get me wrong – my kids still say 'Nothing' if I happen to say 'What did you do in school today?' Nothing works all the time!

16

ANSWERING THOSE IMPORTANT AND SOMETIMES EMBARRASSING QUESTIONS

'What's the Kama Sutra?' my niece Laurie piped up in a voice that brought the conversation at adjoining tables to an immediate halt. Laurie was five and we were in a restaurant crowded with thousands of stern, disapproving types. Or so it seemed to my sister and I as we exchanged pained glances and told Laurie to 'speak a little more softly, dear'. (Actually the 'dear' was said through clenched teeth. Why do they always find the most public time to ask the most embarrassing questions? I guess it's a gift children are born with.)

I patiently and carefully stepped through an answer. 'Well, you know that men and women have sex . . .' Laurie interrupted, 'To have babies,' she said brightly. 'That's right. There's a book that is kind of like a reading book with pictures, that gives men and women ideas about different ways to have sex.' Laurie listened carefully, along with all the people at every table within 100 yards. 'Oh,' said Laurie, 'but why did King John have to sign it?'

Magna Carta, Kama Sutra – they do sound a bit alike. Poor Laurie, she couldn't understand why we were weak with laughter, tears streaming down our cheeks. As Art Linkletter, television personality from the Forties and Fifties said, 'Kids ask the damnedest questions.' Looking back with the benefit of hindsight (Laurie is now twenty-six), my first response should have been a casual, 'Where did you hear about that?' It would have saved Laurie a lot of confusion and us some embarrassment, but it has made a great family story over the years.

How can we avoid the pitfalls, but still answer the important questions children ask us? I asked all my friends who are parents to come up with the questions their children had asked which were the most awkward or unusual or difficult to answer, and I've added suggested replies. In most cases, the children had asked the question in a loud voice in a supermarket queue, in the middle of a solemn religious service or on a very quiet crowded bus. I'm sure you have many examples of your own that could top these!

1. What's Sex?

If possible, start when your children are very small and explain sex to them in simple terms when the opportunity presents itself – a pregnancy in the family is ideal. If you do this, you are less likely to receive this question out of the blue. If your child does ask, find out where he or she heard the term sex, just to make sure someone has not been using it to explain abuse. One child sex offender I talked with said he told children that he was teaching them 'sex' so they would know what to do when they grew up. Most likely your child has come across the word on the television, or heard it discussed on the playground.

Explain that when grown-ups love each other they sometimes show it by having sex. This means that the man puts his penis into the woman and they hold each other very close and they like it. For a young child, this is usually more than enough explanation before they look at you in complete disbelief and go 'Yuck!', followed by 'Why?' When you explain that that's the way babies are made, but that having sex doesn't always produce babies, they say something like: 'You and Daddy don't do that!' For older children a more complete description is in order, usually with books and drawings. I found the books by Claire Rayner, which have wonderful illustrations, very helpful with my sons when they were about four. As they grew older, we answered more and more questions until they got to the age when they'd rather giggle with friends than ask us.

I remember one evening sitting with my five-year-old on my lap watching a programme about a seal cow being mated by a huge bull seal. I thought we'd done a good job of explaining the facts of life, especially when he said confidently, 'I know what they're doing. They're having sex.' 'That's right,' I replied. 'With animals they call it mating.' He watched for a few more minutes, then looked up at me and said in disgust, 'Is *that* what you and Daddy do?' Back to the drawing board . . .

The important things about questions about sex are that we answer them as completely as necessary for the child, and that we are straightforward. I think it is a good idea to teach children the correct names for the parts of their body and to try not to be embarrassed by the mention of sex. This is the best way to ensure that our children have a healthy and natural outlook about sex. Most adults I know got their 'sex education' from books left lying around by their parents in the hope that their children would read them and not ask anything. Usually, parents put the books out about five years too late.

2. What's Safe Sex? What's a Condom?

Because of the publicity about some diseases which can be sexually transmitted, like herpes and the HIV virus, children now ask questions about things many of us didn't even know about until we were adults. If children ask this before they know what sex is, you will need to start at the beginning with an explanation about sex. Then explain that, sometimes, a germ or virus can be transmitted or 'given' to a person through sex, but that there are ways to make sure this doesn't happen. One way is for the person with the virus not to have sex with anyone. Another way is for the people having sex to use something to keep the germs from spreading – like a condom. Then draw a picture or show the child what a condom is and how it works. As your children become teenagers, it is imperative that you bring the subject up with them for their own protection. With the younger ones, I would wait until they ask.

You may, on the other hand, find yourself in the situation of the teacher who overheard two children on the playground. One child, aged about six said to the other, 'I found a condom on the patio.' Her friend replied, 'What's a patio?'

3. What's Oral/Anal Sex?

For older children and young teenagers, explain that some people like to have sex in different ways. One way to have sex is called oral sex – people kiss and suck on the genitals. Another way is called anal sex – this involves putting a penis into someone's bottom. For younger children, you could say it is when people 'have sex with each other's bottoms'. I don't think we need to go into lots of detail with young children. It is better to give information until they are satisfied with the answer. Too much detail can be counterproductive.

4. How Do Babies Get Into the Tummy? How Do They Get Out?

Explain that sperms rush up to the egg in the mother's body and that the sperm and egg are very tiny, like the head of a pin. Then the sperm and egg get together and form the very first cells of a new baby. As this new little baby grows, the mother's stomach grows with it. When the baby gets big enough to live outside, the mother's body has a tube-like place wide enough to let the baby out. Of course, you can go into as much detail with drawings and videos and books as you wish. Many children think that the baby comes out with the 'pee pee', so I made sure my children knew it was a different tube! What I didn't tell them was that having a baby was like passing a watermelon.

5. What Will Happen to Me When We Get a New Baby?

A wise midwife friend, Audrey, told me never to tell my older son that when the new baby came, my older son would become my 'big boy'. Children don't want to become the big boy or girl when it means they won't get all that wonderful attention they had before.

Audrey said to say, 'You'll both be my babies. You'll always be my baby, even when you're grown-up!' She was right, and it worked a treat.

6. What is the Matter with That Person?

Children are often quite direct when they see someone who has a deformity, is in a wheelchair, is blind or has a birthmark or burns. Children don't mean to be hurtful; they are just curious. Try to prepare them in advance so they won't embarrass someone. Explain that we don't stare at people just because they are different to us. If they make the comment in public, take them aside and explain that some people are born that way and some people have accidents or diseases which cause them to look that way. It isn't funny or weird, it is just how they are. It is like some people have blue eyes and some brown. They can't help it and we should remember that no-one likes to be stared at or made fun of, so we should treat them just like everyone else.

7. What Does It Mean to Be Gay/Lesbian/Homosexual?

Most men fall in love with women and most women fall in love with men. There are some men who fall in love with other men and there are some women who fall in love with other women. If you are a man who loves a man, some people call that gay or homosexual. If you are a woman who loves a woman, some people call that lesbian or homosexual. With older children, explain that heterosexual means different sexes, while homosexual means same sex.

8. What's AIDS?

My eldest son, then eight, came home from school one day and declared that he wasn't sleeping with his little brother anymore because you could die from sleeping with someone. He had got the wrong message from a campaign to prevent the HIV virus spreading. As far as he was concerned, sleeping meant just that, and he wasn't taking any chances. Older children will often have a better understanding of AIDS (Acquired Immune Deficiency Syndrome) than we adults, because of informative teaching in schools and youth clubs. Younger children need to know that AIDS is a disease that affects mainly grown-ups, and that it is difficult to 'catch' the 'germ' that causes AIDS. To go further and explain that AIDS is only one consequence of infection by the Human Immuno-deficiency Virus is more than children need to know. It may be the most correct explanation, but it is too confusing. Children need to know that you and they are not going to die from AIDS – that is often their overriding concern.

If a child or adult they know has AIDS, then seek professional help from one of the AIDS trusts or from your GP.

9. Why Do People Hurt Children?

If a child is kidnapped or abused or murdered, it makes headlines, and children ask questions. I used to say that people who do this are sick, until a friend got sick and my children wanted to know if the friend would turn into a child abuser. Now I say that most people love children and would never harm them, but some people have bad problems and they might hurt a child.

10. Should I Worry About All the Bad People Who Might Hurt Me?

Reassure your children that there are very few bad people who want to hurt children. The problem is that you cannot tell by look-ing at someone if they might be bad, so it is best not to talk to people you don't know if you are on your own. Draw up a list of 'safe' people with your child – it is easier to have a 'I can talk to these people if I'm on my own' list than for a child to determine who is safe. Or make a blanket rule that your child should not talk to or go off with anyone unless they check with you.

11. What's Rape/Incest/Sexual Abuse?

Find out where your child heard the term and then give enough information to satisfy him or her. For example: with a young child, rape can be described as someone touching your genitals or 'private parts' in a way that you don't like or want. Incest or sexual abuse could be described as a relative or another adult or teenager touching genitals and asking the child to keep it a secret. For an older child, the term would have to be described more fully. With the many programmes and news articles referring to rape, incest, sexual abuse, AIDS, etc., children will be asking questions whether we're ready or not.

12. Why Don't They Have a Baby?

When friends or relatives don't have children, your children may think it strange and ask awkward questions. Daphne, a nanny of many years' experience but no children of her own (probably because of her many years of experience!), was approached by one of her young charges, Sarah. 'Nanny, I know why you haven't got a baby. You've got to sleep with a man. I don't know what you do when you sleep but that's the only way you'll get a baby.' Nanny laughed. Some people, however, are sensitive about the issue, so we need to tell children that not everyone wants to have children and that some people cannot have children. Also explain that it is a private matter and we don't ask people about it because it might make them feel bad.

13. What Happens When We Die?

How you answer this depends upon your beliefs. Some parents tell their children that you go to heaven or hell, or you become part of the universe, or you come back in another life. Others say that there is no afterlife and that when you die there is nothing. I think children find it more comforting to believe that a loved one who has died has gone somewhere like heaven, rather than just 'gone'.

Another aspect of this question is what happens to our bodies. I think we have to say that our bodies go into the earth and become part of nature and that it doesn't hurt. See Chapter 31 p. 296 – about Grief – for more ideas.

14. What's That?

Your child comes into the bathroom pointing to your penis, or vagina or breasts, etc. and asks what it is. Without embarrassment, tell them what it's called and what it's for and carry on. The only real problem here is that some fathers get worried that the child might then go to school and say, 'I saw my Daddy's penis' and start into motion a social work investigation of child abuse! As long as you don't tell children to 'keep this a secret', it is highly unlikely this would happen. If you are worried, then be sure to lock the bathroom door.

There are hundreds of questions children ask, and we will never get it right all of the time. But there are some pitfalls we can try to avoid when talking with our children.

Pitfalls to Avoid

If a child, particularly a young child, asks a question which startles you because it doesn't seem appropriate to his or her age:

1. Swallow Your Surprise or Embarrassment

Parents have to be fairly good actors or our kids will never ask us anything remotely embarrassing. They'll remain in the dark or ask another child, who will either misinform them or tell them too much. My sister and I should not have laughed – Laurie must have thought we were nuts. Although she continued to ask questions as she grew up, we could have easily put her off. I console myself with the fact that we were young and Laurie was the first child we had to experiment on, but we didn't handle it well.

2. Find Out the Real Question

If we had asked Laurie where she'd heard of the Kama Sutra, we would have answered her real question about the Magna Carta. Laurie's class was having a story book read to them, and she somehow confused it with one of those throw-away lines overheard from adult conversation. However, it was remotely possible that there could have been a more sinister reason for Laurie's question – that someone was abusing her and had shown her pornography. Most questions turn out to have an innocent explanation, but it always pays to find out.

3. Don't Avoid the Questions

Probably the worst thing we can do when children ask us questions is to say, 'I'll tell you when you're older,' or 'You don't need to know,' or 'Don't worry about that.' Children ask when they need to know or are worried about something. If we avoid answering or indefinitely postpone our replies, then they have learned an important lesson – not to ask us. If we answer them now, later they may come to us with questions which could literally save their lives – about drugs, or safe sex or drinking. They may also feel more comfortable about telling us if something untoward happens, such as someone abusing them, if we have established that we are willing to listen and try our best to answer their questions and concerns.

4. Honesty Is the Best Policy

Although we have to keep our amusement or horror to ourselves when children ask certain questions, it is a good idea to admit that we don't always know the answers. But we should always say that we'll find out, and let them know as soon as we can. This also gives you time to think about how to respond to questions that throw you, or to check out your ideas with someone else.

5. Give Age-appropriate Answers.

If Laurie had been asking about the Kama Sutra, then the answer we gave was enough information for her. The rule of thumb is to give children the facts gradually until they are satisfied with the answer. Let them keep asking questions, rather than bombarding them with tons of information they don't need or want.

Keep these last few points in mind and you'll never be in the position of the father I heard about from a speaker at a conference. He told of a four-year-old boy who came into a room full of people and asked in a loud voice, 'Dad, where did I come from?' His father excused himself and took his son into another room, sat him down and patiently explained about love-making, how the sperm and egg got together and how the baby grows inside his mother's womb and then comes into the world. The son listened intently and then said, 'But where did I come *from*? Fred says he's from Newcastle.'

17

THE MORAL MAZE

Teaching Values

Horrifying newspaper reports of children robbing or even raping or murdering makes us ask what is going wrong with parenting. Do today's parents find it too difficult to teach right from wrong?

When Your Child Disappoints You

Jenny was driving her nine-year-old son's friends home after a great day. The boys were giggling in the back seat of the car. 'Did you see it trying to fly away?' whispered Paul. She heard flapping noises and more giggles. Not wanting to be left out, Jenny asked 'What's so funny?' Suddenly there was embarrassed silence and her son Alex said, 'Oh, nothing.' Jenny was curious, but didn't pursue it until she had dropped off the other boys. On the way home, she noticed that Alex was quiet. 'What was all that about?' asked Jenny again.

Alex squirmed. Jenny could see he didn't want to talk about it, but this only added to her growing sense of unease. 'Come on, tell me about it,' Jenny urged. 'Well, we found this bird when we were playing and it had a broken wing. It was flapping around. Paul said we should put it out of its misery, so we started throwing stones and things at it.' Alex bit his lower lip and stopped. 'Go on,' said

Jenny. She listened, but dreaded what she was going to hear. Alex took a deep breath, 'We chased it and killed it.'

Jenny was thunderstruck. Her sweet, gentle Alex, who she thought she had raised to be kind and compassionate to all living things, was confessing to heartlessly killing a poor wounded creature. So much for the values and morals she thought she had instilled in him.

Values? Morals? Are we allowed to mention the words, and is it politically correct to do so? (Speaking of which, recently I read about a woman cellist who resigned from her orchestra because they were playing *Peter and the Wolf*. You remember that wonderful children's story I mentioned in Chapter 9, in which each character is represented by a different musical instrument? Anyway, the cellist thought the story was not politically correct because it was 'unfair to wolves'. I ask you, am I nuts or is it the rest of the world?) Anyway, if we teach our children to be kind and generous to others, will someone be offended because we aren't teaching them to be self-aware enough and are exploiting them? Should we come down on them like a ton of bricks if they steal something from a shop, or do we ignore it because 'it's a stage and we don't want to upset their psyches'? Have we become so understanding of people with problems that we can't take a stand on morals and values? If we teach our children four basic values, I think the rest will follow:

1. Kindness and Compassion

Which brings us back to poor Jenny and Alex and the first value to teach children – kindness and compassion. It wasn't that Alex didn't know the value of kindness; he did and he felt bad when his mother confronted him with her disappointment. His friends were another story – when Jenny told the boys' mothers, they were unconcerned and even a bit annoyed that she brought it up. 'It was only horseplay – don't get your knickers in a twist,' said one.

Jenny discovered that it wasn't enough just to tell Alex he should be kind and compassionate, it was necessary to discuss why and to show him the right way to behave. She had a long talk with Alex and gave him ways to get out of such a situation, should it arise in the future. She also took him to an animal sanctuary (which he later raised money for by doing a sponsored walk) and impressed upon him the importance of humane treatment of animals and other living creatures. Although he still plays with his friends, they have never repeated their cruel actions, as far as Jenny knows. Jenny hopes that Alex will influence them, rather than the other way around. Although she can't change the attitudes of the other families, her discussions with Alex and having him take the consequences of his actions in a positive way by raising money for the sanctuary, were brilliant ways of helping him to learn a better way to behave. Jenny did not tell Alex that he was a terrible person, but she did make it clear that what he had done was terrible.

If I were opting for values to teach children, I think kindness and compassion would be at the top of the list. Too often we read of criminals, murderers and rapists who have at one time been bullies or who had killed or tortured animals. I know from my work with young offenders that many were bullies, cruelly tormenting other children, and no-one stopped them. In fact, one young lad said to me that everyone was very understanding of all his problems, but no-one tried to develop any kindness in him. Certainly, he had been neglected as a child, but with everyone so careful not to blame him, he felt he could just carry on being horrible.

2. Understanding Consequences

If someone had given the young offender I spoke to cause to think, and there had been consequences to his actions, perhaps the young mother that he mugged would not have suffered a broken shoulder and jaw. The idea of consequences seem to be quite unpopular at the moment. Why? Because some people feel that there are so many social injustices that no one should be blamed for anything. But I think that children who develop an understanding that there are consequences to actions are well equipped to deal with life's ups and downs.

Take the case of Daniel Jewell, the fifteen-year-old who was beaten by three boys and kicked as he lay on the ground. He staggered home and was taken to the hospital by his widowed father. The doctor said that internal bleeding had left him within ten minutes of death. The boys who beat him had been bullying him for some time, and it escalated into this tragedy. The boys were convicted of grievous bodily harm, sentenced to young offender institutions and they were publicly named by the court.

Logical consequences to actions, you might say, especially if it had been your child beaten nearly to death. Yet a 'training officer' who goes round to schools teaching a 'no blame' approach to bullying, stated in the newspaper that 'naming the accused is an awful thing to do and is counterproductive'. I beg to differ! Why should you keep the names of the offenders secret when they have done something so wrong? Surely, one of the consequences to these actions should be to realise you have done something against the values of the community, and *be ashamed*. Yes, it is shaming to be named in public, but isn't that productive rather than counterproductive?

What would be counterproductive would be to humiliate and degrade the culprits. In my opinion that would serve no purpose except to make the offenders even more vindictive. However, a little old-fashioned shame might bring about a change in attitude.

Fortunately, very few of our children will ever be involved in such a horrific case, but we can help them along with their understanding of consequences by our own example and by discussion. If you are in a shop and the assistant mistakenly gives you £5 extra, it is very tempting to grab the money and run (and spend it on the National Lottery). But this would be an excellent opportunity to help your child think about consequences. Say to the assistant, 'I think you gave me too much change,' and subsequently explain to your child that, otherwise, the assistant might have to put the money back from her own purse, or she may even lose her job. You could also explain that taking the money is stealing from the shopkeeper and how, if everyone did it, the shop would have to close. Then ask your child what she or he thinks. You can at various times expand the discussion to other issues which might be important to you, be it war, the environment, poverty or whatever. But don't try to do it all at once, or you will find your child running for the nearest exit or hiding under the bed to get away from old moralising mummy or daddy! And I would be right there with him – no-one likes a self-righteous bore.

It's always a good idea to talk about good consequences and to reward children when they do something well, too. It is vital that they know there are good, as well as bad consequences to actions. When our sons were recognised for outstanding achievements or work, we took them out for a treat. I guess we just have to hope that there are more times we can salute the good than deal with the bad!

3. Honesty

When I asked several friends (all parents) what were the most important values they would teach children, honesty was mentioned more than anything else. I feel that if we teach our children about consequences and help them to develop a conscience, then helping them to be honest should be an easier task. On the other hand, there are so many ways to be dishonest – pinching change left around the house, lying, cheating from someone else's homework, etc. And it does make it more difficult for us ordinary mortals (who, of course, never do anything wrong!) when many of our so-called leaders are setting bad examples with headline-grabbing news about marital cheating, politicians 'forgetting' to mention gifts and money, and important people making lots of money from insider trading.

Still, there are ways to help children learn to be honest. When one of my sons, then age seven, took a trinket from a shop, I scolded him and marched him back to the shop with the illicitly gained item. He begged me not to make him go, but it was vital for me to ensure that he understood the consequences of his actions. I was very careful not to call my son a thief, and I told him that I did love him, but I did not like what he had done. He then knew he shouldn't have taken it.

Yes, he was miserable and ashamed and vowed never to do it again. Good! I was pretty miserable, too, though I have a dim memory of having done something similar as a kid. Had Fagin been his guardian, I am sure my son would have been praised for his nimble fingers!

I think we can help kids think about honesty by asking them questions such as:

- why is it wrong to lie?
- who is hurt by lying?
- why is it wrong to cheat on a test or to copy someone else's homework?
- why is it wrong to steal?

If your child answers, 'Because you get caught,' he or she may be honest, but you've got a lot of work to do! Explain that:

a) Lying, stealing and cheating hurts other people, as well as the person who does it. The culprit has to continue lying to cover up the lies, the stealing and the cheating, and will probably feel bad inside. Certainly, the parents and friends would be disappointed if they knew.
b) Sometimes children can't figure out a way to stop because they get into the habit of doing these things, but that you will always try to help them if they need it. That doesn't mean bailing them out of the consequences, but it does mean you will do your best to think of possible solutions and ways to change behaviour.
c) Honesty *is* the best policy. Stick to your principles, but also try not to punish your child if she or he does tell the truth, even if they have done something wrong. It might be worth skipping the wrong behaviour in favour of praising their honesty!

4. Developing a Conscience

I like to think my son developed a conscience because of that little stealing episode, but then there is never a guarantee that, when our children are out of our sight, they will do the right thing. If I were given the option of teaching my children just three values, developing a conscience would be one. Still, I reckon it was easier for us when we were growing up, because it always seemed as if a little voice inside nagged at you if you did something wrong. My father told me the voice was my conscience, and a persistent little creature it was. I'm sure I needed it and, luckily, it was reinforced by the teachers in school and by the church I attended.

It certainly seems harder today to help my own children develop a conscience. To give you another example of my shortcomings as a parent: about two years ago one of my sons came home with a roll of film to develop. When the photographs came back, there were several of my son and his friends, but also photographs of an Asian family having some sort of celebration. Since we did not know the family, I asked him about the photographs. My son looked distinctly uncomfortable and tried to change the subject (a sure-fire way for a parent to know that something stinks). After a while, I found out that a friend of my son had found a camera on the street and had finished taking the roll of film. He then asked my son to get the film developed, while he (the friend) took the camera and sold it! I was beside myself and got quite angry with my son. I threatened to ground him for life and asked him to think about the poor family who did not now have their precious photographs. I told him I was calling the other boy's mother.

At this point, my son broke down and said that the boy was very popular and that he would be a social outcast if I rang David's (not his name) mother. I didn't care, but promised to wait for an hour so that I could cool down. During the hour, I thought about what had happened when Jenny rang her son's friends' mothers, and I confess to backing off slightly. David's mother had a reputation for being difficult and I really didn't want a mouthful of abuse. So what did I do? I told my son that he had to ring David and tell him that I was upset about the camera and photographs, he had to turn the photographs into the local police station near where the camera was found and that David was not welcome in my house for the time being. Also, I expected that my son would work with the local soup kitchen for a couple of days to make up for what I considered to be immoral behaviour. I wasn't happy with the outcome, and my conscience tells me I should have rung David's mother. But that is how I negotiated that particular moral maze.

Here I confess that we don't go to church, except for special occasions like Christmas, and therefore my children don't have that tradition. But that is our choice. Also, the teachers seem to be far too busy teaching the National Curriculum to spend time on moral issues. So, for many families like ours it means we take full responsibility for trying to instill a conscience in our kids. I will keep working at it – my conscience won't let me do otherwise! You know, it still bothers me worrying about whether that family got its photographs . . .

Ways To Teach Values

There are so many things we want to teach our children: fairness, responsibility, courage, humanity – the list goes on and on. But it seems to me that if we start with kindness and compassion, honesty, developing a conscience, and an awareness of consequences, then these other values will naturally follow. There really are only four specific ways I can think of to get our values across to our kids, and they are all based on old-fashioned communication:

1. By Example

There will be occasions when we can teach values to our children through our own actions. And we can reinforce good morals when we hear about various good deeds, such as people who risk their lives to save others, people who try to help starving children, people who speak out for their beliefs, people who excel in music, sport, academics, etc. Stories like this abound in the media every day.

2. By Explanation and Discussion

We mustn't be afraid to express our approval or disapproval of what is going on, and to explain why. If you give money to a cause, tell your children why you are doing it. Equally, if you do not approve, explain what your values are. Discuss with your children what their opinions are – encourage them to start expressing their own values.

3. By Using Books, Films, Television

Use books, films and television programmes as a point of discussion. In C.S. Lewis' *The Narnia Chronicles*, children encounter love, hate, loyalty and deception. In *The Lord of the Flies*, the child characters deal with cruelty, loyalty, honesty, courage and responsibility, as well as countless other values. Little Lord Fauntleroy shows courage, compassion and kindness and brings out the best in his grumpy old grandfather. And, of course, *Oliver Twist* has larger-than-life issues, with its child thieves, murder, revenge and the shining courage of Nancy in saving Oliver from a life of poverty and degradation. If you are religious (and even if you aren't), *The Bible* has some riveting tales, and there are numerous other religious books you can use. (See p. 173 for a list of books for teaching values.)

The wonderful thing about books is that they offer heroes and heroines to emulate, villainous actions to despise and distance yourself from, and characters to stimulate thought. And, if you are working through a particular problem with your child, you can ask the librarian for books about subjects such as lying, courage (*The Diary of Anne Frank* and *The Red Badge of Courage* were childhood favourites of mine), friendship, etc. All of the books I have mentioned are also films or television plays, so you could watch them with your children and discuss them, if reading is a problem.

4. By Asking 'What If?' Questions

Posing dilemmas is another excellent way to involve children in learning about values. This came home to me quite graphically when I asked my children what they would do if they saw someone lying on the pavement. Soon after, we were travelling in the car and one of the children pointed out a man who had collapsed on the street, and asked us to drive around again 'to see if he was OK'. We did, stopped the car and watched in amazement as people literally stepped over him, presuming that he was drunk. My sons and I got out, went over to him and discovered that he was having an epileptic fit. Other people then stopped and joined in to help when they saw the man was convulsing. Thank goodness an ambulance passed by and we waved it down. We never found out how the man fared, but my kids felt good that they had helped.

Changing Values

I know I didn't handle the stolen camera situation as my parents or previous generations would have. Nor have I adopted all the values I grew up with. I don't, for example, teach my own children that they will go to Hell without passing Go if they do something bad. Nor do I insist that they kiss all their relatives goodbye so they won't hurt their feelings. My kids' feelings about owning their own bodies are more important to me.

We used to place a value on children being seen and not heard. We used to 'value' children working down mines and up chimneys. In some countries, they still value children as slave labour – I recently saw a documentary in which a man said, 'Of course we use children to tie the tiny knots in the carpets. They are valuable because their fingers are so small.' Another person defended the use of children to make and pack matches for the same reason, in spite of the fact that the children were suffering, going blind and dying of malnutrition. I felt like hitting the television (I quite often feel like hitting the television, actually). So, I guess it is a good idea to question values, especially if they hurt someone else. But that doesn't mean we have to have a moral vacuum, or that we should be afraid to stand up for what we believe and know to be right. It seems to me to be just plain common sense to say loudly and clearly that we want our children to have values, and that we're proud if they do.

Our values might not be exactly the same as they were in the distant past, but I suspect that my grandmother would agree with ninety per cent of what I've written. One thing that has changed that she would definitely not approve of is pregnant women and old people standing on public transport while young, healthy, strong children and young people sit. I always get up and offer a seat, because it was one of the values taught to me. It drives me wild when children push past to sit down, leaving their elders tottering.

There is a slight twist in the tale, though. Recently, an elderly, white-haired gentleman at least twenty years older than me got up and offered me his seat. What was the correct thing to do? The man was being kind and compassionate and had probably been taught to give up his seat to a lady, so I graciously accepted. A conflict of values, if ever there was one. On the other hand, maybe I looked older than him?

It Sometimes Works

I know we don't always get it right, but we try our best and, once in a while, something happens that makes you feel it was worth it. I will remember until my dying day a Saturday morning just after the James Bulger murder trial had ended. I was driving my eleven-year-old son to football and was stopped at a traffic light when the pedestrian light went out and our light turned green. Frozen in the middle of the road was a blind man who had obviously become slightly confused. It was single-lane traffic and the driver behind me could not see what had happened. He began honking.

Before I could say a word, my son was out of the car. He escorted the man across the road and jumped back into his seat. In the meantime, the light turned red for us. As we finally pulled off and turned the corner, a taxi driver in a black taxi pulled up next to me and signalled for me to roll down the window. I did so, half expecting to be told off, but the man smiled, handed something to my son and said, 'Have a treat on me. I wish we had a million more like you.' As he drove off, my son looked at the pound coin in his hand and asked why the driver had done that. I knew the driver and I were contrasting my son's actions with those of the boys who had murdered Jamie and that my son was the same age as them, but I couldn't say a word – my eyes and heart were too full. Maybe, just maybe, my son had a few good values to see him through.

PS: Perhaps I should have urged my son to give his pound to charity, but I told him to keep it and buy a treat. Virtue may be its own reward, but a little reinforcement never hurt.

Ten Important Values

If I had to pick out the most important values that I really hope my children will take through life, they would be:

1. *Compassion.*
2. *A conscience.*
3. *An understanding of consequences to actions.*
4. *Honesty.*
5. *A sense of responsibility.*
6. *Courage.*
7. *Respect.*
8. *A sense of fairness.*
9. *Sportsmanship.*
10. *Sympathy for others.*

Eleven Ways to Help Them Develop Values

To sum up the best ways of ensuring those values are taught, I would try:

1. *Praising their good actions.*
2. *Teaching by example.*
3. *Discussing issues about values.*
4. *Pointing out good actions of others.*
5. *Using 'what if?' questions to bring out value judgements.*
6. *Asking children for their opinions and ideas and listening when they talk.*
7. *Using books, radio and television to reinforce values.*
8. *Letting your children know your values and expectations.*

9. *Using consequences to both good and bad actions to teach children.*
10. *Showing your disappointment if your children slip up, and helping them to learn the right way to behave.*
11. *Being a parent and being willing to take a stand.*

Have you ever had a 'values' dilemma, or have you a great way to teach children a way through the moral maze? Let me know and I will include it in the next edition. And I will use it with my own kids!

Books for Teaching Values

Young Children

Pinocchio	Loyalty, conscience, lying
The Three Little Pigs	Hard work, loyalty, courage
Snow White	Cruelty, kindness, love, loyalty
The Tale of Peter Rabbit	Lying, disobedience, love
Dr Seuss – The Sneetches	Prejudice
Dr Seuss – The Grinch	Greed
Dr Seuss – Horton Hears a Who	Everyone is valuable
Dr Seuss – The Lorax	Environment
Charlotte's Web	Helping each other
The Wind in the Willows	Kindness, loyalty
Please & Thank You,	Manners, consideration
by Richard Scary	

Older Children

Aesop's Fables	Full of tales of wisdom
Watership Down	Courage, environment, evil, loyalty
Little Women/Little Men	Respect, responsibility, caring
The Wizard of Oz	Courage, love, intelligence
The Beech Tree	Love and understanding
The Secret Garden	Kindness, caring, assertiveness
A Christmas Carol	Consequences, kindness, conscience

The Trumpeter of Krakow	Courage
Kes	Courage, prejudice, kindness, caring
Black Beauty	Kindness to animals
The Adventures of Tom Sawyer/	Conscience, respect, loyalty, kindness,
The Adventures of	Consequences, honesty, prejudice
Huckleberry Finn	

18

WAYS TO MOTIVATE YOUR CHILD TO BE A WINNER

Have you ever wondered why some children seem to develop certain traits or skills, and wished that your child could do the same? 'I just wish Will would learn to play the piano – I always regretted that I didn't,' or 'My children don't enjoy reading, but my nieces and nephews seem to love it,' or 'Sally is so popular and funny, if only my Judith were like that.'

Why do some children seem to succeed, while others with equal ability just get by? It isn't always the brightest who excel, or those born into families with power and influence. We only have to look to certain members of the aristocracy who are constantly in trouble with the law to know that just having money or privileges, or even being intelligent, counts for very little if you aren't motivated to succeed.

There are some ways we can help our children to become winners, each in their own way:

1. Share Your Own Interests and Skills

Charlie is an excellent saxophone player. He plays with the school band and has won honours in many contests. Everyone comments on how lucky his parents are to have such a talented son.

Shelly loves science. She has won prizes in school science fairs ever since she first started school. Her science teacher foresees a promising future for her at a top university, and then in the field of research. Maybe she will find a cure for some dread disease.

James is the star soccer player in his school. He gets his work done so he can practise his skills every day. No-one pushes him, he does it for the sheer joy of playing.

If Lisa has a spare moment, she is either reading a book or writing a story. She is full of ideas and is a bright, popular girl who is seen as a class leader. 'Wish we had more like her,' is her headmaster's comment to her parents.

These four young people have different interests and skills, but they have one important thing in common. Each child has a parent who also excels in or is interested in their child's particular skill. And each child's parent has helped their child to foster that skill. A parent's interest and support in a skill or subject can be a very powerful influence on a child.

Charlie's mother loves music and, although she can't play a note, there have been music and singing in Charlie's home. His mother remembers dancing around the kitchen, 'Pregnant, singing away to the radio.' When Charlie was born, his parents played music to him and sang him to sleep at night. Charlie himself grew up associating music with warmth, love and fun. His parents could not afford a piano, much to Charlie's mum's regret. She would have loved for him to play the piano. But an elderly relative died, and when an old saxophone was found amongst his possessions, it was given to young Charlie. His parents had it refurbished and Charlie taught himself to play with a do-it-yourself book. Charlie, now sixteen, plans a career in music.

Shelly's mother teaches science. Shelly's room seems at first glance to be a complete mess, but on further inspection you see experiments going on everywhere. Her mother says she was, 'Pulling apart toys to see how they worked as soon as her fingers would let her. I was half afraid that I would come down one morning to find her taking apart the refrigerator.' But Shelly's mother didn't tidy up the messes Shelly made; instead she sat down with her daughter and complimented her on what she was doing. She was always interested in Shelly's experiments. 'I didn't try to turn her into a scientist, it just came about naturally,' she says.

Jamie's dad played soccer with his local club, and Jamie and his sister were taken to matches from the time they could walk. The whole family went along, and often spent the entire day out with picnics and lots of fun and laughter. Their father spent loads of time just 'fooling around and kicking the ball about with the kids'. Not surprisingly Jamie and his sister ended up loving the game.

Lisa's parents don't watch much television. When Lisa was little, her parents read to her and let her play with books. Although she is thirteen, Lisa still enjoys cuddling up to her mother or father while they each read their own books. Sunday morning is an orgy of newspaper reading, with everyone in the family competing to read out the most humorous, bizarre or interesting story of the day. Debate over issues brought up is often boisterous and good-natured. Clearly, that family emphasis on reading has paid dividends.

None of these parents put pressure on their children. They simply spent time and had fun with their children around what turned out to be a shared interest. There were no hidden messages that 'You'd better do this' – just loads of attention, approval and support attached to the activities. Try:

a) Spending time with your children in the activity you wish to encourage.
b) Making the activity as fun as possible, so children will want to carry on with it.
c) Paying lots of attention to your children when they show an independent interest in the activity.
d) Praising and rewarding your children's efforts.

2. Build Your Child's Self-esteem with Praise

'Clever girl!' Two-year-old Sarah's mother scoops up her daughter and gives her a big hug. Sarah squirms with delight. What has brought about this jubilation? Sarah has put her jumper on by herself. The fact that it is back to front and inside out doesn't matter. She feels proud of her achievement and her mother is starting her on the road to self-esteem.

When Jamie missed an important goal and felt really terrible, his dad's comment was, 'Never mind, there's always a next time and you did your best.' Jamie still wished he had made the goal, but he knew that his dad still had faith in him.

School results for Lucy were not as good as she'd hoped, but she and her parents knew that she hadn't given it her best effort. In fact, there had been angry words about how her study habits took second place to her desire to go out with friends and talk on the telephone. Lucy was depressed about the results and her parents wanted to say 'told you so'. Nevertheless, her parents bit their tongues and said, 'We know you aren't happy with what you've done, but we believe you can do better. How can we work together to make sure this doesn't happen again?' At least they were giving Lucy the message that they knew she had it in her to do better, instead of telling her that she was a failure.

Children who feel good about themselves are much more likely to become winners. I think that building self-esteem is one of the most important things we can do for children, and we can start from the moment they give us that first smile. When we smile back and say to our babies that they are brilliant (even if it was just a burp that produced that smile), they don't understand the words, but they soon get the idea. Of course, it will need to be tempered with kindness and compassion and all those other things discussed in the chapter on values, but a child with self-esteem is ready to try anything.

Try using some of the following messages with your children:

When It Doesn't Quite Work Out
- *Nice try, I'm proud of you.*
- *You've really improved.*
- *You're doing much better.*
- *Great effort.*
- *I can tell you've been practising.*
- *You're getting the hang of it.*
- *You really stuck to that.*
- *You've come a long way.*
- *Every day it's getting a little better.*
- *Things take time, don't be discouraged.*
- *Rome wasn't built in a day.*
- *You're learning a lot.*

Praise for Achievement
- *Brilliant.*
- *Well done.*
- *I'm so proud of you and what you've done.*
- *Clever girl/boy.*
- *Fantastic.*
- *You deserve to be very proud.*
- *You're a winner.*
- *You're a star.*
- *You're first rate – couldn't be better.*
- *Marvellous achievement.*
- *You've outdone yourself.*
- *I'm so proud that you're my son/daughter.*

I am sure that you have a million things you could say – these are just to get you going. Praise works wonders to build self-esteem. Try it!

3. Encourage Curiosity

'Why doesn't the moon crash into the earth?' asked Tony. 'That's a very good question, young man. It's to do with gravity,' replied his grandfather. 'What's gravity?' 'Well, it's the pull of the earth and it keeps us from falling off and other things from falling down on us,' said grandfather. 'But, I don't understand,' said Tony. 'I've got a great idea, Tony, let's go to the library and find a book which can explain it a bit better.' Tony and his grandfather found a book and then did a couple of experiments which were at the right level of understanding for Tony. But, more importantly, Tony's grandfather showed Tony that there are ways to find out information and that everyone goes on learning. He fostered Tony's curiosity instead of giving him a perfunctory answer and getting rid of the pesky kid. Telling Tony that his question was a good one will also make Tony want to ask more questions.

We can encourage children's curiosity by:

a) Answering their questions as best we can.
b) Saying things like, 'I am really pleased you are asking questions,' instead of sighing and rolling your eyes.

c) Comment to others in front of your children that you love it when they are curious about things, instead of saying 'He drives me nuts with all his questions' – this is a sure way to stop curiosity dead in its tracks.

d) Involve your children with you in finding answers – don't just tell them to 'go look it up' themselves. Your involvement makes it more likely that they will ask again, and that their curiosity will grow.

e) Never say 'Curiosity killed the cat!'

4. Encourage Lots of Different Experiences

Tom loved the Science Museum. 'I finally had to drag him away in order to pick up the other children on time. He burst into tears because there were masses more levers, buttons and wheels to push and turn, and he wanted to do it all. I promised to bring him again next week. I never thought he would enjoy it so much.' Tom's father was pleasantly surprised that his son would be so excited about the museum. He thought that it might be tame after things like amusement parks and computer games.

Children's intellectual horizons will be expanded if they have the opportunity to experience as many different activities and interests as possible. By making the effort to get your children to as many different places and activities as you can – exhibitions, museums, plays, cinema, concerts, railway journeys, sports events and anything else you can think of – you will increase their appreciation of life's experiences. Although many children get information about the world from television, and though much of that information is excellent, television is a poor substitute for hands-on experience.

When Jane took her five-year-old god-daughter to a concert for the first time, she was amazed that the little girl thought music came from tape cassettes. She really did not know that people played the instruments. 'I just assumed that somewhere along the way she would have realised this,' said Jane. 'The good thing is that she now wants to try an instrument, though I do think the tuba is too big for her!'

What you are doing is giving your children a variety of things which might inspire them to try something new and different, and which could give them another opportunity to shine and to develop a new skill. Perhaps Tom's parents will get him a science experiment kit for Christmas instead of another computer game, and set him on a different path in life. You never know.

Here are a few ways to widen your child's horizons:

a) Find out what is happening locally that might be interesting, and try to arrange to take your children.
b) Check on the free days at museums and go with your children and friends. Make it a fun excursion and take your lunch and some treats.
c) Check on interactive children's theatres in your area.
d) Enrol your child in a pottery class or tap dancing or cooking – check with your local authority.
e) Find out about half-price tickets for plays, and support your local theatre groups.
f) If your children have never been to a soccer or cricket match, take them.
g) Watch out for specials from the railways when you can take your children on a day outing for a very small price, or even free, with your ticket.
h) Get your children a library ticket and take them often.
i) Often, there are concerts in parks or churches or libraries. Many children have never heard instruments played live.

The more things children try, the more likely it is they will find something they enjoy and which will improve their self-esteem.

5. Help Your Children Assess Their Strengths.

'I just don't know what to do for my project,' Gareth told his mother. Gareth's teacher had asked the class to write about what they saw themselves doing in ten years' time. 'Let's think about what you like to do and what you're good at, and then see what kinds of things you could do with those strengths,' replied his mother. A wise woman, Gareth's mum. She was helping him to think for himself and to appreciate his own abilities. Together they made a list of Gareth's strengths:

Reading
History
Writing
Thinking of ideas to save the environment
Loving animals
Playing rugby
Good balance
Good eyesight
Gets along with friends
Likes travelling
Skiing
Swimming
Happy most of the time
Feeding the goldfish
Good hand-eye co-ordination

When they had compiled the list, they looked up a variety of jobs and activities in books in the library, knowing full well that in ten years' time there should be lots of other jobs not even thought of today. Gareth thought that being a vet was a great idea because he loves animals, but his lack of interest in science would probably be a hindrance. The idea of writing and broadcasting about environmental issues was very appealing as was becoming a coach for sports, because he enjoys games and likes working with people. Being a travel guide was rejected because of Gareth's indifference to languages, but he thought he might *write* a travel guide.

Gareth eventually decided to do his project on being a broadcaster who played rugby with his local club at the weekends! He felt quite good about his project and learned that his strengths and interests now would probably influence what he did in later life.

If children can be helped to realise their own strengths, it can make a difference in their attitudes towards school and other activities. Gareth's mother posted his strengths on the front of the refrigerator and noticed that Gareth would sometimes pause beside the fridge and read them over with a smile on his face.

Help your children by:

a) Making a list with them of their strengths.
b) Posting the list and updating it when necessary.
c) Encouraging them to think about their strengths.
d) Praising the things they do.
e) Finding examples of people who have used similar strengths to do exciting or interesting things in life.
f) Giving them biographies of people who have achieved things which you think your child might be interested in.
g) Encouraging them to ignore any weaknesses they can't change or which don't hinder them. Too often, people focus on what they can't do rather than what they *can* do.

6. Help Your Children Decide What They Want to Accomplish

In the summer before the beginning of each new school year, Angela sits down with her children individually and helps them think of what they would like to accomplish that year, academically, socially and in other activities. It isn't a great long list, but includes goals for the year and sometimes more long-term, like eventual career plans. One of her children's lists included:

> Get to school on time
> Get a better mark in French
> Turn in homework on time
> Get to know at least one new student
> Keep my friends
> Do at least one good deed for someone
> Improve in gymnastics

Angela goes over the list with her children, listens to their concerns and makes suggestions. She also notes things that might signify a problem. Because her daughter had mentioned 'Keep my friends' on her list, Angela asked if her daughter was happy about what was happening with her friends. It transpired that there had been some problems and her daughter was quite worried about starting the new year because she was feeling left out. As it turned out, they decided to invite the girls over before school started and the problem was nipped in the bud.

Put the list in a safe place and go over it once a term to see if the goals are being achieved, and how you can help if they aren't.

Try:

a) Helping your children think of what they want to achieve.
b) Discussing with them how to reach their goals.
c) Helping them set realistic targets. Being elected to Parliament at the age of eight might be a bit ambitious (although it could be an improvement on some Members), but visiting Parliament and finding out how to go about becoming an MP is realistic.
d) Helping them to break the goal into manageable bits – saving whales is a great idea, but perhaps it needs to be done in stages.
e) Updating their goals with them on a regular basis.

7. Help Your Child Cope with Disappointment

Susan was desperate to get the main part in the school play, but when the roles were announced, she was playing a minor character. She fled the school and came home, bursting into tears as she entered the door. Her father knew how much she had practised and rehearsed for the audition and how much it meant to her. 'We all know that there are disappointments and discouraging things which happen in life. I've certainly had my fair share, but somehow it always seems worse if it happens to your child. You want to take the hurt away, take it on yourself instead of on them.'

A completely understandable reaction – I feel the same way. But part of learning to be successful inevitably includes setbacks. If our children learn to deal with these disappointments they will be less likely to be pulled down by depression and life's curve balls.

Susan's father didn't know what to say, so he wrapped his daughter up in a big hug and told her soothingly that he was so proud she had auditioned for the play because he himself would never have had the courage. He didn't care what part she had, it was better than he had ever done as far as drama was concerned. To his delight, his daughter stopped crying and looked at him in astonishment. Her father was an executive with a large company and was always making presentations, so this was news to her.

What Sarah didn't realise was that her father had always been terrified of getting up in front of people and had to steel himself even now. He also told her about the time when he was in school and had wanted to run for a student election. He practised and practised what he was going to say, but never went through with it – nerves got the better of him. But her father had taken a course in public speaking, because he was determined to go into a business that demanded this skill. So, even if he didn't enjoy it, he could do it.

Sarah's father said he didn't know how to help Sarah cope, but he instinctively did the right thing for her. By sharing his own sense of failure at not trying out for the student election, he showed her that people get through these things and are sometimes motivated to change things. He also made her feel good that she had been brave enough to audition for the play in the first place, something he had been unable ever to do. Telling her he was proud of her achievement, even if it wasn't as great as she wished, was like a balm to her.

To help children cope with disappointments;

a) Accept that it is important and don't say 'It doesn't matter' – it obviously does matter to your child.
b) Say you are sorry it happened.
c) Give them hugs and attention, no matter how big they are. Inside, they feel about two, and they want your support.
d) Tell them about times when you were discouraged or disappointed, but try to mention how something good followed. No point saying something like, 'I never got over what happened'. *Wrong!* Choose your examples to help your child cope, not to encourage him or her to give up.

8. Help Your Child Learn to Relax and Enjoy Life

'Gill is always wound up like a top,' complained her mother. 'If she is like this at her age, I hate to think what will happen to her when she gets out into the real world.' Gill's mother is right to be concerned, but the funny thing is she is ten times worse than her daughter, and doesn't know it. Guess where Gill has learned her behaviour from? No prizes for right answers, sorry!

I have a friend who drives us all to distraction. She never relaxes, and wonders why we all make excuses to leave after being with her for less than an hour. She cannot sit down and talk, and always finds something to do like make a fifth cup of coffee, plump up the cushions, fiddle with the cord of the telephone – it's perpetual motion. An hour in her company leaves me feeling slightly more hyper than the cartoon character the Road Runner. The most noticeable problem she has, though, is that she is so busy being busy that she doesn't listen to anyone. She simply cannot relax long enough to engage in meaningful conversation. Sad, but true.

Back to Gill. Why do we care if our children relax or not? Because when you're relaxed you are receptive to other people, your mind is clearer and ready to accept information, your body isn't at war with itself and you can tune into your own feelings and thoughts.

Of course, there are times when you might function better if you are slightly tense and the adrenalin is flowing, perhaps before a big game, or before a performance or test. But functioning on that level all the time just leads to burn out and children need to know how to relax. You can help them by:

a) Teaching them to sit or stand very still.
b) Asking them to close their eyes and think of something calm, like a clear lake or a sunny meadow or a peaceful experience they have had (like sitting on Gran's lap and having a story read to them).
c) Teaching them to breathe deeply, slowly and calmly.
d) Asking them to hold the thought that is relaxing them and to focus on it until they feel quite calm and still.

e) Explaining that they can use this technique whenever they feel themselves getting upset, or before they have to try to do something difficult or of great importance to them.

The ability to relax helps children (and the rest of us) to put aside worries or distractions and to focus on what we need to do. Believe me, it helps in writing as well – mind you, just now I felt like relaxing and not carrying on, so I guess I'd better focus!

9. Pay Attention to Your Child's Work and Work Habits

My youngest son came in the door, threw a pile of papers in my direction and waltzed out of the room. I knew he was dying to talk with me about them, but he wanted me to make a fuss and look at them first and then to come and find him to tell him how brilliant I thought he was. It's a kind of ritual in our house – passed down from generation to generation, I think. I used to do the same with my parents and grandmother. I didn't want to appear to be too pleased, but I couldn't wait for the adulation I knew would come. Some papers, I confess, never made it home, but then you can't expect a kid to ask for trouble, can you?

When Johnny or Louise bring home their work or reports from school, take the time to go over them and read them. Comment about specific things you like and ask them what they think. Make a fuss, put the work on the refrigerator (why don't they make stronger fridge magnets? Papers end up on the floor whenever we take out the milk), ring their grandparents and brag about them, tell them how proud and pleased you are.

When dealing with your children's work habits, ensure that there is a place they can do their homework in peace – not in front of the television. For some children, it is essential that they have a quiet place; others seem to function quite well in a busy, slightly noisy kitchen. My eldest son informs me that he *has* to have music or his brain withers. I'm not convinced, but he is doing fine, so I won't complain – yet.

Ensure that your children have all the information they need to do their reports or homework. Check to see if they need any help, but never do their work for them.

Make sure that your children get to school on time and go with something in their stomachs. A recent study showed that children who eat breakfast function better than those who don't.

Don't come back from holiday three days after the start of term – it isn't fair for your child to have to start from behind. Try to make appointments with doctors and dentists outside school hours.

Encourage debate and discussion about issues. The dinner table is a great place to bring up subjects which tie into what your children are studying (bad place to bring up biology experiments, however).

So, to summarise:

a) Take a real interest in papers and reports that come home.
b) Ensure your children get to school on time.
c) Don't take extra holiday which means your children miss out on the beginning of term.
d) Ensure that your children have the right information at hand for doing their work.
e) Create a place for doing homework.
f) Send them off with a full stomach.

10. Encourage Self-congratulation

I know, I know . . . it's very un-British to encourage self-congratulation. I can just hear you saying, 'We'll end up with precocious little monsters bragging about themselves – insufferable!' That isn't what I mean, actually, though I see nothing wrong with being able to say, 'I did that well.' No, what we're talking about is teaching children to *tell themselves* that they did well or that they can do a brilliant job. Ask your children to practise saying to themselves that they are great, wonderful, fantastic and that they are going to do it (whatever it is).

This is exactly the sort of thing top athletes and business people and actors and musicians do. They jig themselves up by saying, 'This is going to be my best performance ever,' or 'I'm going to get that commission because I have the best product,' or 'Today I'm going to win that medal because I deserve it after all my hard work.' Sort of like – watch out world, here I come. I'm a winner! Try it!

19

THE TEN WORST AND TEN BEST
THINGS YOU CAN SAY TO YOUR KIDS

For all parents with badly bitten tongues, here are some ideas about what *not* to say to your kids.

Lisa comes through the front door, drops her books on the floor, deposits her jumper on the kitchen work-surface, steps in the dog's bowl of water and grabs a handful of jelly babies on her way out of the room. 'Lisa come back here, you stupid girl. How could you be so inconsiderate? Why can't you do anything right?'

You're on a longed-for holiday. All you want to do is relax by the pool. Then it starts. 'Did not.' 'Did.' Whack! 'Muuuuummie – he hit me.' 'Out of my sight, both of you. I wish I'd never had children.'

How could we say such things to our kids?

Give me a break – we've all done it. We've all said things we wish we could take back. Let's face it, children *can* drive you crazy, and none of us says the right thing every time. Of course, we feel annoyed at times – even murderous – and we do make hurtful comments.

Not that the occasional remark will wound them for life, but we'd all agree that it isn't the best way to talk to children or to teach them how to behave. In fact, a barrage of negative comments could destroy your child's confidence altogether.

Marcia still remembers her mother's favourite put-down. 'I'm glad I had your sister – you're nothing but trouble.' At thirty-five

Marcia is nervous, worried and feels she is worthless. She has been divorced three times and has four children who are unhappy little creatures. She is still afraid of her mother and cannot stand her sister. Marcia is one of the casualties of parental power gone wrong. Even so, she admits to saying much the same thing to her children as was said to her in childhood . . . and so the sad pattern continues.

Usually, when we make hurtful comments, it is because we are frustrated and angry, and not because of deep psychological problems. But even if it might be a natural reaction to lash out, we need to remember the effect that it can have.

Try asking your friends if they can remember something said to them as children which still rankles. Forty-year-old Michael is hurt to this day by his father's comment. 'He told me I was an idiot, with such contempt that it really hurt. I still get a tight feeling when I think about it.'

Take heart, we all make mistakes along the way. But what we say to our children does have an amazing influence on them. Just think how often we hear ourselves repeating something our parents said to us. If we *can* break the cycle, our children and grandchildren will be the real winners.

Read on for the ten worst and best things we can say to our children. And see if any of them rings a bell with you . . .

The Worst

1. 'You're So Stupid!'

Parents can often say this in exasperation or in panic.

Karen's four-year-old daughter dashed into the path of a car, which squealed to a halt just inches from the terrified child. Karen grabbed her daughter and shouted: 'You're so stupid!' Of course, this was blind fear taking over. Karen said she gave her daughter a hug later and apologised, but she had thought her daughter was going to die, and couldn't believe it when the car stopped. I doubt her daughter will remember the exact words Mummy used – no real harm done.

Sara, on the other hand, uses: 'You're so stupid' as a weapon. Her children hear it frequently and say it to each other and to friends. More important, they believe it. They are downtrodden kids who do badly at school and who feel they cannot win. Surprise surprise – they can't. Inside, they are saying to themselves: 'Doesn't matter, I'm just stupid anyway.'

'Stupid', 'dumb' and 'idiot' are such negative words. They destroy confidence and initiative. Children learn to value themselves from those around them. If we tell them they are stupid, they will always feel inadequate.

Sometimes kids do stupid things. (Sometimes, so do we.) If we could remember to respond to the action, not the child, as in 'That was a stupid thing to do,' not 'You're stupid,' then we'd be doing well. It helps to have some phrase like: 'When you do that it drives me up the wall,' so you won't blurt out something you'll later regret.

2. 'You Could Do So Well, if Only . . .'

Keith said that his parents were constantly told by his teachers that 'He could do so well, if only . . .' in other words, that he had potential. 'That meant I wasn't doing enough to please them. But then I never could do enough to please them.'

Have you ever noticed that the word 'potential' is never used positively? As Keith says: 'Having potential is like having an illness. When I was little I thought I might outgrow it.'

If your child has abilities he is not using, don't despair, just plot. Wait until your child does something you can praise. Then say: 'You have really improved. That makes me really happy.' If you can praise what he does right, you may be able to bury that word potential and he may even finally live up to it.

3. 'Why Can't You Be More Like . . .'

This is never said as a compliment. Think about it – if you want your child to be like someone else, then you want him to be less like himself.

'I was always told to be more like my brother,' said Stephanie. 'I ended up hating my brother and not feeling good about myself, either. It seemed he did everything right and I was a dud – sometimes I wished I hadn't been born.'

Stephanie's parents could have focused on the behaviour they wanted her to change. Why did they want her to be more like her brother? If he was neater, they could have given her specific ideas, such as cleaning up her room. If he was better at maths, they could have homed in on her talents and praised what she did well. As it was, she just felt generally anxious and was sure she could not live up to anyone.

Stephanie was four years younger than her brother. What probably happened was that her parents forgot how long it took her brother to learn to walk, talk, and so on. It quite often happens that parents make unfair comparisons between older and younger children.

4. 'I Wish I Didn't Have Kids'

We may all wish this at least once in a while, but we should never say it, ever. It is the ultimate rejection for children and one of the most devastating things to hear.

If you do feel angry enough to say this, take a deep breath and say: 'Sometimes you make me mad enough to spit.' Or use the intellectual approach: 'When you do that I feel very angry.'

If things get to the point that you want to lash out verbally like this, take yourself out of the situation. Leave the room – it's called 'time out for grown-ups' and is a valid way to deal with extreme frustration and the desire to be single and carefree again. (Those were the days, you must admit.) It's normal to feel you want out sometimes, but it's *not* 'OK' to tell the kids! They'll find out on their own one day.

5. 'Look at All I've Given Up for You'

Groan! This is a comment most adults remember with a mixture of anger and guilt. In other words: 'If you hadn't been born, my life would have been better and I could have accomplished so much. It is your fault that I am a failure.' It's a trite saying, but children *don't* ask to be born. Parents are there to take care of children and that can mean sacrifices. But kids don't need to be told and are not interested anyway – what can they do about it? Disappear? Some have tried . . .

Sharon ran away from home when she was fifteen. She could no longer take her mother's continual stream of abusive remarks about how difficult it was having children. 'I decided that I would be doing her a favour if I just left.' Now married with three children of her own, she rarely sees her parents. 'It is too painful – my Mum still plays the same record over and over and she doesn't know she does it. I say to my children that they are the best thing that ever happened to me, and I mean it.'

If you have given up a lot for your children (and, let's face it, who hasn't) and are tempted to tell them, stop. Don't ever say it.

6. 'You're a Liar, a Thief and a Lazy Good-for-nothing'

Seven-year-old Larry took his brother's toy soldiers and then lied when asked about it. 'You're not only a liar, but a thief as well,' shouted his parents, enraged that a son of theirs could steal and have the audacity to lie about it.

Most kids steal and lie. They learn from it, outgrow it and move on *unless* we label them. Kids believe what we tell them, and if we say they are lazy, thieves or liars, they begin to think of themselves that way.

Try saying that you don't like laziness or stealing or lying – attack the behaviour, not the child. Sometimes, though, you can get away with calling your child a 'lazy good-for-nothing kid' as long as everyone knows you don't mean it and that it just reflects an off-beat family sense of humour. In fact, humour can forgive a lot, as long as it isn't at your child's expense.

7. 'Don't Be Silly, There's Nothing to Be Frightened of'

Eight-year-old John woke up in the middle of the night, screaming. His dad hurried to comfort him. 'There's a monster in the cupboard, Daddy.' 'Don't be so silly, there's nothing to be frightened of,' he replies.

By saying this, we give our children potentially harmful messages. It's silly to be scared. Is it? Parents know there aren't monsters in the cupboard, but they are very real to John. It's far better to say: 'It's all right to be scared. All children get frightened sometimes. I know there is nothing in the cupboard, but let's look together.' Telling a child it is silly to be scared won't make the fear go away, but may prevent the child telling you about his fears in the future.

By saying that it is all right to be frightened, you are also acknowledging that the world can be a frightening place and that you will support your child through his fears.

8. 'I'm Going to Leave You'

You are in a hurry and Lucy is dragging behind looking at the toys in the shop. 'If you don't come right this minute, I'm leaving,' and off you go towards the door. Lucy panics and runs behind, crying. The thought of Mummy leaving reinforces the basic childhood fear that you may disappear and never return. Andy, fifty-five, still remembers his mother getting in the car and driving away, just to stop him always dawdling. It worked – he never dawdled again. Instead, however, he became clingy, whiny and was terrified to ever leave his mum in case she left for good. Try giving your child a few minutes warning and then giving them the choice of taking your hand or being carried. Bribes will also work: 'If you come now, we will have time for a story or a treat.'

9. 'You Must Always Obey Grown-ups'

A mother from Wales wrote: 'I was sitting in the park reading while my three-year-old daughter played. I glanced up to see her being led away by a man. I ran after them and found myself in an isolated place with this man. Knowing we were both in danger, I just chatted to him, took my daughter's hand and edged away. When I asked her why she had gone with him, she replied: "He told me to obey him." I shudder now to think that my insistence on always obeying adults could have had such terrible consequences.'

By all means teach children to respect adults, but also explain that there may be times when it isn't safe to obey.

10. 'Wait Until Your Father Gets Home'

To set one parent up as the disciplinarian is an awful thing to do – bad both for the parent and the child.

Peter still shudders when he remembers this threat. 'Whenever we did something wrong as children, Mum would threaten: 'Wait until your father gets home.' We knew that meant a spanking, and dreaded Dad coming in the door. Can you imagine living all day with that fear and hating our father because he administered the punishment?'

Whatever form of discipline we use with our children (and I am against hitting them), it is better done at the time and by the person who is with the child. If Matthew hits Sam and the punishment is a set time, when books and/or TV are not allowed, then do it while Matthew still remembers what the punishment is for. It is much fairer, it will get the message across and is kinder to the child.

The Best

1. 'You've Always Been a Plus in My Life'

Tell your children how important they are to you. It's a wonderful thing to hear. For a child to know that she is the best thing to happen to you sets her up for life with good feelings about herself.

2. 'Telling Is OK'

'Mummy, Jessica pushed me.' 'Don't tell tales,' you reply without skipping a beat.

Jessica isn't 'telling tales', she's saying what happed and wondering what she or you should do about it. She's testing her new-found independence to see how to respond to the world; how should she react if she has been taught not to fight or hit.

Why do we tell children to be quiet, not to tell tales, keep the code of silence? It's probably because we were told the same thing when we were growing up. Next time, think twice and say; 'Let's see what we can do about this.' This will give Jessica some strategies on how to deal with similar situations in the future and show her that you are interested in what is happening to her.

3. 'I Am Proud of You, You Did That So Well'

Jenny had just tied her shoe for the first time. 'Jenny, that was wonderful,' said her mum. 'I'm proud of you.' Jenny beamed at her mother's praise. It is lovely to think that someone is proud of you. It gives a child the incentive to try anything. Don't be afraid to praise and to praise often.

4. 'I Said NO'

Nancy wanted more than anything to be friends with her children. She remembered how her parents had always been so negative, and how frightened she was of them. Determined not to let that happen with her family, she allowed them everything. She never said 'no'. By the time her kids were teenagers they were rude, demanding and wouldn't listen to anyone.

What her children *wanted* were limits, they needed a mother with grown-up judgement, not a benevolent older sister. However much they protest, children need guidance. It's great to treat kids with respect, but they need our maturity to put them on the path to responsible behaviour. It took some time for Nancy to realise it was OK to get angry and to say 'no'. In fact, her kids were secretly relieved to blame Mum for 'not letting me do it'. They didn't lose face and were saved from having to act beyond their years.

5. 'It's All Right to Cry or Feel Sad or Scared'

On holiday, we were walking behind a young family. Their three-year-old son was wobbling along on a bicycle with stabilisers and fell off just in front of us. He howled loudly. His father crouched down, took him in his arms and said: 'That hurt, didn't it? You have a good cry until it feels better.' Give children permission to cry, to feel sad or frightened. It lets them come to terms with their own feelings, not just our ideas about how they should feel.

6. 'It's OK to Make Mistakes'

Well . . . some mistakes. Being calm when Kathy spills indelible red ink on a white wool carpet may be beyond most of us, but helping children to learn that everyone makes mistakes is not. Some mistakes will have consequences, such as having your fifteen-year-old come in an hour after an agreed curfew. She may be grounded for a particular time, but it isn't the end of the world.

Children will make mistakes growing up. Keep them in perspective, or kids will be so scared of making a mistake that they won't try anything. So, if your four-year-old picks the rare orchid your husband has been cultivating and presents it to you, smile, keep your cool – and leave town!

7. 'You're So Clever to Have Worked That Out'

Giving a child the chance to sort things out on his own will give him the confidence to try. If your child tries and fails, you can say: 'It's really great that you tried. I'm so pleased you did.'

8. 'You Don't Have to Do Anything'

Nowadays, children have every waking hour filled with 'meaningful activities' – ballet, art, music lessons, tennis lessons, chess, football training – you name it and children are able to sign up for it.

When my children say they've nothing to do, I reply: 'You're lucky.' What about time to be, to think, to wonder? When my sons go to Andrew's house, his mum always has the day planned. First the cinema, then pizza, then supervised tennis. It is all right once in a while, but Andrew has his whole life planned for him. It destroys creativity and the play kids need. When Andrew comes to our house, he loves it. 'You don't have to *do* anything here,' he says wistfully.

Continually entertaining kids doesn't help them to develop. 'Don't *do* anything' might just startle them into their own activity. What a good idea!

9. 'I Like You Because You're You'

Wouldn't you love it if someone said that to you, with no 'ifs' or 'buts'? A child needs to feel that he is 'just right' as he is . . . today, this minute, now. You're also saying that your child doesn't have to prove anything to you; it's enough that they are there.

10. 'I Love You'

For children, these are the best three words in the English language. As parents, we should use them at least once a day, if not more often.

20

WAYS TO KEEP YOUR SANITY
AS A PARENT

(Assuming You Had Any to Start with)

'Why didn't anyone tell me it would be like this?' wailed Cynthia, mother of three children under the age of five. She was up to her ears in paint, plasticine and pooh. I waded in to help with the paint and plasticine, but let her take care of the pooh – friendship only goes so far with me, I'm afraid.

Several fraught minutes (or hours, I forget) later, we were commiserating over a cup of tea.

'No-one tells us how stressful it all is because otherwise we'd never have kids,' said Cynthia. 'Then, where would the human race be?'

An hour later, when the little monsters were peacefully sleeping, we decided that it wasn't really so bad after all – we could cope with all the stress. Until they wake up, that is.

I think every new parent should be given a leaflet offering advice on how to cope with parenthood. It could be entitled 101 Ways to Get Through the Next Ten Minutes. There are parents who say that they sailed through it all and their children never caused them stress for even a moment. How splendid for them. They are either zombies or saints or liars!

If I were writing this leaflet for parents, I would start from the premise that, sooner or later, we all go through a time when we just want to forget the whole parenthood business and find a desert island immediately. Here are some tips culled from all my friends and acquaintances about how they coped when the going got rough:

1. Fantasise

Anna, thirty-four-year-old mother of two, said there were times when she was so stressed that the only way she could cope was to pretend she was somewhere else. Remaining sane through fantasising might not seem like such a good idea, but I think she was clever. She said she sat at the kitchen table and just imagined herself on a Greek island with no one else around (no Shirley Valentine, our Anna). She saw herself swimming, drinking Ouzo and walking barefoot in the hot sand. Excuse me while I take a little break here . . .

When she returned to her kitchen table, Anna was one laid-back mother, and her kids seemed easier to deal with.

2. Take Up a Class

Sign up for a class with your local authority. I decided last year to take up tap dancing, though I had never done it in my life. I now look forward to getting away from it all on Wednesday nights with my class of similarly middle-aged new friends. (Don't expect Singing in the Rain, however.) Learn a new language, how to sing (my next project), play an instrument, sew, cook, type, become computer literate – you name it, they've got it, and it is cheap or even free. All it takes is time.

3. Escape to the Park

Perhaps you can't even carve out a few hours a week to take a class. In that case, take thirty minutes. Go to the park, sit on a bench and watch the people go by. Better yet, lie on the grass and watch the clouds.

4. Visualisation

A psychotherapist friend of mine, Dr Brian Roet, uses a technique called visualisation which can relax you in minutes. When I asked him to try it out on me, I was surprised and delighted with the results:

- Close your eyes and think where in your body you might feel happy. Let's say you choose your chest.
- Visualise going inside your chest and seeing the happy feeling. Think in colour and see what colour the feeling is. Let's say you choose yellow and red as the colours.
- Visualise what the feeling looks like. Is it crystals, softly lapping water, clouds, snow, rainbows? Let's say you decide that your happy feeling is crystals and they are yellow and red. Look at those sparkling crystals and try to visualise them even brighter yellow and red so that they shine and glimmer.
- So now you have a happy feeling associated with colours and crystals. When you feel stressed again, close your eyes and think of those crystals and relax.

This may sound a bit hocus pocus, but it only takes a few minutes and it works wonders. It is also something you can help your children to do when they are feeling anxious about something. One of my children had a teacher who really did not like him. She didn't appreciate his humour, his charm and all those things that I thought were great. Unfortunately, she was the only one teaching that subject, so despite all my best efforts to put her on a slow boat to China, we were stuck. My son calmed himself before his class with his visualised coloured crystals and eventually did quite well in the subject. But I can feel my stress levels rising just writing about her! Anyway, when things get on top of you, try it. I think you'll like it.

5. Join a Parent Group

It is no accident that groups of parents end up being friends because their children know each other. An important way to stay sane is to realise that you are not alone in the parenthood field.

There really is safety in numbers, and in exchanging gripes and ideas. If you can't find a group in your neighbourhood, contact your local authority and find out where the nearest one is. Or just start your own, if you have the energy. Ask at your local schools, and check with the secretary or dinner staff because they are most likely to know what is going on in the local area.

6. Drop-in Centres

Some areas have Drop-in Centres where parents can meet and get support. Again, check with your local authority.

7. Treat Yourself

Go out for scones and tea, or lunch. Take a friend and discuss anything except children.

8. Go to the Cinema

Most cinemas have cheap tickets before three pm, and some have certain days when films cost next to nothing. Find out, and if you're a parent who is at home, take yourself to the cinema in the middle of the day.

9. Take a Peaceful Walk

Go for a walk, pack a picnic and find a nice place to have a peaceful lunch.

10. Enjoy a Luxurious Bath

Pour a bubble bath, close the door and announce to everyone that you are not to be disturbed for half an hour. Try it by candle-light with a glass of wine, it's heaven!

11. Do Something Different

Go swimming, have a sauna, sit in a jacuzzi, go ice-skating or roller-skating.

12. Garden for Fun

If you are lucky enough to have a garden or a balcony, or even a window box, dig around and plant something. But only do this if it is fun and not because the garden needs doing. Then it's a chore instead of an escape.

13. Relieve That Tension

Really treat yourself – have a massage or a facial. This could count as one of the greatest pleasures of all, as the stress is soothed out by an expert.

14. Go on a Journey

Pick a town that is accessible by train, buy a day-return ticket and wander around exploring the shops, museums and ancient buildings. Treat yourself to lunch, as well.

15. Read

Curl up with a good book, ignore all the work waiting to be done and immerse yourself.

16. Write

Put aside an hour a day and begin that book you've always known you have inside you. If you wrote one page each day, by the end of the year you would have 365 pages.

17. Draw

Get a sketch book and start drawing or painting. Even if you think you have no talent, it focuses your mind on other things besides the fun and games of parenthood.

18. Be Creative

I tried this once and ended up with a blob of useless clay and dirty fingernails. However, for those with patience and talent, it is very satisfying to make something and it is a great escape.

19. Fellowship

The Winston Churchill Trust in London gives 100 fellowships every year to ordinary people who would like to learn about something which might help them or others. There are different categories each year. I found out about it and applied under the heading of Bullying, and to my immense delight was chosen. I spent six glorious weeks in Norway on my own, wrote a children's book and learned some excellent ways to deal with bullying (see Chapter 29, p. 275 – What to Do About Bullying). It really was one of the highlights of my life so far (excluding my children, of course). You do not have to be a university graduate or a professional person – the Trust seeks people from all walks of life. You just have to be enthusiastic and put a good case for the category you are interested in that year.

20. Sleep

Not very exciting, I know, but if you feel stressed and exhausted, then sleep when your kids sleep, if they are young. If not, take a nap when they are at school. You will be a better parent if you aren't in a zombie-like state. The best advice about this was from Stephanie, who said, 'Take a hot bubble bath, get your favourite book and teddy bear, and go to bed. Read until your eyes can't stay open, cuddle the teddy bear and sleep for two hours.'
Sounds wonderful.

21

CREATE HOLIDAY MAGIC WITHOUT A PRICE TAG!

Eleven-year-old Steven is desperate for a special present – a new pair of trainers that will ensure that he runs faster than Mercury. They cost £99. Fourteen-year-old Richard just knows that he is going to be given that fantastic music centre. It's a bargain at £299 . . .

As the holidays approach, the advertising campaigns are in full swing, aimed straight at the children's hearts and our wallets. The children see, hear and tell each other about so many products, and we as parents long to make all their dreams come true.

Yes, they know that money is tight. But they have all seen the ad on television in which the father tells his son they can't afford a bike this year. The son sits around looking wretched when, presto! – the new bike arrives. The look on the boy's face is enough to make us all want to rush out and buy our sons the mountain bikes they yearn for. Then we remember, with a sickening thud, the bank balance, the leaking roof, the washing-machine that cha-chas across the kitchen during the spin cycle, and come to our senses and decide he doesn't need a mountain bike – there are no mountains where we live!

Questions, Questions

Have Christmas and other holidays become 'gimme' seasons? And, if we accept that they have, should we try to stop *our* children wanting things? What about parents who simply cannot afford it all? How do we handle our child's disappointment? If we could wave a magic wand to get our kids everything they wanted, should we? How do we keep the magic of Christmas and our sanity?

1. It Is OK to Want

There is nothing wrong with wanting nice things. Perhaps we long to have that beautiful car, those designer clothes and a swimming pool in the back garden. (Or maybe just a back garden?) Years ago we might not have thought about them, but now we see wonderful products to covet in magazines, on our television screens, in the cinema, at railway stations, on the sides of buses – you name it, it advertises. I would love to have thick, plush carpet and a Dulux dog. I have carpet tiles and a hamster.

In fact, I am an advertiser's dream – it all looks good to me. So, naturally, I think it is OK to want things, but not to expect that we will always get them. That goes for kids, too. It would be unrealistic to let children think we get everything we want. Life just doesn't work like that. But I also think it's OK to dream, so why can't kids dream, too?

Jane found that if she said to her children, 'Yes, that toy really is fantastic and I can see just why you want it,' that made them feel at least one need had been met – mum agreed with their judgement. She then went on to explain that there are lots of things we want and don't get, which helped them set more realistic expectations. (See Chapter 7, p. 71 – Money Madness.)

2. Everyone Has One

'Mum, everyone in the whole school has one!'

Words guaranteed to tug your heartstrings, especially if it is true. If only you could, you would happily produce whatever it is that leaves your child in a minority of one. Parental misery sets in.

Wait a minute! Let's keep this in perspective. Children are incredibly resilient. Once they know the full facts, they often respond very nobly and even buck up the adults. When my youngest son was about four, I stepped on and smashed his favourite plastic pull-toy. Tears from him, tears from me. Guilt! Then a little voice piped: 'It doesn't matter, Mum, it's only a toy.' It was a moment to treasure.

Give kids a chance to show their stuff. Tell them you'd love to be able to give them that special present, but you just can't this year. It isn't easy, but the sooner they know, the better. Anticipation only increases the disappointment. You may be surprised at how mature and understanding they can be after they've had time to think about it.

But don't forget, either, that children might be willing to settle for something second-hand, but which doesn't *look* second-hand.

Sean, who was unemployed, told his children that he could not afford the computer and games they had seen advertised on Saturday morning television, but he said he would try to find a used model. This he managed to do and, although it wasn't the exact model they wanted, his children were delighted.

The irony is that Sean's children took much better care of their computer than the neighbour's children – who were given the latest, most expensive model of that and everything else they wanted.

3. If You Promise, Deliver

Tony's kids weren't promised anything, he just said he would try. Mary's children have something much worse to contend with every year.

Whenever they ask for something, Mary says, 'Wait until Christmas,' thinking that they will forget. So her children dream and hope and come charging down the stairs early on Christmas morning. Maybe this time she really meant it? No . . . Mary's children are consistently let down. And disappointment hurts more than dreaming.

Mary isn't being malicious or purposefully cruel. She just

doesn't realise how much children rely on us to be 'straight' with them. If we promise, we should deliver. The world's unsettled enough, and kids need us to do what we say. Otherwise, who can they trust?

4. Wishful Thinking

There are times when children should not be promised things or given everything they want. Fulfilling their every wish can create bored, spoiled, 'gimme' kids who don't appreciate anything and, worse than that, don't have anything left to wish for – no excitement or anticipation in their lives.

We all know adults who are continually looking for something new, who don't appreciate anything they have and are never satisfied. They flit from job to job or spouse to spouse.

I think they probably had the kind of childhood in which their every desire and wish was fulfilled, and now they are wondering why life is no longer like that. Well, it isn't and we do children no favours by giving them the impression that their every wish is our command.

My children have a friend whose father is quite wealthy. Jason has a room filled with toys and all manner of gadgets and games, yet he likes nothing better than to come to our house, help with small chores, have a water-pistol fight and stay up late, chatting. There is nothing he wants for, except attention and the wonderful gift of wishing. Because he gets everything, he is never surprised. How sad for him.

5. Disappointments

It seems such a shame when kids are disappointed on birthdays or at Christmas. After all, it should be a time of joy and fun. So how can you cope when you find your daughter crying alone because she didn't get the special present she wanted? (It was simply too expensive or unobtainable). You comfort her the best you can, but you feel just as bad or even worse. What can you do?

a) Tell her it is all right to feel sad that she didn't get what she wanted. Too often we try to stifle feelings, but it is important that children should learn to cope with them. Crying, feelings of anger, resentment and unfairness are natural. And it's better that they should come out into the open, than be buried and cause bitterness.

b) Explain to her why you couldn't get the present – not in a defensive way, but factually: 'We just didn't have the money' or 'The shops had none left' or 'We think it is a present for older children and you should wait.'

c) Give her space to deal with it in her own way (as long as she isn't torturing the cat or kicking her baby brother). Having a cry can be good and she may want to do it in private, without a guilt-ridden parent fawning all over her.

d) Help her keep it in perspective by gently pointing out some of the good things she has. But remember the 'gently'. Some parents continually ask their children to think how lucky they are 'compared with all the little starving babies' and tell them not to be so silly. Of course, they are right – our children have incredible wealth compared with those in many countries, but that's hard for a child to take in when they are desolate. Better to say this when they are feeling more generous to mankind/womankind/peoplekind. It can backfire even then, though. I repeated my grandmother's 'remember all those poor children' to my sons, until the youngest squished his sandwich into an envelope and addressed it: To: the pour, stravvings.

Parcelling up squished sandwiches aside, try to ensure that your children do something for others during the holiday season – helping at a fund-raising event, passing on outgrown clothes, collecting toys for homeless children and choosing something of their own to give, and so on.

6. Real Holiday Magic

However, I don't think Christmas or other holiday magic comes from gifts at all. They are soon discarded, broken or outgrown. The real magic is in the family traditions you create. For some, this includes religious ceremonies; for others it is the time the family spends together at home, or it is a combination of both.

On birthdays in our house, it is the tradition that the birthday person gets to choose what the family has for dinner and how to celebrate. It might be reading a favourite book aloud, renting a special video, going to the park, ice-skating – whatever. The treat of the day is that the decisions are up to the child, within reason, of course (the request for a day trip on Concorde was a non-starter!) In our family, the birthday person does no chores, has breakfast in bed, is allowed to dictate television viewing and goes to bed when he or she feels like it (unless there is something really important happening the next day, and then the going-to-bed time is deferred to another chosen date). We always have balloons attached to the door, regardless of age. And singing and candles are obligatory! Presents can be homemade or inexpensive, and they can be wrapped in painted newspaper or the coloured cartoons from the Sunday paper. Cards are much more fun and personal if they are made by family members, especially if you can think of funny verses or limericks. I have kept all my children's homemade cards, but none of the store-bought ones.

We lived in America when I was a child and I loved the autumn holidays of Thanksgiving and Hallowe'en the best, just as my children love Guy Fawkes night. None of these holidays involve presents – they are family times with good food, good company, games, face painting, cosy fires or fireworks. I always remember playing charades and card games and dancing. These are the things that make holiday magic.

I suppose that my all-time favourite holiday is still Christmas. On Christmas Eve, we always went out to choose the tallest tree we could find. We listened to Christmas carols as we set up the tree in the living-room. The ornaments would be unwrapped, exclaimed over and clipped on: glass birds with tails made from stiff, white bristles; painted baubles; fairies; glass icicles that sparkled when the old-fashioned, large, coloured lights were finally lit. The strands of silver tinsel were hung one at a time. Finally, the electric train was set up to run around the base of the tree, and for us that completed the magic.

Then out would come the Christmas biscuits, baked into shapes – Christmas trees, wreaths, reindeer, Father Christmases, all decorated by us, the children, with different coloured icings. With only the lights of the tree on in the dark room, we would look at the patterns on the ceiling, sing and munch biscuits until it was time to go to bed.

When we were tucked in, my dad would read the children's poem, which begins:

> *'Twas the night before Christmas, and all through the house*
> *Not a creature was stirring, not even a mouse;*
> *The stockings were hung by the chimney with care,*
> *In hopes that St Nicholas soon would be there . . .*

When Dad got to the end, out would go the lights.

My children are teenagers now. Too old, you may think, for such simple traditions. But we make red-nosed reindeer biscuits, put up the tree with carols playing, and set up the electric train set to run in never ending circles . . .

You know, I don't remember many of the gifts I got as a kid, but the warmth, fun and joy of Christmas have stayed with me to this day. If you don't yet have family traditions, start some. The marvellous thing is that you will find your kids love them and insist you repeat them year after year.

We continue to add new traditions, including one inherited from my husband's family. Just before the kids go to bed, we set out a glass of milk and a decorated biscuit for Father Christmas. On Christmas morning we find the glass half empty and the biscuit gone, but for a few crumbs.

I suspect that, in years to come, when my sons bring home their families for Christmas, the same traditions will be carried out to the letter. I am looking forward to reading *'Twas the night before Christmas* to them when they're forty. The only difference might be a glass of brandy left out for Mother Christmas – that is, if the roof is fixed by then and we can afford it.

22

WHAT YOU AND YOUR CHILD NEED TO KNOW WHEN YOU GO OUT WITHOUT THEM

There will always be times when you have to go out or want to go out without your children. If they are old enough, you leave them on their own with lots of instructions and hope they don't have wild parties. If they're younger, you leave them with a babysitter or childminder.

How Old?

How old should children be before you leave them home alone? In England there is no law stating a specific age, but you can be prosecuted for leaving your children alone *if* they subsequently come to harm. In Scotland it is against the law to leave your children home alone if they are under the age of twelve. Each country has its own laws, but that doesn't mean that children are never left home alone, regardless of what the law says. How often have you had to slip across the road to buy some milk, and left your kids for just a couple of minutes? Most parents have found themselves in this position for one reason or another and, fortunately, nothing untoward has happened. When something horrible does happen, we read the headlines and wonder just how those parents could have left those children alone, even if we've done it ourselves. I talked with a group of five-year-olds in one school and found that fifteen out of twenty of them had been home alone at least once in their lives.

So, I guess there is no set time when it is OK to leave kids home alone. It depends upon where you live and who is nearby and, of course, the maturity of your child. Certainly, leaving children as young as five home alone scares me to death. Personally, I worry about things like fires or accidents or the possibility of intruders when I consider leaving kids at home. So what should kids know about if they are to be left alone?

1. Fire

Practise fire drills with your children and make sure they know exactly what to do and how to get out in case of fire. Seek advice from your local fire department.

2. Emergency Telephone Calls

Practise making emergency telephone calls with your children. Well, don't really practise or you will have the police at your door. Use a toy telephone, or unplug the telephone and then put your kids through their paces. Explain that they should never make a call unless it is an emergency and that the number they ring from can immediately be traced. Also explain that the operator will ask them their name and number and which service they want – police, fire, or ambulance.

3. Obscene Telephone Calls

Tell them to hang up and not to respond. Then to immediately ring either you or whoever they have as a contact and arrange for help.

4. Intruders

If your children are home and someone tries to break in, they should immediately ring the police. You may want them to try to get out of the flat or house to a place of safety that is close by, like a neighbour's. Do ask your local crime prevention officer to check your home and give advice on making it as safe as possible.

5. List of Contacts

Work out a list of people your child can contact and put their names and numbers near the telephone. Also work out what to do if you do not have a telephone, or it is out of service for some reason. There should be someone your child can get in touch with without using the telephone.

6. Answering the Door

If someone your children is not expecting comes to the door, I suggest that they don't answer. If it is a delivery, it can be made later; if it is a friend he or she can telephone and come again. If there is an emergency involving the police or the fire service, the officers will give your children an identification or, in extreme cases, break down the door (to save children from a fire, for example). In most situations, children can simply be told to ignore the doorbell. If someone persists in trying to get them to answer the door, instruct them to ring you or their contact number and explain what's happening.

7. List of Do's and Don'ts

Children need to know what they are allowed to do when they are home alone. Obviously, this will depend upon their ages. For example, you may make a blanket rule that cooking is not allowed, to eliminate the possibility of them burning themselves or the house down. You might ask them not to use the iron for the same reason (if you are lucky enough to have children who are dying to iron their clothes!). Knives and scissors could be off-limits, along with blenders. It is not a good idea for children to take baths in case they scald themselves, or use the washing-machine because of floods.

You may say to your children that they can eat foods, such as fruit and cereal, that require no cooking, and other snacks you put out. Also, they can watch television, do their homework (yippee), talk on the telephone with their friends, etc. We all need to work out the most detailed instructions possible, if kids do have to be left home alone, and hope that their common sense will prevail.

Choosing the Right Babysitter

If you are leaving your child with a babysitter, there are several things you need to consider. When choosing someone to babysit for your child:

1. Check Them Out

Be sure to find out who has recommended the sitter, and what do you know about him or her? In a study recently completed for the Nuffield Foundation, we found that forty-eight per cent of the male child molesters we interviewed made contact with their victims by babysitting! That certainly doesn't mean that all babysitters are child molesters, just that babysitting is an excellent way for child molesters to be alone with children. I am not trying to frighten you into never leaving your child with a sitter, but it pays to know as much as possible about who this person is.

2. Take Care with Babysitting Ads

Never use babysitters from local adverts without taking refer-ences, and actually talking to other mothers who have used this person.

3. Look for Signs

How do your children react to being left with the person?

- Are they happy to have the person return as a sitter?
- Do they cry when left with the person?
- Do they beg their parent to stay home and not go out?

4. Can They Cope with Emergencies?

Does the sitter know basic first aid, or what to do in case of emergency. Ask the person to tell you what s/he would do in case of a fire or a child getting burned? And what would s/he do if your child was injured?

5. Get To Know Them

Meet the sitter before you leave your children with her/him. Make sure you can ring the sitter or know where s/he lives.

6. Use the Element of Surprise

Ring home or come home unexpectedly to check that everything is all right.

7. Ask the Children

Ask your child about the sitter, even if it is someone you know and like. You need to make sure your child liked the person and didn't feel unsafe in any way. Since people who molest children often ask the child to keep secrets, you might casually ask your child if the babysitter asked her or him to keep any secrets. This doesn't mean that you have to be madly questioning your child, rather that you be aware of what could happen so you can prevent your child being harmed. In all probability, your child will be quite safe with the babysitter!

8. Leave a Contact Number

Make sure the babysitter knows how to reach you or the person you have designated in case of emergency. And ensure the baby-sitter knows what to do and who to contact should anything happen to *you*. Who would you have come over to take care of the children if you had an accident, for example?

What to Tell Your Children

Having decided on a babysitter, you can now go out without doing anything else *except* giving instructions in advance to your children if they are old enough. They may need to know some of the same things listed above under How Old?, but these are two especially important points to remember:

1. Telephone Numbers

Even if the babysitter knows how to contact you, make sure that your children do, as well. They should also have another emergency contact – who should they contact if the babysitter gets sick, for example? Even though this is unlikely, better safe than sorry as far as I'm concerned.

2. Arrange a Secret Code

Arrange a code with your children so they can let you know if something is very wrong and you need to come home. For instance, one parent I know worked out with his children that, if they rang him and asked how to do a maths problem, something was amiss that they couldn't say for some reason, and that he should return home immediately. Fortunately, they have never had to use the code. Something like this would be vital if the babysitter was drunk, or doing something to threaten the safety of the children.

Go Out and Have A Great Time

We all need to get away from our kids once in a while, if for no other reason than to maintain our sanity. Don't get me wrong, I love my kids, but it is wonderful to escape and have a good time without them. I think it's also good for them to learn to be independent of us. I just want to make sure that they are as safe as possible, and I will certainly let them be completely on their own – in about thirty years!

23

WAYS TO BRIBE YOUR CHILD

We know, of course, that it is wicked to corrupt innocent children by implying there's a commercial value to every act. How about washing-up out of noble concern for your mother? Or minding your little sister because you love her? By talking about bribes, I'm not trying to imply that children should never perform selfless acts. What I'm suggesting is that, by admitting that we use bribes anyway (who hasn't bought a toddler a packet of sweets so he will stay in the supermarket trolley while you struggle with the shopping?), we can actually use them even more constructively – and everyone wins!

Would you work – on a regular basis – for no reward? It's certainly true that we do many things in life out of a sense of duty, or out of fear for what will happen if we don't do them, but we work with most spirit when we're highly motivated. We work for money or job satisfaction; learn a foreign language for fun or to get a better job. So why not, when a child needs motivating, set up appropriate reward 'traps' – and turn the sometimes tedious processes of learning and co-operating into a winning game. If you still think you're not – and never should be – a briber, consider how often we use 'negative bribes' such as smacking, not allowing the child to play with friends, taking away a privilege or possession, shouting, sarcasm, counting to three with the threat that something dire will happen, or criticism. These do work, but they only turn kids into 'non-losers' as opposed to 'winners'.

Here, I've included ideas for 'good' bribes, many from my own or friends' experiences. It's important to remember that the younger the child, the more immediate the reward should be. Asking a four-year-old to wait until next week is like asking an adult to wait until the end of next year.

If the word 'bribe' bothers you, substitute the word 'reward' when you're reading this chapter!

Collectables

1. Stars on a chart

2. Tokens

3. Money

4. Stickers

Children love to collect things just to see how many they can get. The final reward, if there is one, becomes secondary to the game of collecting. Stars can cost you nothing – with a small child, letting him draw a coloured star in a space on a homemade chart every time he goes to bed without complaining, for example, can be sufficient. Stars have value provided they aren't given for nothing.

For an older child, say an eleven-year-old who does not want to do her homework, you could use something more tangible. Agree with her how much time homework should take. Put on a timer and offer her ten tokens for working the set period. When she gets 100 tokens she gets an agreed reward: a friend to stay the night, a visit to the cinema, whatever she chooses that both of you think is worth so much effort.

Money is a more controversial bribe. Although adults consider it perfectly acceptable to work for money, many think children should do things for the joy of it. The problem is that many of the tasks we set children are not joyful.

If you use money with small children, give them lots of little coins each time they succeed. With teenagers, the promise of a certain amount at the end of the task will work better than lots of change. A young friend of ours, Jennifer, bit her nails until they were sore. Her mother offered her 20p for each nail that was a certain length by Easter. Jennifer soon stopped nibbling at her nails and by Easter, when she had £2, she'd lost the habit of biting her nails all together.

Money bribes can teach children to respect your own budget. Learning that money comes through effort helps them understand when you say: 'Sorry, I'm broke this month – how about washing the car for love?'

Stickers and cards are things children collect and swap, but they do seem to go in and out of fashion. Find out what, if anything, your children are interested in and try to get them special stickers or cards they really want. Sometimes there are albums to put the stickers in, which might be another bribe.

Edibles

5. Satsumas

6. Sweets

7. Favourite pudding

8. Take-away pizza or burger

With food, it's a case of identifying the 'currency' which motivates a particular child. My friend's little boy, Malik, was such a dedicated satsuma-eater that he got through a week's rations in a day. It wasn't such a good idea for her budget or his digestion. I suggested restricting him to one a day, with 'extras' on condition he did whatever she needed him to do that he found difficult. If a child wouldn't eat breakfast before school, for example, use an extra satsuma as a 'carrot' (so to speak). Even young children enjoy planning their own food treats.

Another friend of mine's two-and-a-half-year-old daughter, Nicky, wasn't interested in using the potty. Her mother wanted her out of nappies for a long journey they were taking in a month's time. Nicky could use the loo when it suited her, but was a bit lazy. Nicky's mum put a jar of Smarties, tightly sealed, near the potty and showed Nicky that every time she used it she would get three Smarties. She was daytime trained in a few days.

Smarties are also useful for teaching colours. If you pick the right colour, you get to eat the Smartie. This needs to be monitored, or your children will have no teeth, but know their colours beautifully!

Personally, give me a pudding or a pizza and I'll do anything (just about). This only works if your children don't have so many puddings and pizzas that they are overdosed on them.

Escapism

9. Cinema

10. Video

11. Pantomime

12. Exhibitions

13. Books

Children, like adults, will work for 'fun'. As we all know, fun doesn't always come cheap. It does no harm to explain to kids that you enjoy expensive outings, but they'll need to help you so you can afford the time and money.

You could sort out specific jobs which are 'Pantomime' or 'Indiana Jones' jobs – from dusting the banisters to cleaning the table after meals for a week. Before you set up this bribe you have to be careful not to say anything you don't mean. In other words, if you really plan to take them to the cinema on Friday, come hell or high temper, then it's pointless making the excursion totally dependent on the tasks you set them. Instead, you can invoke moral bribery: 'I need you to help me now, if we're going to make it to the cinema on Friday.'

A trip to the video shop and the promise of an extra video can also work wonders. Combine this with the promise of staying up late to watch the videos and you will probably be able to bribe your children for a month.

I think that being given a book or a book token is the best bribe going. I would do most anything for a new book, but I realise that some children would rather have a new computer game. Notice that I don't include this as a bribe because, not only are computer games too expensive, they are mind-numbing in my humble opinion.

Extras

14. Extra TV

15. Staying up late

16. Extra pocket money

17. Tapes or CDs

18. Special clothes

Have you noticed how angelic children are just before birthdays or Christmas? The stocking is, if you like, the bribe of the year – and it works. You can use the Christmas factor to good effect at other times, too. If a child starts wheedling for extras, you should give his desire the importance it deserves and suggest that he might like to work for it.

Joan wanted her nine-year-old daughter Emily to play the piano, and she was initially keen. After several weeks, however, Emily said it was boring to practise, and she would rather watch TV. Joan and her daughter worked out an agreement. For every ten minutes that the girl practised, she would be allowed to watch ten minutes of television. This only worked because Joan usually restricted Emily's TV watching.

If you are desperate to get your child to do something and are meeting with little or no success, then by all means try a little extra pocket money, if you can afford it. Pamela's nine-year-old son had the really nasty habit of burping all the time. His friends encouraged him and laughed whenever he did it, but it had got beyond a joke with his parents. The trouble was, he sometimes did it without thinking – great loud belches which were incredibly embarrassing. As they were going away on holiday in four weeks, Pamela really did not want to be stuck in a nice restaurant with a burping son. Nothing seemed to work, until she offered extra pocket money for the weeks leading up to the holiday, so her son would have more to spend when they got to the resort. It did the trick, and the burps subsided!

Tapes, CDs or special clothes are much sought after, but they are a fairly expensive bribe. Try telling your child you will match what she saves towards the CD or hat she wants if she stops fighting with her sister for a set amount of time, or whatever you are trying to get her to do.

Funnies

19. Ping-pong ball in the loo

20. Musical potties

21. Mum painting her face

22. Mum standing on her head

23. 'Getting' dad with a water pistol

Anything which involves humour helps make tasks lighter. A good, amusing way to encourage small boys to aim straight when they learn to pee standing up is to put a ping-pong ball in the loo as a target. Musical potties have the same function at an earlier stage.

I once rashly promised my children that if they brushed their teeth every night for a week, then I would stand on my head in the park. It was worth it – just!

In the Name of Love

24. Cuddles

Children deserve love and affection as of right, regardless of how they behave. But *extra* cuddles, or words of praise, show children that their efforts are especially valued.

Grasping Little Creeps

So, if you bribe your children to do what you want them to do, will they turn into nasty, grasping, horrible people? I don't think so. In fact, children are generally more noble and moral than we give them credit for. They might not need much to motivate them to change or help. And you can't use bribes all the time, anyway. If you find your child won't do anything without a bribe, then you need to stop and reconsider your methods. I am only advocating that you use them to get children started, not forever. If a child continually cries or acts out and then demands sweets, you firmly say no. Otherwise you are rewarding bad behaviour. If your children will only be 'good' when bribed, then you should have a talk and explain that you will occasionally give them something, but they won't know when so they have to try all the time. Then surprise them. After a while, the behaviour will be so ingrained that the bribe isn't necessary – a word of praise being the best reward.

Helping Others

As a final word, remember that children can be motivated or bribed in very simple ways to help others, an important trait to try to instill in children. Every year on the first day of December, my grandmother would bring out the Christmas crib, with all the figures except the baby Jesus. Next to it, she put a pile of short pieces of straw. For every good deed that my sister and I did between December 1–25, we were allowed to place a piece of straw in the cradle. Our reward was an increasingly soft bed for the baby. The one thing we were not allowed to do, however, was tell anyone about our good deeds. It was to be our own little secret. My sister and I pursued our task with relish, though I confess we did brag once in a while to each other about what we had done. A little one-upmanship did occur, but I suspect that was also part of the plan. My grandmother was a master of bribery – I will always love her for it.

PART III

Getting Through A Crisis

24

WHAT TO DO WHEN YOUR KIDS SCREW UP

'Your son has been stealing money from children at school. Would you please come in so we can discuss what happens next?'

'We have just found out that your daughter has been spreading nasty rumours about another girl and causing great distress.'

'Your school rang me today. You've been playing truant!'

'I'm sorry to tell you that your daughter has been caught shoplifting. Can you come to the police station?'

'I've got a note from your teacher about that homework you said you didn't have last night.'

'Your children have been harassing my children, and now my children are afraid to go outside and play.'

Rare is the parent who has never had to deal with their children 'screwing up'. We are lucky if our children are called to task for such relatively minor problems as not doing their homework. Most of us can cope with such things by monitoring our children, restricting television, grounding or the like. It isn't a crisis, only a drama that will soon pass.

However, what happens if our children do something which does create a crisis, like injuring another child, being brought home by the police or being sent home from school in disgrace?

Ten-year-old Jon played truant one day from school with some older children. They got bored and decided to hang around the local shopping centre. One thing led to another and they ended up forming a club which you could only join if you successfully shoplifted something costing at least £5. The older children managed to 'succeed' and taunted Jon for being a baby and a sissy for not trying to steal. Jon nervously went into a shop, was instantly spotted by security staff and caught as he left the store. The other children scattered when they saw what was happening, leaving Jon to fend for himself. By the time Jon's parents learned what he had done, everyone else knew, as well.

'We were mortified and very angry,' his father told me. 'Jon let us and himself down very badly. He really isn't a kid who does things like this. He usually does well in school, he has enough pocket money and doesn't want for anything. We've tried to be good parents and teach him right from wrong. We can't understand how this happened.'

Jon's parents felt terribly guilty, but they were good parents. You can't be with your kids every minute, nor can you control all the outside influences in their lives. The bottom line is that kids make mistakes, big and small, and we have to figure out how to help them learn from those mistakes.

If our children are accused of screwing up somehow, here are some suggestions about what to do.

1. Keep Calm and Find Out the Facts

This is easy to say and hard to do when faced with awful, embarrassing accusations about your child. Sometimes we react by immediately assuming what we are told is correct. It may be, but until we find out the facts from all concerned, it isn't fair to judge. Things are not always as they seem at first sight.

Helen told me about the time another mother rang to say that Helen's ten-year-old son, David, had been rude and hurtful to her son, Max. The mother told Helen that David was spreading rumours that Max had 'poohed in his pants'. Since Max and David had been friends and she knew Max's mother, Helen apologised profusely. Max's mother wanted David to apologise in front of the class and to admit that he had lied about Max. When Max's mother asked to speak to David, Helen called him to the phone. She heard David dissolve into tears as Max's mother yelled at him for being so horrible to Max. Helen, thinking that David had been naughty, felt he deserved to be told off.

Helen said, 'I should have told Max's mother that I would ring her back, but I was so embarrassed and annoyed with what David was supposed to have done, that I wasn't thinking straight. It was only when I sat down with him that I found out what had really happened. Then I really felt horrible. It turned out that the boys were fooling around and that Max had farted several times to the delight of all the boys. Everyone, including Max, had been giggling like mad about it. David had said, "You poohed in your pants," which again made them all laugh. Max was not upset. One of the other boys told his mother what David had said and neglected to say how it had come about. This mother rang Max's mother and Max's mother rang me. The kids were actually fine – the mothers had got it wrong!

'I was angry at myself for allowing David to be yelled at, and furious at Max's mother. Poor David – he probably shouldn't have made the comment, but he was tried and condemned quite unfairly. I apologised to him and still cannot talk to Max's mother. Next time anyone tells me something I will look carefully before I leap to conclusions.'

It may be that you find your child has done what he or she is accused of, but try to make sure you:

a) Ask (calmly) for as many details as you can.
b) Don't make any rash promises about what you will do.
c) Give yourself a breathing space to take in what is happening. If someone rings you, listen with as little comment as possible and then tell the person you will ring back to discuss it.
d) Talk calmly with your child to find out his or her perception of the matter.
e) Find out information from other sources, such as other parents, witnesses, children, teachers, etc.
f) Seek legal advice if your child is in trouble for having broken the law. Contact an organisation such as the Citizens Advice Bureau, unless you have access to your own solicitor.

g) Take no action until you have had time to reflect, even if that just means taking a walk to clear your head, or having the proverbial cup of tea.

h) Have the best support you can muster for both you and your child.

2. Act Decisively

Once you have all the information, act as quickly as possible to sort out the mess. If your child has done something wrong, it is best that it be faced up to and dealt with immediately. One of the things that cools down situations is the feeling that something is being done. Delaying action once you know the facts will only add angst to the situation, and may make it worse. If your child has purposefully spread rumours or somehow hurt another child or stolen from a shop, then restitution is in order.

a) Your child should apologise to the victim and, if necessary, others who were affected by what he or she did.

b) If goods have been taken, they should be returned or replaced and the child should make up the cost by doing extra jobs, if necessary.

c) You may wish to apologise, as well. This is especially helpful if your child has harmed another child in some way. At least the victim and his or her parents feel their needs are being considered.

d) Work out a plan about how all this can be accomplished in the most constructive way. There is no point in humiliating your child – the purpose of the exercise is to make the victim feel better and to help your child learn this is not the way to behave.

e) Tell your child what you expect to happen next, including whatever punishment follows, such as restricting privileges. If the police are involved, explain what is expected to happen.

f) Explain that when your child has made the necessary steps to correct his or her mistake, you know this behaviour won't be repeated.

g) Make sure your child knows you don't think she or he is condemned for life, and that we all make mistakes.

h) Make sure that your child is not so devastated by what has happened that he or she does something silly, like running away from home, or, worse, trying to commit suicide. Even young children can make these dramatic gestures, which sometimes go tragically wrong. One eight-year-old felt he had done something so terrible that he would never get over it. He stood in the road waiting to be hit when his older brother saw him and dragged him to safety. Assure your child that you love him or her in spite of what they have done. Remember the old adage: 'I don't like what you've done, but I still love you.'

i) Make sure your child understands what will happen if he or she transgresses again. For example, Linda's teenage daughter Shelly came home one night well past her curfew. After grounding for life, Linda relented and let Shelly out again with the proviso that, if she was late again without good reason and didn't ring her frantic mum, her curfew would be pushed back an hour for every five minutes she was late.

j) Don't hastily give out punishments which turn out to be so severe that you have to back-pedal. And don't stick to a punishment you've meted out if it is too severe – be willing to admit that you've made a mistake. After all, beheading is a little over the top!

As I was writing point h) above, the telephone rang. It was the mother of a five-year-old boy, Blake. She had just come from an emergency meeting with her son's headmistress. It seems that Blake was caught in the toilet with another five-year-old boy and they were touching each other's penises and doing some other, more serious things which were quite inappropriate for their age. She had to act decisively.

Even though the headmistress was reassuring and said that children do experiment, Blake's mother was very worried about Blake, about the other boy and about what the other children and parents would think. We went through the process of finding out the facts mentioned above. It seems unlikely that Blake was himself abused, given the information about him. He is doing well in school, has never been inappropriately sexual before, is bright, articulate and well-adjusted. A few weeks before this incident, however, he did find a pornographic video (not homemade and not violent or degrading) which was hidden away. Blake's father had the video from before their marriage and had put it out of sight and forgotten it. At the time, his mother, horrified when her son innocently asked her questions about it, destroyed the video and told her son not to think about it.

It seems Blake didn't forget it, but decided to try out some of the things he'd seen. The concern here was not to label Blake as a 'sex abuser', nor to have him feel badly about his body, and to counteract any rumours in the school which might start. There was also some concern that Blake might have done these things with other children during the two or three weeks since he saw the video. After we talked, Blake's mother decided to:

a) Tell Blake that she loved him, but didn't like what he had done.
b) Make sure that Blake understood that sex was not a bad thing, nor was he bad.
c) Ask Blake if he knew why the headmistress had asked her to come in today. Trying to get Blake's perspective on what had happened was important. I think he just thought it felt good and it was naughty – two things guaranteed to spark a kid's interest.
d) Try to find out if anyone has done anything sexually to him.
e) Talk to Blake about the video and explain that what he saw was acting, and that people don't necessarily do what they see on film.
f) Explain that he can do things to his own body, but that those things are private and that he should not be doing them with other children.
g) Explain that he would get into trouble if he did sexual things at school with other children, and use the example that teachers don't go into toilets and touch each other (you hope!).
h) Explain that touching is nice and that it should not be kept secret, and that keeping touching private is different from keeping it secret.

Finally Blake's mother was going to meet with the mothers of the other children to ask their advice, and to explain what had happened before rumours started to fly. She and the other mothers are friends of long-standing, so this would make it easier. In a situation such as this, which could result in a child being ostracised or even asked to leave the school, it is vital to act immediately. Trying to sweep it under the carpet only makes things worse.

3. Follow-up

Jon was cautioned by the police and turned over to the care of his parents. He gave the item he had stolen to them. They also had to go to the school and sort out his truancy and his relationship with the older children. Jon was grounded for several weeks and forbidden to see the other children (who escaped police action because they were not caught, but who were in trouble at school) with whom he had truanted. His parents, with the help of the teacher, encouraged other, more positive and age-appropriate friendships. Jon had played truant once before this incident, but I think he now prefers the relative safety of school, even if he still gets bored once in a while. Jon came through his experience wiser and more cautious. His parents say they've learned a lot and are now paying much more attention to what is happening to Jon.

If your child has done something wrong, which you have managed to sort out, be sure to follow-up your actions:

a) Give your child lots of praise for good behaviour.
b) Keep an eye on the situation and ask the school, if involved, to help you.
c) Don't continually bring up the transgression, unless you want to make your child feel guilty and useless.
d) Keep in contact with other parents, if more than one child has been involved.
e) If other children have been influencing your child to get into trouble, then either forbid contact (if your child is young enough – much harder when they are teenagers) or arrange for contact with them to be supervised, perhaps at your home.
f) If your child has been bullying another child, keep in contact with the parents of the victim to make sure it has stopped. In

some cases, the bullying continues, but the bully becomes more subtle.

g) Try to create opportunities for your child to shine, and praise, praise, praise.

Most messes that kids get into are fixable, even if they are a pain for us parents to deal with. Reassure your child that everyone makes mistakes, and that *even you* have made a few – unless, of course, you are one of those perfect people who never has. Hah!

25

WAYS TO DEAL WITH LYING, CHEATING AND STEALING

'Tell her I've just gone out – I'm not home,' you hiss to your daughter, Vicky. It's your dreaded Aunt on the telephone and you know you can't bear to listen for forty-five minutes to the same old complaints about how all her children, your children and the world in general are going to hell in a hand basket.

'Um . . . Mum says she's not home just now, Auntie. She's just gone out.'

Great! Vicky can plausibly come up with twenty completely false excuses for not cleaning up her room, but she can't handle one lame lie to your Aunt. You grab the telephone and resolve to cut her pocket money allowance by 100 per cent.

'Hello Auntie, how are you? I was closing the front door when I heard the telephone ring and thought I better come back to see who it was. Yes, I know what Vicky said. I told her just as I was leaving to tell anyone who rang that I was going to be out for several hours, but luckily I heard the telephone. Lovely to hear from you.'

Lovely, my foot. You hate talking to her and will do anything to get out of it. Anything except tell her the truth – that she's a bigoted, silly old cow and always has been. Well, she is an old lady now and you can't hurt her feelings.

Does that make you a liar? Well, perhaps a *kind* liar. Were you trying to get your daughter to lie for you? Yes. Have we all lied, cheated or stolen occasionally? Of course. But we know it's wrong, and we certainly want our children to be honest. In fact, most of us believe that honesty is the best policy, unless we have to spend two hours listening to grumpy old Auntie.

Why do our children lie, cheat or steal, and how can we instill in them a sense of right and wrong?

Why They Do It

Children have the same motives as adults for the things they do. They may lie or cheat or steal:

- because they don't understand
- to seek revenge
- for personal gain
- to get friends
- to get out of a difficult situation
- because they fear the consequences
- because of peer pressure
- to please someone
- because they want something very badly
- because of the thrill of it
- because they get into the habit
- for attention

With luck, our children will pass through the 'phases' of lying or cheating or stealing without harming themselves or someone else. If it is any comfort, most children do go through these phases and come out as honest little critters at the other end. Still, it is upsetting to be told that your little Sarah is a marauding thief or shameless liar and you wonder where you went wrong.

Let's take the issues one at a time, lying, cheating and stealing, though sometimes a child is managing to do all three at once. Don't despair, in all probability your children will turn out just fine. Here, nonetheless, are some hints to help you through the worst.

Lying

How can you tell if your child is lying? My grandmother only had to look me in the eye to know that I was not telling the truth. I used to think she could see right inside me, and I would go scarlet at the very thought of lying to her. Not that she ever beat me or struck fear into my heart. No, she would just look at me and I seemed to curl up with guilt. It is no surprise to me, looking back, to see why she could tell I was lying. My red face, evasive answers and refusal to look at her were rather striking clues. For years, I thought she was Sherlock Holmes, but I guess I was such an open and shut case that there was no need for detective work. Mind you, that doesn't mean that I never tried to get away with things! It just means that I did my best not to have to explain it to her.

Although these signs may have other reasons, your children may be lying if:

- they shift around uncomfortably and twist their hands
- they refuse to meet your eyes
- the story they are telling doesn't fit
- they change their explanation several times
- they seem afraid
- they are vague
- your intuition tells you something isn't right – parents (or grandparents) are usually quite tuned in to their children and 'know' something is amiss

Of course, if you always over-react to things and your children are frightened of what you will do or say, then they might be nervous even if they are telling the truth. It may be that you are always suspicious, or that they have been wrongly accused in the past and therefore feel uncomfortable the minute they have to discuss anything with you. They are afraid and vague because they are so worried.

On the other hand, if you have a good relationship with your children and can usually discuss things openly and in a good natured manner, then the above points are useful clues.

What to Do

Storytelling

If your child is lying, try to sort out the reasons before grounding him or her for life. A young child may really not know the difference between reality and fantasy. Whenever I work with young children, it is refreshing to see how much imagination applies to their everyday world. If you ask a group of five-year-olds what they did on holiday, there are always some who have had the most marvellous adventures, which become even more fantastic as they listen to others. When my son, then aged five or six, was telling his friend William about our trip to the Eiffel Tower in Paris, Wills went one better. His family had been to the Eiffel Tower in Norway and had seen all the way to London! He wasn't lying so much as wishing, dreaming and spinning tales. Wills always came up with inventive stories, and still does occasionally. Perhaps he will be the next Hans Christian Andersen! He certainly is *not* a manipulative little liar, and should not be branded as such.

One way to handle the child who continually makes up stories is to say: 'I understand how much you wish what you say would come true, and wishes are a very good thing. I wish for lots of things.' The child knows you know, but you aren't making him or her feel like a liar. The next step is to bring the conversation back to reality and focus on something the child can talk about without storytelling. For example, you could switch the topic to the wonderful time the child had at the park on the swings, or planning what you will have for lunch – anything that lends itself to a factual based conversation.

Making Up Imaginary Friends

Many children have imaginary friends when they are young. These friends are fun and a great comfort to children, as well as a handy source of blame. Pauline, aged four, decided that her bedroom walls would look pretty painted with rainbow colours – like the painting she did at nursery school. She busily got out her paints and dabbed blue, yellow, red, green and purple all over one wall. When her mother walked into the room to tell Pauline that tea was ready, she couldn't believe the mess. She began shouting. Up to that point, Pauline thought that she was improving the dull decoration of her bedroom. Her mother's reaction convinced Pauline that it was time for her imaginary friend Susie to come out and take the blame. Many's the time I've longed for an imaginary friend to shoulder the blame for something I've done, but I guess I'm too old!

When Pauline's mum settled down, she asked Pauline to explain herself. 'Susie thought it looked nice, but Susie's naughty,' said Pauline, who was too frightened to own up.

'Tell me what Susie did,' asked Pauline's mother. Little by little she coaxed the truth out of Pauline.

'I know you think Susie was naughty to paint on your walls. I understand it is hard to tell me what happened when I was so angry. I'm not angry now, so you don't have to pretend that Susie painted the walls. You can tell me.'

Pauline tearfully explained that she wanted rainbows on her walls and that she hadn't meant to do something bad. Her mother told her that she should ask before embarking on interior design as a career and made it clear that painting was for paper, not wall paper.

Did Pauline lie? In a way, but it was only a brush fire, not a full-scale inferno. By treating it as a learning experience (if you don't include the cost of repapering the wall!), the child won't grow up thinking she's a liar. Thank goodness her mother didn't call her a liar and make matters worse. She took exactly the right view: that her daughter needed to learn the difference between truth and falsehood and that this was an opportunity to help her.

Deliberately and Persistently Lying

Leaving aside the kind of things mentioned above, let's turn to the little blighter who is lying his or her head off. We are talking about the child who sets out to deceive and is making a habit of it. Why is the child doing this? There may be many reasons, but the most likely cause is a child who is not functioning very well in real life and finds it better to lie. Perhaps the expectations placed on the child are unobtainable, perhaps the child is terrified of parental reaction, perhaps the lying gives him or her the only relief from an awful life, or perhaps lying has become a bad habit or has developed because the child cannot figure out how to stop lying.

Ian was the eldest of five children. His parents were loving, but strict. If Ian brought home a poor report from school or got into trouble in any way, the consequences were swift and non-negotiable. Ian felt he was always wrong and could not succeed, so he started lying to cover up. Of course, he didn't always get away with his lies, but he found that if he stuck to his story and was charming, he could get away with some things. Ian could look you right in the eyes and, without a hint of discomfort, tell his parents and any other adult exactly what they wanted to hear. Ian lied, cheated and squeaked through school, but everyone loved him. Nothing was ever his fault and he has now come to believe that so strongly that he cannot separate fact from fiction. He is a charming, compulsive liar.

So, how might his parents have handled the situation differently and how can we learn from their mistakes? Remember the story at the beginning of this chapter? It turned out that Ian's parents expected absolute honesty from their children, but their children saw that they were not always honest themselves. Ian's father, a businessman, was often 'not at home' to telephone calls, sometimes stayed home sick when he wasn't, bragged about the deals he pulled on other people to their disadvantage, and took the family out to dinner as a 'business expense'. Ian was actually learning through example, regardless of what his parents said. Try:

1. Checking your own example. If you lie and your children catch you out, admit it and apologise. Explain that, even if someone doesn't always tell the truth, admitting a lie is the next best thing. Either be a paragon of virtue or handle mistakes in a way that gives a model for your children to follow.

2. Staying calm if your child is lying. Your child may be confused, or using fantasy, or be scared to death about something. Shouting only makes it worse.

3. Gently questioning without immediately placing blame. The more forcefully you approach the child who is lying, the more likely it is that the child will cling to the lie.

4. Biting your tongue when you want to berate your child for lying. You cannot shame and humiliate children into responsible behaviour. If a child is continually lying, it is often because of a lack of confidence, and ridicule will only increase his or her bad feelings.

5. Finding out what it is that is making the child fearful of telling the truth. A question like: 'What is it that you think would happen if this was true?' might elicit the reason why the child is lying. It may be that self-protection or protection of a friend is the over-riding concern and not a desire to be malicious.

6. Changing your child's perception of himself or herself by saying: 'I know that inside you are an honest person and that's why I am so disappointed by your lying. Once we've sorted this out let's work on not doing it again.'

7. Telling your child in a matter-of-fact way that you know he or she lied, if you are absolutely positive of your facts. If you see your child pull the dog's tail, don't *ask* what happened, *state* what happened. If there is denial, don't get into a slanging match, it will only make the child lie more in a desperate attempt to prove innocence. Say: 'You go away and think about it. You can even write me a note, if that's easier, and then we'll talk some more.'

8. Letting the child face the consequences of lying. If, for example, your child has not done his or her homework for no good reason, don't write a note letting them out of the situation. A small lesson now will prevent big trouble later.

9. Following through. Although it is sometimes easier to let the child off the hook because you are tired, or it just doesn't seem worth it, do follow through so that the situation is finished for the child. Forgetting about something or letting it slide sends the message that lying isn't really that bad, after all. So, if your child writes you a note as in point 7 above sit down and have a chat about it, or decide on the sanction.

10. Letting it end. After you have finished dealing with it, do just that – finish it. Don't bring it up again and again or you will end up with a child who is a liar – a self-fulfilling prophecy.

11. Explaining that sometimes it is kinder to not say anything, or just to tell a 'little white lie' if the truth is very hurtful. When a friend of mine had radiation therapy after surgery for cancer, she lost her hair and wore a wig, which made her self-conscious. Every time she came over, she asked if I could tell it was a wig. 'It looks amazingly like the real thing,' was my reply, though it was obviously a wig. She certainly didn't need me to say something that would undermine her confidence any further. In my opinion, it would have been cruel. So I guess I am saying that sometimes it is OK either to lie a little or be silent. I don't want my children to blurt out truths such as, 'You're smelly,' or 'This is the most boring time I've ever had,' at the difficult relative's house. Maybe I'm a coward and you wouldn't agree with me, but I think that there are times when people's feelings are more important than the absolute truth.

12. Negotiating – don't force your child into lying by being totally unreasonable. Ian's parents actually put Ian in a situation where he couldn't win. He felt the only way to get through life at home was to lie, because he couldn't live up to what was expected. There was no room for negotiation.

    Deborah's eldest son, Chris, was invited to go to a disco with a group of his friends, but knew from past experience that curfew would be an issue. He wanted to go so badly that he arranged to spend the night at a friend's house rather than tell Deborah he needed to stay out late. She found out from another mother and was ready to turn Chris into mince, until she realised that something was amiss if Chris did not feel he could come to her with a problem like this. They negotiated, and Chris has never once let her down since.

13. Not going overboard about small things. It will make it harder to deal with the more important issues.

14. Making sure that the consequences to lying are known if possible, in advance. For example, if you lie, then you won't get to watch that favourite television programme. Or you will have to tell anyone you lied to what you did, and apologise to them. It will not be possible always to set consequences in

advance, because each situation is different. But generally knowing what will happen might be a deterrent, if it isn't too draconian.

15.   Admitting if you make a mistake and make amends. If you wrongly accuse your child of lying, apologise, offer to get a new, more perfect mother or father and keep trying. No-one gets it right all the time – if they say they do, they're lying.

16.   If your child is older than pre-school age and is a compulsive liar, and you've tried everything you can think of, then do get professional help. There are some underlying reasons why they are trying so hard to lie, and it does take effort to keep up a lying lifestyle. Whatever you do, don't ignore the problem and hope that it will adjust itself in time. It won't. Check with your child's school or your doctor for a referral to Child Guidance.

Cheating

Kids are bad losers. So are some grown-ups I know. To make sure they don't lose, they cheat. When I first started teaching my children card and board games, their ability to cheat was breathtaking. Cards would miraculously appear from up their sleeves, Monopoly money and property cards mysteriously ended up in their ownership, extra scrabble letters suddenly popped up from nowhere, and the rules shifted ominously in their favour. There were tears, cries of 'that's not fair' if they lost, and sulks combined with threats of 'I'm not playing with you ever again'. Yet, somehow, both boys have turned into avid and fair game players. At times, I despaired of this ever happening and I thought only my children were such horrible monsters. Not true.

All children cheat, especially when they are young. Cheating comes naturally when you want to win and haven't yet learned that other people have feelings, and fairness doesn't just mean fair for you.

The trick is to help them through this selfish stage and to make sure that they don't turn into habitual cheats who get into trouble when they are older. I guess we are trying to give them a sense of fair play.

What to Do

Starting when your children are first learning about games, sports and rules:

1. Always explain that cheating is wrong, because it is not fair to everyone. Try to get children to see that they would not like it if someone else cheated on them. Give concrete examples such as: 'If Alan took away your card, would you like it? Would it be fair? Then it isn't fair to take away Alan's card because he doesn't like it.' I think young children work better with examples than with abstract ideals.

2. Explain each rule clearly in terms your child can understand. 'Everyone takes seven letters. If they take more, it is cheating and we all know that is wrong. But I know everyone is going to play fair because that is more fun.' (I know they may not buy it 100 per cent, but keep saying it until they do.)

3. With very young children, you might let one or two things pass if everything else is going smoothly. However, it is best to try to stop cheating whenever you see it. Sometimes, a quiet word with the culprit works better than embarrassing him or her in public. Other times you may have to resort to shoot-out-at-the-OK-Corral-type tactics and pick them up on their cheating. Usually, one of the other kids will begin the 'shoot-out' and you'll have to mediate.

4. If it is not clear what happened, the game may have to end. This is unfair to those who weren't cheating, but sometimes it can't be helped. Always follow up this kind of outcome with a discussion, and reinforce your disapproval of cheating.

5. If your child cheats and you know it, then supervise any situations with other children as much as possible. Play games with them. Wander into the room where they are playing and observe. Use what you observe to discuss with your

child how to behave. Play games alone with your child, and help him or her model good behaviour.

6. Notice and comment on fair play. Give kids lots of praise when they do it right and say how proud you are that they are turning into 'fair players'.

7. Look for books and videos with fair play as a theme, and use them as a way of showing your children how people should behave.

8. Teach your child to apologise for cheating, but don't make it so humiliating that it is counter-productive. A quick 'Sorry' is good enough in my books, if it is followed by no more cheating.

9. If your child is cheating at school or in sports, you will soon find out about it, either from the teachers or from other children. First, find out all the facts (as in Lying above). If it is true, then make sure your child apologises, accepts whatever sanctions are set, makes up for the cheating in some way and then starts again with a clean slate. This may be difficult if all the other children know, and you will need to support your child through the bad times. Let him or her know that you understand people make mistakes, and that you know it won't happen again.

10. Make sure that your child isn't cheating at school because the pressure is too great. If your expectations are too high, you might be inadvertently pushing your child into cheating.

    That doesn't mean you shouldn't have expectations. It does mean that you should check with the teachers and check with your child that what is expected is realistic. This is very important. I have dealt with several cases of suicide and attempted suicide of children under the age of twelve who felt completely out of their depth. Far better to ease off than to have to cope with such tragedies.

11. If your child is self-imposing pressure which leads to cheating, seek professional help. If you feel you cannot cope with what is happening and your child's cheating behaviour does not stop, don't ignore it. Get help. (See point 16 in Lying above.)

Stealing

When young children see something they want, they take it. As far as their little egos are concerned everything *is* theirs. The sun isn't the centre of the universe – they are. That is why they get so hysterical when someone takes something that belongs to them. One mother in a panic consulted me because her two-year-old was 'stealing' from shops, from her, from relatives and neighbours. She thought she had a budding Great Train Robber on her hands, and wanted to put it right before her child fulfilled his early promise! After reassurance that this was quite natural behaviour and that she was not a terrible mother, she went home relieved. I wish all my cases were as easy.

Just because children do think that anything within reach belongs to them, doesn't mean that we let them get away with it – not by a long-shot. With little ones, we watch like hawks in shops, put back ill-gotten gains and pay for those consumed in seconds. We keep a look-out for objects that don't belong to them which have materialised out of the air and into their pockets. And we tell these Fagin's children that those things belong to someone else, even if they don't want to hear it and don't really believe it.

As children get older, say six or seven depending upon their maturity, we might have to march them back into shops and enjoin them to apologise for taking something without paying. Most kids try it at some time, and we have to make sure they don't get into the habit. It is highly embarrassing for parents to have to do this, believe me, but it is effective.

What to Do

To help children learn that stealing isn't something you'll put up with, you might want to:

1. Make sure they know that you think stealing is wrong. If you are clear about this in discussions and show them by example, then they will know the ground-rules. If you are given too

much change in a shop, give it back and then explain why. If you see someone shoplifting, report it. Use books and films to make sure they understand why stealing is wrong.

2. Make sure that if your child steals something, he or she gives it back. It is best to ask them what they think they should do. If they don't come up with the right answer (ie: give it back!) tell them. Help them make arrangements to return or make restitution for what they've taken.

3. Make sure you are giving your child enough pocket money for his or her needs. It may be that your child cannot go out with friends or manage on what he or she is given, and that this is the reason for the stealing.

4. Try to find out any other reason why your child is stealing. It may be for the thrill of it, or because of peer pressure. In at least six cases we dealt with at KIDSCAPE, children were stealing to pay off bullies who were threatening them. It could also be some underlying problem, such as unresolved hostility or jealousy or anger, which requires some counselling. Or it might just be plain, everyday greed.

5. Use common sense to help the child stop, whatever the cause. If your child steals because friends are pressuring him or her to, then try to help them get new friends. Or contact the parents of the friends and have a meeting to bring about more parental control. If it isn't possible to change or cut out these friends, then arrange supervised playtimes or outings so that your child can't get into more trouble. If your child is paying off a bully, contact the school or the police. If your child needs counselling, contact Child Guidance. If your child is stealing because of greed, arrange for him or her to do a little community service and get a different perspective on the world. Perhaps a local soup kitchen needs volunteers, or a home for the elderly could do with someone to help weeding or serve tea.

6. Use all the help you can get. If you are really desperate because your child seems to be continuing to steal no matter what you try, contact your local community liaison officer in the police and get some advice. Sometimes a talking to or a

little reality therapy goes a long way when it comes from someone in authority.

7. Work with the teachers and staff if your child is stealing at school. If the other children know about the stealing, then your child will be labelled a thief, which will make it more difficult to have friends. Other parents might not want your child to come over to their homes. You may try talking with one or two other parents and explain that you have dealt with the problem and would appreciate their support. You may find them quite understanding. Perhaps the teachers could help by choosing books or projects around themes such as people changing their behaviour, or forgiveness, or not being judgemental. The lessons should not be obviously aimed at your child, but it is a positive way to give kids a second chance.

8. Make sure that you don't leave money lying around which might tempt your child into more stealing.

9. Tell your child about a time when you took something, and the consequences and what you learned from it. It helps kids to know that everyone makes mistakes and that they are not condemned for life.

10. Praise your child for good behaviour. Let him or her know that you believe they are capable of not stealing and that you are proud of them for trying so hard to stop.

11. Reward honesty. Too often we focus on what children do wrong, instead of what they do right. So look out for little acts of honesty and give lots of praise. When your children bring you change from shopping or give you something they found, make a fuss and tell them they are wonderful.

Fortunately, most children do not turn into compulsive liars, thieves or cheats. They dip briefly into these vices and quickly learn it isn't the way to behave. Some children, I am told, never do any of these things and are little saints, though I've not met one. For those of us who don't have saints for children, I think the best things we can do to help them grow up to be good, honest adults are:

- to keep their transgressions in perspective
- to catch them being good

- never to label them as thieves, liars or cheats
- to be patient, firm and loving
- to set a good example

I suspect that setting a good example means that if you get stopped for speeding, you should get out of the car, tell the officer that you knew you were speeding, admit that this isn't the first time you've done it and that you were just lucky not to be caught before. *And* you have to talk to your aunt when she phones instead of pretending not to be home. Now *that's* what I call honesty.

26

WHAT TO DO WHEN YOUR CHILD IS IN WITH A 'BAD CROWD'

What can you do if your child chooses friends you hate? Or worse, if you spot your round-faced, dewy-eyed pre-teenager hanging out with a bunch of shaven-headed, multi-earringed weirdos who make the mods and rockers of your youth look like Venture Scouts? It's a situation all parents face sooner or later. Unfortunately, we seem to be facing it sooner with younger and younger children. Should we live with 'the gang' or take drastic action.

Here she is at last, the girl your just-turned twelve-year-old has waxed lyrical about for the past three weeks. 'She's just great,' your daughter said last week. 'Some kids don't like her, but they're just jealous because she is so popular with the boys. She's got some really *rad* friends.'

'Invite her over some time,' you said.

She arrives in black fishnet tights, heavy white make-up, frizzy bleached hair and a skin-tight mini skirt that even you wouldn't have dared wear in the Sixties. This is your innocent twelve-year-old daughter's new best friend. (Did she say her name was Lolita?)

Suppressing a desire to giggle and scream at the same time, you offer your hand. Fingernails from hell come towards you, each one a different colour and an inch long. Perhaps you're only dreaming. Muttering something about finishing your report for the office, you retreat to the loo and close the door.

Where did you go wrong? Oh, for the days when you invited her friends over and served jelly and biscuits . . . Then you remember your neighbour's boy, David.

David was such a lovely kid when he was small, but he fell in with the wrong crowd at just this age. He refused to go to school, stayed out late, got into trouble with the police for shoplifting and caused your friend to age ten years. Whatever happened to him? Was it Strangeways he ended up in? Oh, that's right, he's married now, with a little girl of his own. He's a dentist or something like that . . .

Yes, maybe you *are* over-reacting, but the truth is that Lolita is here, now, in your daughter's bedroom. What does your ordinary, nice child see in her?

Why They Choose 'Bad' Friends

When I was about twelve I did well at school, helped around the house and was a goodie-goodie. My friends were the stalwarts of the school, until Denise came into our class. Denise, it was rumoured, knew how to French kiss. I desperately wanted to learn how the French kissed, and I thought Denise was wonderfully grown-up. I looked up to her. I loved her. My parents did not. I was attracted to Denise for the same reasons today's kids are attracted to 'unsuitable' friends and gangs. These reasons are:

To Test Values
Because then they'll find out what they really believe in. David, now the dentist, stole for 'kicks' with the gang. It was fortunate that his gang didn't do anything worse which might have affected him for the rest of his life. His parents were far-sighted enough to stand by him and not label him a thief. Ultimately, he discovered that his family's values were more important to him than the gang's.

To Act Grown-Up
We adults drink to celebrate, maybe smoke and stay out late having a good time. We tell our kids to wait until they're grown-up to do these things. Then we are shocked, hurt or angry when we find our kids trying out these things 'before their time'. The gang tells them they *are* already grown-up, and proves it by doing all the forbidden things that adults enjoy. Even to be on the fringes of a group that tries drinking and smoking is exciting, especially if you think you're more grown-up than your parents think you are. With Denise and her gang, I once tried smoking. My career as a *femme fatale* was, however, short-lived, as I somehow dropped the lighted cigarette into my blouse. It is hard to look cool while dancing around beating at your breast and screaming.

To Meet Needs
Eleven-year-old Andy was so shy he could hardly look people in the face when he talked to them. He was bullied and had no friends. So his parents were delighted when Andy started hanging around with a group and getting telephone calls. Delighted, that was, until the head teacher rang to tell them that Andy and his group had been picking on the younger kids.

Horrified, they confronted him. Andy fiercely defended his new friends and said they were only playing. But at their meeting with the head teacher, his parents found out that Andy had become one of the ring-leaders of the gang.

Andy was striking back against all the slights and hurts he had received over the years. In a gang, he felt safe enough to vent his anger. With the right groups of kids, he might have found a more positive way to express himself.

To Be Accepted
Being accepted by their age group is vital to children. It gives them the structure and safety to make mistakes, to develop their personalities, and even to become a little humble (we wish!).

A 'good' group helps reinforce the values parents like; a 'bad' group can make life intolerable for us. To be accepted, kids will do almost anything, including experimenting with illegal drugs – which seem to be available even to primary-aged children in some areas. Kids may also try alcohol, cheating, smoking, vandalism and shoplifting. If the gang does it and you want to be in the gang, you do it.

At my son's school, the teachers were shocked when they found out about the activities of a ten-year-old boy in one of their classes. Over the weekend he invited some other boys to his flat and they drank all the alcohol they could find and accidently set fire to the carpet while lighting up his father's cigars! Don't ask me where his parents were, but I am just thankful that my son wasn't there. I can only hope that if he had been, he would have left, but I will never know.

I think we have to keep it in perspective. Remember some of the things you tried in order to be accepted by a group: clothes; hairstyles; bad language? The dangers of drugs and solvent abuse which threaten our children probably seem a world away from the danger we faced. Feel for them.

To Experiment

When they only experiment with growing penicillin cultures on discarded snacks under the bed, or never hanging up their clothes, you're lucky! When they experiment by getting into the wrong crowd and try joy-riding or illegal drugs, you're not. And then, of course, there's sex.

Thirteen-year-old Jenny looked and acted nineteen. She attracted the attention of some older boys, who invited her into their gang. She was flattered by the attention and by being told that she was 'sexy'. The young girl soon found her status in the gang depended on having sex with the leader. When Jenny's parents heard what was happening, they intervened. Jenny had been having some other problems, and the family did need some help, so this did not come as a bolt out of the blue. There followed long, often heated discussions, with Jenny subsequently being kept in and forbidden to see the boy and the gang. She did sneak out once or twice, but it was more to test her parents' resolve than to get back in with the crowd.

Her parents could have called the police, because the older boy was breaking the law by being sexually involved with Jenny, who was under age at the time.

Jenny later told her parents that she was secretly glad to be able to blame them because she just didn't know how to get away.

Jenny needed help. And that's usually where parents come in. Don't be put off by your children's protests that they are grown-up and can handle whatever happens. They aren't and they can't.

What Can We Do?

There are some strategies you can try when you are worried about your kids' friends. Some may work, some may not, but at least you'll have done your best.

1. Invite Those Awful Friends Over

It may get on your nerves having Lolita, Jungle Jim and Mono-syllabic Bill around, but better to have them where you can see them, than out of sight but always on your mind. Impossible though it may seem, you may even grow fond of them once you get to know the person behind the horrendous exterior.

Suggest places to go, like bowling alleys, cinemas, discos, swimming. So much of the malaise children exhibit is due to being at a loose end. Those kids who seem to have the easiest 'passage' as teenagers, are often the ones with lots of interests, many developed from an early age: music, art, drama, sports. Kids look for excitement, which can lead to car stealing or shoplifting, or can be channelled into something more useful.

2. Try to Withhold Judgement

When I brought my friend Denise home, the only comment I remember was Dad saying he cared too much about me to let me go out dressed like her. His comment was not against her so much, as protective of me.

Denise let down her guard with us. My parents did not hesitate to say what they thought and felt, but they never made it seem as if they were judging. No-one ever said how much they liked Denise, but no-one ever said she was a terrible person.

3. Help Them Set Limits

Often, teenagers are afraid to hurt someone's feelings, or do not want to look foolish in front of others. Then they end up in a dangerous situation. If you can help them decide their limits in advance, they will be in a better position to make judgements about what to do. Talk to your children about what they'd do if they were with a group which wanted to get drunk, take drugs, shoplift, sniff glue, crash a party, and so on.

4. Help Them Stick to These Limits

The old 'My mean old Mum won't let me . . .' routine is useful whenever they're asked to join in something they think is dubious. (I don't mind the mean, but I object to the old!) We shouldn't be put off by our children's rebellious poses; they may complain, but many are secretly grateful to be able to place the 'blame' on their parents.

5. Tell Them to Trust Their Intuition

Often, children, particularly young teenagers, do not trust their own feelings and judgement. Though they are getting into a difficult situation, they go along with it so they won't appear silly in front of friends.

Max was talked into having a party while his parents were away for the evening. His friends said they would help clear up, and that his parents would never know.

Everything went well until a group of troublemakers gate-crashed. Max knew immediately that he should get help, but thought that by handling the situation himself he would appear a big man in front of his friends, and that his parents wouldn't find out. The troublemakers began to beat the boys, molest some of the girls and wreck the house. Finally Max called the police.

If Max had trusted his initial judgement not to hold the party, none of this would have happened.

6. Arrange a Code

Regardless of whether you love or hate your child's group of friends, arrange a code which can be used to rescue him or her from any situation.

Twelve-year-old Heather was at a party. She had lied to her parents about where she was (she was supposed to be spending the night with a friend) and she needed rescuing. She and her dad had worked out a code to be used in case of emergency. If she rang and asked: 'Has Pat called me?', her parents would know that she needed them to get her. Dad had promised her he would pick her up any time, night or day, with no questions asked.

She decided to give it a try and it worked – she told him where she was, he came, collected her and restrained himself from asking anything. Soon after, Heather gave up this gang of friends. Her dad will never know for sure if it was his non-judgemental attitude that helped her break away, or whether she just outgrew them.

The hardest part for her parents was sticking to 'no questions asked'. Better, though, than Heather not ringing in a potentially dangerous situation. Even better would have been for Heather's parents to have rung the parents of the friend Heather was supposed to be staying with, even though some kids consider this 'checking up on them'. Well, so be it – we do need to talk to another adult if our kids are going to be in someone else's care. For that matter, what if we need to contact them in an emergency and find they are not there?

7. Find Time to Be Alone With Them

Try to establish a time with your child when just the two of you can talk privately. If possible, do this away from the home so that you have a neutral place to talk. Perhaps you can go to a cafe for a hot chocolate or coffee, or even out to lunch, if funds permit. You don't have to bill it as a time to talk, but that is usually what ends up happening. I've noticed that when our family is travelling or eating out together, our children seem to be much more willing to talk than at home. I guess it's because the lure of the television, telephone or other distractions are missing and it frees them (and us) to focus more on one another.

8. Encourage Interests

It may be that your child is stuck into this crowd because she or he doesn't have interests or skills in common with other children. Find out what is available which your child might like to get involved in, and which will also open up other friendships. Music, sports, martial arts, dance, computers – there are many possibilities either at school or within your local area. It may be a pain to organise, but it is worth the effort if it gives your child a way out of the crowd he or she is in now.

9. Give It Time

The policy we usually have to follow when our children fall in with the wrong crowd is simply to wait it out. Nerve-wracking and heart-stopping though this may be, it almost always works. The group just outgrows itself and no longer meets anyone's needs. Kids drift off, find new friends, leave school, move, and suddenly the problem has resolved itself.

10. Get Tough

There are times when parents need to make their positions quite clear. That is when your child is in real danger from a bad crowd. I am sure Denise wouldn't have been welcomed into our house if she had been using drugs. If your children are in danger, it goes without saying that your first responsibility must be to them.

The first line of defence is to know the signs of gambling, drug, alcohol or solvent abuse. I know it seems impossible to have to consider this with children, as well as teenagers, but consider it we must. I never really thought I had to worry about any of this stuff until my children were older, but that's not true any more. A recent survey of 5,000 children in Staffordshire showed that almost forty per cent of four-year-olds and ninety-three per cent of eleven-year-olds knew about drugs. In the same survey, fifty-three per cent of the eleven-year-olds felt that drugs could be good for them. More comforting was the fact that ninety per cent also knew that there was a potential harmful effect of drugs. The point of this is that our children often know more than we think they do, and that some are being offered drugs and others are already taking them before the age of eleven. If you think your child's crowd is into drugs, stealing from shops or playing truant, then forget the non-judgemental, sit-back-and-wait attitude. Here's what to do:

a) *Keep an adult perspective* and don't feel it is necessary to get on the same level as your children or teenagers by acting 'cool'. They have enough of the other point of view from their group.

b) *Don't be afraid* to say that using drugs, shoplifting, playing truant or gambling are wrong and that you disapprove whole-heartedly and you will ensure that it stops. Talk about your family standards and values. Tell your child that it doesn't matter to you if her friends and their families have different standards. Explain that you expect your child to uphold your family standards. Children may rail against this outwardly, but often it gives them the inner strength they eventually use to break away from the 'gang'.

c) *Get it together* with parents of other members of the group and agree rules, pocket money, and any other guidelines which make it harder for your children or teenagers to say 'but everyone's doing it'.

d) *Keep communication open*, because although it's worrying and we are angry, the more we withdraw, the more they will – it's a downward spiral.

e) *Use a last resort* if your child is in extreme danger and you have the option to get him or her out of the situation. Ask your parents, in-laws, sister or brother to let the child move in for a month. Or take your child out of school and educate him/her at home (it is legal, but places quite a burden on you). In extreme cases, consider moving house in order to get away from the gang once and for all.

None of these will work, though, if your child really *needs* whatever the gang provides.

Sometimes it is just bad luck that the child ends up with a wild and weird group. Other times, a child has a very real problem and the choice of group reflects that.

If all your efforts fail, then it's time to seek counselling to try to unravel things before they get any worse. Contact your local Child Guidance centre.

Take Heart

Children need to break away, to change, grow and find their own paths. Groups help them do that. Sometimes even the 'wrong crowds' help them find their own values, which turn out to be not a million miles from your own.

We laugh about Denise now – she and I together, that is! Through our friendship she grew to adopt the values of my family. (Now she complains about 'kids today'.) I used our friendship to find out if I wanted to keep those very same values.

I did. And I just hope I have a tenth of the patience which my parents showed me when, and if, my two boys get into the 'wrong crowds' or start to bring home a Lolita Liz or Acid House Annie as the latest girlfriend.

Symptoms and Signs

If your child exhibits signs of drug abuse or gambling, forget the 'it'll soon pass' attitude and take action. Get involved, and call on experts (see Where to Get Help, p. 314).

Symptoms of Drug or Solvent Abuse

- *inexplicable personality change*
- *frequently changing moods*
- *becoming secretive, vague or withdrawn*
- *alternately very drowsy or hyperactive*
- *paranoia*
- *slurred or slow speech*
- *paraphernalia left around, such as burnt foil, needles, pipes*
- *glue on clothing*
- *red eyes, spots, red nose, jerky movements*
- *stealing, lying*

Signs That Your Child Might Be Gambling

- *money disappearing from home*
- *truancy*
- *possessions disappearing or being sold*
- *lying*
- *bloodshot eyes*
- *behaviour that is aggressive or completely withdrawn*

27

WAYS TO STOP KIDS SWEARING

Penny, aged eight, and her brother Ben, aged six, were playing with their friends in the park. Their father, Brian, was talking with some of the other parents while keeping an eye on them. He noticed a few older children playing with the younger ones, but thought nothing of it until Ben came running up to ask if they could get an ice-cream.

'Sorry, I don't have any money with me,' explained Brian.

'Oh, sh—!' said Ben in disgust, and started to walk off.

'What did you say?' exclaimed Brian, who was incredibly embarrassed and shocked as he made it a point never to swear around his children.

Ben stopped short and turned scarlet. 'I said "Oh, sh—."'

Brian thought all the other parents were looking at him and judging him to be a rotten, foul-mouthed father. In fact, they were sympathising – they'd all heard their children repeating words they themselves didn't use.

The reality is that children swear, adults swear and who knows what the dog is really saying when he barks his head off at the doorbell. That doesn't mean, however, that we have to condone or put up with it.

Poor Ben – he had just been playing with older kids who were busy proving how much more grown-up they were than the little kids by swearing a blue streak. Now he was in trouble and not getting any ice-cream either. What could Brian do, and how can we make sure kids don't turn into trash mouths?

1. Explain

If your children use swear words which they don't understand, explain to them what the words mean. Children may use the f–word, for example, without knowing that it is slang for sexual intercourse. So, if your children are old enough and you have explained to them about sex, then tell them what it stands for. Likewise, many of the offensive words used to swear refer to sexual parts of the body, or to bodily functions.

Also explain that some words are considered offensive for religious or cultural reasons. When I first moved to the United Kingdom in 1971 from the United States, I was amazed when someone took offence at the word 'bloody'. In the UK it is a swear word, supposedly coming from a contraction of 'by our Lady', and is blasphemous. In the USA it just means someone is being difficult!

2. Give Them Substitute Words

Many swear words are short and emphatic and easy to get into the habit of using, especially when we are angry. Help children come up with a list of acceptable words which serve the same purpose. I had an acquaintance who used to say things like 'Oh, poopy doo' when she was angry. To tell the truth, it almost caused me to swear at her. Don't make the words so bizarre that your child won't use them. Try words like 'blast' or 'darn' or 'drat' or 'heck' – one syllable and easy to shout out when they are annoyed.

3. Set a Good Example

Obviously, if we swear our children will copy us, so we have to set a good example. I remember swearing once in front of my then three-year-old son, who proceeded to repeat the word from his car seat until I thought I would scream. When I told him to stop, he just said, 'But Mummy, you said it.' Out of the mouths of babes and all that . . . Believe me, there is nothing like a parroting three-year-old to make you clean up your language quickly.

4. Friends Swear

Even if you don't swear, your children will have friends who swear, or will go to homes where swearing is a normal part of the conversation. If your children come home and say, 'But Jay Smith's brother swears and he doesn't get into trouble,' tell them that you know other people swear, but that isn't what is done in your family. Or tell them that your last name isn't Smith (or invite them to go live with the Smiths if it becomes too much – just kidding). Stick to your guns and don't let them swear around you. It is more difficult to ensure that they don't swear when they are away from home, unless you have an army of spies.

5. Shock Value

Children do swear to shock and to get attention. Say, 'I don't like or appreciate that language,' and then get on with what you were doing. Don't react by getting angry or shouting, as that will only make the child realise that swearing can be used to upset you. If you think it helps, tell your child that he can swear to himself in his own room, but you don't want to hear that language.

6. Ignore Them

Some parents just ignore bad language entirely and pretend they didn't hear it. They carry on with what they were doing as if the child said nothing unusual at all. Parents I know who use this method say that the child then uses the words louder and more frequently for a time, but eventually gets bored trying to get their attention this way. Debbie told me that her child kept saying, 'Did you hear what I said?' in a not very subtle attempt to see if she was shocked. Debbie didn't over-react, explain, correct or punish, and her child did stop swearing – there was no point in carrying on because no-one paid the slightest bit of notice.

7. Play Dumb

When eight-year-old Khalid came home and used profanity, his
father looked up from his work and quietly asked him what the
words meant. 'I'm afraid I don't understand, Khalid, what does that
mean?' Needless to say, Khalid's sojourn into profanity was quite
short. Can you imagine how embarrassing it is to actually have to
explain to your parents what a swear word means?

Asking a child to explain the words he or she knows are nasty
embarrasses the child, but you can use that embarrassment to
advantage by explaining that that is how other people feel hearing
swear words. Go on to explain that it is not right to use words
which embarrass people.

8. Monitor Television/Films

I remember getting into terrible trouble because I saw a film which
used the words 'damn' and 'hell' and told my grandmother about
it. It seems that I should have got up and left when the first 'damn'
was uttered, but the film suddenly became much more interesting
just because those words were in it. The same applies today, except
the words are several degrees stronger. Words that I would have
been killed for using are now standard fare, making the parent's
job more difficult. If your children are exposed to bad language on
television or a film, explain that the language is still not acceptable
and that, sometimes, the people who write films like to shock and
use swear words. Reiterate that it is still unacceptable, just as
murder might be portrayed in films but that, too, is unacceptable.

9. Consequences

When I was growing up and a child swore, the bar of soap came
out and little mouths were left foaming. Ugh! I guess it worked, but
it does seem a cruel and unusual punishment – I would never use
it with my children. If children do continue to swear in spite of your
best efforts, warn them that there will be consequences and tell
them what they are. Try:

a) Taking away a privilege such as watching television.
b) Giving extra privileges if they don't swear.
c) Asking them to leave the room and not come back until they can talk in a more civilised manner.
d) Telling them to repeat the word 100 times (boring!).
e) Fining them a certain amount every time they swear. This works best if you are giving them pocket money and can either deduct at source or ask them to put the money into a jar, kept for that purpose. If you use this method, grown-ups have to pay up, as well!

10. Praise Clever Use of Words

Some people swear because they have a limited vocabulary and, in my opinion, limited intelligence. Encourage children to use descriptive words instead of swear words. If they hate that '@*!~' homework, help them look up and use more clever words, such as 'onerous' homework, and then tell them how clever they are.

I once endured a two-hour train ride with a group of young men going to a football match. They were well-dressed and seemed quite nice until they started talking. I have never heard the f–word used as much in my life, and I have heard it used. A typical sentence went something like: 'Did you f— see how that f— player f— kicked the f— ball into the f— net?' Although I moved further up the carriage, their voices were loud and there was no escape. I guess I should have said something, but they probably would have been amazed that anyone would care how they talked, and I wasn't feeling all that brave. Anyway, it was kind of sad because they weren't trying to shock, they just had no other adjective to use.

Ben knew the word he used would shock his father, even though he was only six. Even much younger children know this, though most are just copying words and don't understand their meaning. Ben was annoyed that Brian wouldn't buy him an ice-cream and was angry. He had heard the older boys swearing and filed it as a possible new skill that he, too, could use. Ben's father took him aside and told him that it was wrong to use that word, and that polite people did not talk like that. When Brian turned back to apologise to the other parents, he found that it wasn't necessary; they were full of stories of their own about their children's language.

Probably all children will experiment with swearing, and I think we have to accept that. What we don't have to accept is their swearing around us or in our homes. They may insist that they have a right to talk as they wish, but, *darn* it, we have a right not to listen.

28

WHAT TO DO ABOUT LOST CHILDREN

'How many of you have ever been lost?'

The assembly of 300 children became a sea of waving hands.

'How many of you have never been lost?'

Four hands shot up.

Amazing? No. Ask any group of children and you will be hard-pressed to find many who haven't been lost.

Six-year-old Alan keeps his hand up, urgently seeking attention. 'Miss, miss!'

'Yes Alan?'

'My mum got lost in the shopping centre. I looked up and she was just gone. Mums shouldn't go off that way – it scared me.' The older children giggled. Sooooo sophisticated, at ten!

Then everyone wanted to tell their stories. It seemed that getting lost was the most common thing that ever happened to kids, and the one thing that caused great anxiety. In fact, ask your adult friends.

'We were at the park and I suddenly realised that my mum had disappeared. I was absolutely terrified. The trees became attacking giants, the wind was swirling around, ready to take me off. Even the passing people looked sinister. I was only four, but I can still remember that awful, sinking feeling of being alone.' Lynn is twenty-seven years old and the look on her face is of being four and lost. This feeling of absolute panic is one parents will know well.

Discovering your child is lost ranks amongst the ten worst things a parent dreads, and is one of the ten most likely things to happen while you are raising children. I don't know a parent who hasn't lost a child at one time or another. Luckily, most children are found safe and none the worse, apart from fear, within minutes. The rescuer is usually another parent, who recognises the signs of distress only too well.

We took our children to a large theme park and were getting lunch when I noticed a little boy, aged about three, looking very forlorn. He was walking slowly around the huge cafeteria, one foot carefully placed in front of the other, as if measuring the edge of the room by the length of his feet. He carefully scrutinised every table as he walked past, and kept anxiously looking at people going by with their families. He reminded me of a caged animal. Something wasn't right. I watched for a few minutes to see if any-one came up to him, but no-one did. Finally, I approached him, knelt down next to him and asked: 'Where is your mummy?' His eyes filled with tears and he gulped, 'I don't know.' He just collapsed into my lap and threw his arms around my neck. I comforted him, told him we'd find his parents and asked my husband to contact the cafe manager. I tried to turn over my new little friend, Miles, to the manager, but he wouldn't let go. I guess he had decided that *I* wasn't a stranger, but the manager was. After the public announcement, a frantic, crying woman came rushing in, followed by an equally distraught father and endless other relatives, and Miles was safely back in the bosom of his family. I wonder how long he wandered around before I stopped, and how many people had not picked up the signs? It scared me, because you hope that your child will be helped by a kindly adult should he or she get lost, and that people will not just turn away. I guess we have to rely on the goodwill of people and give our children some suggestions to follow just in case. But what can we do to arm our children if they get lost? How do we give them strategies without scaring them to death?

1. Arrange a Meeting Place

When you take your children to any public place, arrange a 'meeting place'. Most of us now do this automatically, whether in a store, shopping centre, park or restaurant. Our local shopping centre is the ideal place to get lost. Lots of eye-catching displays and distractions. The most noticeable feature is the large water fountain, so we always tell the children, 'We will meet you at the fountain if we are separated from each other.' We say it *every* time we go to the shopping centre, so our kids interrupt to say 'I know' or 'Boring'. Good! I drum it in to those little heads until it is second nature.

2. Give Instructions About Public Transport

The same goes for public transport. Helen was getting on the underground with her baby in a push chair, carrier bags and her three-year-old, Peter.

'I let go of Peter's hand for all of thirty seconds. When I turned to gather him in, the doors closed with him on the outside and me inside. Both of us started crying and screaming, but the train pulled out just the same. I got off at the next stop, with a kind woman who came along when she saw what happened. We ran across the platform, waited what seemed like an age and got on a train going the other way. We ran back to our original platform, where a group of adults was comforting my very distressed son. I grabbed him and held him close and just wept with relief.'

Give your children very clear instructions about what to do if you are separated on a bus or train. You may decide to tell the child to wait at the stop, or platform and you will come to them. Or you might want them to stay on the bus or train and tell them to talk to the guard or driver, and ask that they be accompanied to the end of the line, where you will arrange to meet them.

3. Accepting Help From Strangers

What about accepting help from people you don't know? This is a dilemma. What if the woman who helped Helen had offered to hold the baby and told her to go and find her son. Well-meaning though she may have been, you do not know if it would have been safe to leave your child with her. She is a complete stranger. Remember the recent case of the 'store detective' who assured the mum that she would look after the children while the mum went back into the store for a refund. The 'detective' kidnapped the baby, who was eventually found safe, thank goodness. We warn children about strangers, but we, too, can become unwitting victims of a kindly face. Most people are genuine, but you never really know. So, always keep your other children with you if you have to look for a missing child. Peter, however, was obviously being helped by a whole posse of kind strangers.

The best advice we can give children is not to talk to strangers if they are on their own. However, if they are lost or need help, tell them they can ask a shop person behind the counter, a police officer or a person with children for help.

But explain to children that they don't have to hold hands or go with the person. They can tell the adult that they promised to stay where they last saw you. This relieves them of having to go off with a stranger. Obviously, in the case of my little friend Miles, he was too young and frightened to keep his distance. He just wanted a mummy figure to hug him, and help find his real Mummy.

How Adults Can Help

My husband said he'd have felt uncomfortable had the child flung himself into his lap, because he was worried about being seen as a child molester or kidnapper! My husband would help a child in distress, but would try to keep the child at arm's length. Unfortunately, this is not an uncommon feeling amongst men because of all the media coverage about child abuse, so I understand how they can feel this way. But I think it is sad, both for men and for children.

Well-meaning adults can help lost children by:

a) Offering to get an announcement made or getting a couple of other adults to go for help while he or she stays near the child.

b)   Talking to the child reassuringly.
c)   Not offering to hold the child's hand or force the child to hold yours.
d)   Giving comfort if the child climbs on your lap or grabs your hand.
e)   Not taking the child away from where you find him or her unless absolutely necessary, or you could be thought to be kidnapping.
f)   If possible, ringing the parents or waiting until they arrive.
g)   Not taking the child somewhere in your car.

What Parents Can Teach Their Children

Parents can help by:

a)   Teaching children their full names, addresses, and telephone numbers.
b)   Teaching children how to use the telephone.
c)   Teaching children that they can dial the operator to ring your home, or they can ring emergency services without having to use money.
d)   Getting a friend or relative to wait by the phone if the child is missing for any length of time.
e)   Contacting the police if you are worried and your child isn't found quickly. Better safe than sorry.
f)   Hugging them tightly when they are found – don't yell or scold them, they are frightened enough.

Helen says: 'The fifteen minutes it took to get back to Peter were the longest in my life. I am just so grateful that everyone was so helpful.' That is the real message – most people will help and comfort a lost child, and we are soon reunited. The world isn't such a bad place, after all.

Practical Advice for Lost Children.

1. *Stay put.*
2. *Know name and address.*
3. *Telephone home or a friend.*
4. *Know where to meet if you get separated.*
5. *If you need to ask for help, go to the shopkeeper or a grown-up with children.*
6. *If you are indoors, don't go outside.*

29

WHAT TO DO ABOUT BULLYING

'Bullying is part of human nature, something children must learn to cope with if they are to survive the rough and tumble of every-day life.' This can be a hard line to swallow for parents of tender five-year-olds; little ones often find the playground jungle a sinis-ter place at first. At least, though, five-year-olds usually tell their parents about events and people that worry them. The further they go up the school, the more likely it becomes that children will suffer in silence; either that, or they reveal so little you're not sure how seriously to take it.

Should we root out the problem, make an un-British fuss if we find our child is being picked on? Or is it usually best to leave chil-dren to sort this kind of thing out between themselves? Bullying is an abuse of power, which has the potential not only to cause short-term misery but can lay the foundations for adult aggression. After all, versions of the playground heavies and their victims are re-enacted in sitting-rooms and boardrooms daily.

Who Bullies?

Before discussing some of the things you can do if your child is being bullied, or if your child is being a bully, let's briefly look at who the bullies are. The stereotype of the big, mean, nasty boy is one that usually comes to mind when the word bully is mentioned.

The reality is that bullies can be any shape or size and that girls are equally as capable as boys of bullying. The kids who frequently bully do seem to share some common characteristics. They often:

- feel inadequate
- are bullied themselves within their families
- come from families which extol the 'virtues' of bullying
- are victims of some kind of abuse
- don't know how or are not allowed to show feelings
- are not succeeding in school
- feel no sense of self-worth

There are also bullies who are self-confident, spoilt children who have always had their own way, expect it as their right and are prepared to bully to get it.

Then we have the children who may bully others once in a while because they have some sort of upheaval in their lives, such as the birth of a baby, the death of someone they love, rejection from a friend, being the victim themselves of bullying, a run-in with a family member or a teacher, boredom, or a whole host of other problems which might lead them to lash out at another child.

What Is Bullying?

Bullying is the use of aggression with the intention of hurting another person. It results in pain and distress to the victim.

Bullying can be:

Physical	pushing, kicking, punching, hitting, or any use of violence
Verbal	name-calling, sarcasm, spreading rumours, nasty teasing
Emotional	excluding, being unfriendly, tormenting, racial taunts, threatening or rude gestures

Possible Signs of Bullying

Parents need to be aware of the signs that a child might be being bullied. If your child shows some of the following behaviours or signs, you may want to ask about bullying.

Children may:

- be frightened of walking to or from school, or change their normal route to school
- not want to go on the school bus
- beg you to drive them to school
- be unwilling to go to school or feel ill every morning
- begin truanting
- begin doing poorly in their school work
- come home with clothes or books destroyed
- come home hungrier than usual (bully has taken dinner money)
- become withdrawn, start stammering, lack confidence
- become distressed and anxious, stop eating
- attempt or threaten suicide
- cry themselves to sleep, have nightmares
- ask for money or begin stealing (to pay the bully)
- refuse to say what's wrong (frightened of the bully)
- have unexplained scratches, bruises, etc.
- begin to bully other children or siblings
- become aggressive and unreasonable

If your child does show some of these signs, then ask him or her if bullying is a problem. Be direct. Say, 'I think you are being bullied or threatened and I'm worried about you. Let's talk about it.' If your child doesn't tell you immediately, say that you are there and willing to listen, night or day, when he or she is ready to talk. Then keep a watchful eye – kids can become quite desperate when they are being bullied, and do dumb things like run away or take an overdose because it all seems so hopeless to them.

Why Bully?

Bullying is intended to humiliate the victim, and most bullies know exactly what they are doing. Bullying makes them feel powerful and in control. There are times, however, when the bully doesn't realise how much harm she or he is causing. Perhaps they go along with the crowd and say hurtful things without thinking through what they are doing. Perhaps they bully because they are secretly frightened that, if they don't, they will be the next victim. Perhaps they bully because they are bored. Whatever the reason, it is no comfort to the victim, whose life has been made miserable.

Who Are the Victims?

In my experience, most victims of bullying are sensitive, intelligent, gentle children who have good relationships with their parents. They don't come from families full of conflict and shouting, so when bullies come at them, they don't quite know what to do. They frequently ask why someone would want to bully them – they've done nothing to deserve it and they haven't been treated this way before. The sad fact is that, from the bully's viewpoint, they make excellent targets because they are nice and won't fight back. They might even cry, a bonus for the bully. If you could point out one 'fault' of these victims, it would be that they are too nice! In a school which doesn't tolerate bullying, they have no problems.

There are, however, some children who seem to get bullied everywhere – at school, parties, activities, clubs – you name it and they are bullied. These are the children who seem to invite bullying, and almost thrive on the negative attention they get when they are bullied. It is as if the bullying confirms their opinions of themselves that they are worthless, and deserve what is happening to them. There may be problems in the lives of these children which are very similar to the problems of the bullies mentioned above. Or they may have been bullied right from the day when they started school, and never recovered their confidence. Whatever the reason, they seem to go through life as perpetual victims.

What Harm Is Caused?

KIDSCAPE, the children's charity which deals with bullying and child abuse receives hundreds of letters and telephone calls weekly about bullying. Children tell of fear, threats, violence, bribery (money or sweets being extorted by bullies), ostracism and sexual and racial attacks. Each letter represents a small personal tragedy.

I have talked with parents whose children have run away, played truant, turned to drugs and solvents, become withdrawn, angry or aggressive, failed in school and even committed suicide because of bullying. It is a heart-wrenching experience to try to help them cope with the unnecessary and senseless death of their child, when you know that, had someone taken effective action, their child would still be alive. The parents blame themselves, which is understandable. But most bullying is school-based and, *if* the school knew about the bullying but did nothing to stop it, then I'm afraid I have to lay the blame with the school. There are many things schools can do. If they don't, then parents should suggest they adopt the following approaches:

Crack the 'Code of Silence'

Bullies depend for their success on a code of silence. It is based, of all things, on honour ('It's wrong to tell tales') or on fear ('Don't tell anyone or I'll thump you'). Either way, it prevents children from telling when they have been bullied or have seen someone being bullied.

To crack the code of silence, KIDSCAPE encourages the schools to:

1. Become 'telling' schools. The headteacher makes it clear that bullying is unacceptable. Bullies will not be tolerated. The children have an obligation to *tell* if they are bullied or see bullying take place.
2. Ensure that the adults do something, too, when they are told. Adults have an obligation to *act*. For this approach to succeed, children must be able to rely on a sympathetic and helpful response if they do tell. In this way, they learn that speaking

out will make things better; keeping quiet will make things worse. Experience has shown that bullying is much less likely to happen in schools which have a clear policy against bullying.

Set Up Student Helpers

The idea of using students to help others is as old as teaching itself. I used this method over twenty-five years ago when I had a classroom of thirty-four children, and a few of the older children were making it their business to bully the younger ones:

1. At the start of the school year, assign new students an older 'helper' who acts as an adviser, protector and mentor. Usually, older or bigger children pick on younger or smaller ones, *who are alone*. This approach eliminated that problem, and the older children took pride in helping 'their' charges. Of course, you had to prepare the older children and instill in them a sense of responsibility, but that wasn't difficult. If a helper was a problem, we didn't allow him or her to be in the programme. The competition to be good enough to be a helper was immense, and quite a positive force in the school.

2. We also set up student counsellors who were chosen anonymously by the children and teachers as 'people you would most likely seek out to talk to about a problem'. They were the natural helpers in the school. We gave them some extra training and they become the liaisons for children who felt they needed more help because of a particular bullying problem. We made sure the student counsellors had a place and time to talk with the children, and privacy to do so. It was a bit of extra time and trouble for all of us, but the results were excellent. Some schools are still using the student counsellors with great success.

Set Up Bully 'Courts'

As with the suggestion about setting up student helpers, I have always found that one of the most effective deterrents to bullying is other kids. In other words, if bullies can be made to feel that their behaviour is unacceptable *to the other children*, they will be much more likely to change than if they are simply told by adults to mend their ways. To bring this form of change about, KIDSCAPE advocates:

1. Setting up bully 'courts', in which bully and victim are brought together, with a teacher and perhaps the parents, to discuss the causes and effects of what has happened.
2. Ensuring that the 'courts' are part of a whole school policy, within an atmosphere in which bullying is stripped of any glamour and clearly condemned as wrong. These 'court' collaborations can change a bully's behaviour and make the children feel they have a direct involvement in stopping bullying.

Help the Bully

Sometimes it is possible to help a bully by recognising that he, too, is a victim; perhaps unloved or mistreated at home, or making up for a feeling of personal inadequacy by dominating others. In these cases, treating the underlying cause may also eradicate the bullying. For example, a child with an otherwise poor school record who is encouraged to work hard and excel at some particular subject – art, photography, computing – may in the process gain enough approval to stop bullying. If parents of the bullied can take a sympathetic approach towards the parents of the bully – acknowledging that any of us could find ourselves a parent of a bully one day – there's more likelihood of co-operation than if they feel accused.

In practise, this sort of bridge-building is not always possible. Bullies, as I have said above, are very often children who are bullied at home; they may be punished for their own weaknesses (such as bedwetting, or something as minor as putting a sweater on back-to-front), so that they come to see weakness in others as something to be attacked and despised. It is almost a form of self-hate, a diagnosis that will be of small comfort to the mother of a bullied child. Reforming the behaviour of a chronic bully is not easy;

power may be the only language they understand. Significantly, when schools organise meetings to discuss the problem of bullying, it is usually the parent of the victim who turns up.

However, if you find yourself as the parent of the bully and are in despair over what to do, approach the school and try to:

1. Remain calm.
2. Find out the facts.
3. Talk to your child to find out if she or he is upset, or perhaps has been bullied and is lashing out as a reaction.
4. Find out if your child realises that she or he is bullying and hurting someone else.
5. Talk with the parents of the victim, if possible, to set things right and to avoid the bullying carrying on.
6. Work with the teacher and show you are concerned.
7. Talk to your child and explain that, whatever problems there may be, bullying is not the way to solve them.
8. Work out a 'behaviour plan' and reward good behaviour.
9. Arrange a daily or weekly report from teachers so you can work together to change your child's behaviour.

Help the Victims

Sometimes parents and teachers have to work around bullies by teaching their children how to cope with threats, and how to avoid attracting them in the first place. Some children seem more prone to bullying than others. This may result from factors beyond their control: the colour of their skin, for example, or some striking physical feature, such as being above or below average height, that sets them apart from the others. Or it may be that, if they are repeatedly bullied, children start acting like victims. If this happens, parents *can take steps* to help overcome the problems. Children can be helped to learn some techniques:

1. Walk tall and straight, in a confident way, rather than hunched over, looking scared and uncertain.
2. A timid, shy child can, as a game, practise looking in the mirror and saying 'No' or 'Leave me alone' in a clear voice, looking

into their own eyes as they say it. A firm rebuff will often deter a bully who is looking for signs of weakness and acquiescence.

3. Role-playing – something I have used with great success in schools, and something you could try at home with your own children or groups of children. Act out the threatening situation and practise responding calmly but firmly. This type of imaginative play can also help defuse some of the anger that builds up inside children who are persistently bullied.

4. Ignore the bullying, pretend not to be upset – turn and walk quickly away.

5. Use humour. It is more difficult to bully a child who refuses to take the bullying seriously. This is especially useful with verbal bullying. However, it could make a situation worse if your child is being physically threatened or confronted by a large group of bullies who might get violent.

6. Avoid places where bullying usually occurs.

7. Try to stay with groups of children, if possible. Bullies usually pick on kids alone.

8. Respond to taunts saying the same thing over and over. This is called the broken record approach. For example, to a chant such as 'You're ugly', respond with 'Thank you'. Then keep saying it over and over – 'Thank you, thank you.' It gets rather boring for the bully after a while.

In order for children to feel confident using some of these ideas, you may want to help them to practise and to come up with other ideas.

Also, try to give your children confidence by:

9. Assuring them that the bullying is not their fault.

10. Telling them that you love them and are 100 per cent behind them.

11. Encouraging them to join groups outside school, such as Brownies, Guides, Scouts, clubs, theatre or music groups, martial arts clubs – anything which might give your child a chance to develop their talents or new friendships.

12. Teaching them relaxation techniques.

13. Inviting individual children over to play.

14. Helping them to stop any bad habits which might be contributing to their being bullied (such as biting their lips or making strange faces because of nervousness).
15. Seeking professional help, if necessary.

Approach the School

Your child may beg you not to talk to the teachers, and this will place you in a difficult position. If the bullying is happening at school, then the school needs to do something about it. You can certainly try to work it out with your child alone, if that is what you both think is best, but rarely does that solve the problem. Try to talk with your child about who would best deal with the problem at school, and then work out a plan together. Whatever you do, don't ignore the bullying as it will most likely get worse, or even lead to your child trying something desperate to get away from it.

If you are going to approach the school, try these steps:

1. Ring and make an appointment with the teacher. Don't just show up, especially if you are angry, as it will start things off on the wrong foot. It is unlikely that the teacher will be able to see you without an appointment, anyway, because of teaching schedules. If it is urgent, say so when you phone, and ask for a meeting within the next couple of days.
2. Bring a written record of what has happened to the meeting, as well as copies of any letters you may have written to the school, and details of any telephone calls. This makes it easier to remember and to check on facts, if necessary.
3. Listen to the school's explanation and say that you want to work together with them to stop the bullying. It is always better if there is co-operation between the parents and the school.
4. If you feel unsure about the meeting, or if there has been any antagonism between you and the school, bring along someone else who could be a witness to what is said.
5. Make out a short list of points you want to cover in the meeting, and use it as a reminder.
6. Ask to see a copy of the school's anti-bullying policy.

7. If the problem has not got out of hand yet, ask that the children work together on a solution. This is a particularly good approach if your child has been part of a group, which has somehow come unstuck. When this happens, the children usually have some residue of good feelings which can be used to resolve the bullying. The best outcome in your child's view may be that he makes up with his old friends, or that they are at least sympathetic and stop bullying.

8. If the problem is one of sustained bullying from someone or a group which has no previous friendship with your child, and it cannot be resolved as above, then find out what the school is going to do about it. They should:

- ensure your child is safe
- investigate what has happened
- interview the victim and bully separately
- interview witnesses
- depending upon the situation, they should take appropriate action such as:

  — obtain an apology
  — inform the bully's parents
  — impose sanctions
  — insist that anything which was taken or destroyed be returned or replaced
  — provide support for the victim and a safe place, if necessary
  — ensure that the bullying stops by supervising the bully
  — give the bully help to change his or her behaviour
  — let you know what is happening

Set a mutually agreed time limit for the action to take place.

9. If you feel that the bullying has not stopped and nothing you agreed is being done, then make an appointment with the headteacher.

10. If the bullying continues, contact the board of governors. Your school has the names and addresses, or will pass the letter or request on for you.

11. If the governors don't help, then contact the local education authority. Complain in writing to the Director of Education. Begin your letter with, 'I am writing to make a formal complaint . . .'

12. If the matter is still not deal with, contact your county councillor or MP.

13. You can also write to the Secretary of State for Education.

Last Resort

If you feel that no one is helping and that the situation with the school has become impossible:

1. Get a sick note from the doctor if your child is really stressed, and keep him or her at home until you can make other arrangements.

2. Remove your child from that school and find another, one which has a strong policy against bullying. In some cases I have dealt with, the child who was the victim of bullying in one school thrives and has no problems in the new 'anti-bullying' school. One can only conclude that it wasn't the child who had the problem, but the school which allowed it to go on.

3. Educate your child at home with the help of organisations such as Education Otherwise. The law says you must educate your child, it does not say it has to be done in a school.

The great majority of bullying cases never reach these later steps. And most schools now do seem to want to deal with bullying, but you may be unlucky.

What if the Teacher or Staff Member Is the Bully?

Some of the most difficult cases we have had to deal with at KIDSCAPE have been when a teacher or a member of staff is reported to be bullying children by picking on them, humiliating them or taunting them. If you discover that your child is being bullied in this way:

1. You should talk with the teacher, if possible, and express your concerns. Perhaps your child has misinterpreted something that was said or done, and it can be straightened out without a fuss.
2. If you feel the situation is beyond this kind of repair, and that you cannot speak to the teacher or member of staff, then see the headteacher and explain what has happened. In some schools you have to go through the head to make an appointment to see teachers, anyway.
3. Keep a written record of the incidents and how they have affected your child. It may be that the teacher is unaware of what he or she is doing and that the bullying will stop. Or it may be that the teacher's way of dealing with children is not suited to your child (or any child) and the teacher needs to be talked with and shown more positive ways of interacting. Whatever the reasons, if the teacher is bullying children, then it should be stopped immediately.
4. If the bullying goes on, then get in contact with the governors and follow the steps laid down above. At all stages, keep written records and, if you can see that it is necessary, bring along someone as an independent witness to meetings.
5. If, ultimately, it doesn't stop and all avenues fail, then find another school.

End the Conspiracy of Silence

One thing's sure: bullying is one of the hardest social problems your children have to deal with – and it's probably been made harder by the conspiracy of silence about it bred into us by our Victorian forebears. At least this tacit approval of bullying is one inheritance we needn't pass on to the next generation . . . and our children need not suffer in silence.

30

HELPING YOUR CHILDREN DEAL WITH DIVORCE OR SEPARATION

When I was nine, my best friend Celeste found out that her parents were divorcing. Celeste was the only child in the entire school to have this happen to her and the shock was enormous, not only to her but to all of us, the teachers and the community. It was spoken of in whispers.

Today, forty years later, we no longer speak in whispers about divorce or separation. Not surprising, considering that over a third of marriages end in divorce – and that doesn't include partners who live together and then separate. Exact figures are impossible to determine, but there must be at least a million and probably more children affected by these break-ups. Certainly, there are more than when Celeste had to cope.

However, the shock for children is still the same as it was for Celeste all those years ago. I was counselling a ten-year-old called Marilyn who told me about how she found out her parents were splitting. She was seven.

'I'll never forget the day my mother told us. My younger brothers and I were playing outside when she came out and asked us to come indoors. She was crying and said she had some bad news. I was terrified. My father was waiting for us. With us all sitting there, my father said he was leaving and divorcing my mum. She was sobbing. All of us kids started crying, too. I asked him why. After a long silence he said that he had fallen out of love with Mum and in love with someone else.

'I screamed "No!" and ran out of the room. My six-year-old brother ran after me. My youngest brother sunk deep into the sofa and cried his heart out. It was like a bad scene from a film and everything was in slow motion. My mother came after us and hugged us while we all sobbed.

'I was crushed. I hated my father for causing this pain. I wanted to help my mother, but I was too upset and angry. I guess I was too little to have been of much help, but I really did want to make her stop crying and become our happy Mummy again. I knew lots of kids who had step-parents, or who commuted between their parents, but I never, ever thought it would happen to me.

'It was awful when Dad left. I couldn't believe that we would never be a family again. I missed him, but I hated him, too. You know, I never heard my parents fight so the whole thing was a shock. I went over and over in my head how I could have prevented it happening. I decided that maybe I should have cleaned up my room or not fought with my brothers. Maybe I should have got better grades at school. I also thought that, if I promised God I would be good for the rest of my life, he might organise it so they would get back together. All I wanted was for things to get back to normal. For a while, I made a secret pact that I wouldn't eat and I would get so sick they would have to put me in hospital. Then my parents would come to visit me and promise to get back together to save me.'

Her parents didn't get back together. Marilyn is coping. Her father has remarried and he and his new wife are expecting a child. Her mother is working full-time and occasionally goes out with friends, but hasn't got a boyfriend. Marilyn no longer hates her father and she and her brothers see him on weekends. They like his new wife, but they are torn by loyalty for their mother and are worried that she is lonely.

Marilyn's story is not unusual. I suppose she is lucky that she is loved by both parents and has maintained contact with her father. Often, the parent who leaves home ends up leaving the family or is pushed away. One study showed that over fifty per cent of non-custodial fathers had completely lost contact with their children within five years of their divorces.

Children are not consulted about the break-up of their families. They usually have no control over who gets custody and how often they see their other parent. Some divorces occur because one parent is trying to protect their children from the abuse of the other parent. More often, divorce happens because parents are trying to protect themselves. They think that 'it's better for me and it must be better for the children'. Sometimes that's true, but often it isn't better for the children. That doesn't mean that parents should stay together in an intolerable situation only for the sake of the children, but they should not kid themselves that their children will thank them for divorcing or separating.

Tell Your Children What Is Happening

In my opinion, Marilyn's parents did the right thing by telling their children *together* that they were divorcing. My concern, however, was that it turned into such a dramatic scene. All the children I have seen can remember in great detail exactly what happened when they were told about their parents splitting. While it is understandable that everyone will be upset, try your best not to fall apart when telling the kids. It may be better to tell them over a period of time, but that will depend upon how old they are and how much the two of you can work together.

Before you do anything, it might be a good idea to go to the library or bookshop and get one of the many books that are available on the subject of divorce and children. There seem to be hundreds of them. Keep in mind that many have been written by parents who have themselves been through divorce, so you may or may not agree with all the advice they give. But it might help you avoid pitfalls that others have fallen into.

From what children have told me, the following suggestions seem to make it easier for them to adjust:

1. Plan in advance what you are going to say and agree to keep personal blame out of it.
2. Tell them together, if possible.

3. Tell them the truth. Whatever you do, don't gloss over the fact that the marriage or relationship is over. That will only prolong the suffering and they won't trust what you say later.

4. Give them time to adjust. For some, like Marilyn, the news comes out of the blue.

5. Allow them to bring out their feelings, even if they are very angry. This is not the time to scold them for their rudeness – you may have to 'take it on the chin' and bite your tongue. This is far better for them than forcing the anger inside where it will eat away.

6. Try to stay calm. It is reassuring for children to think that adults are still in control when their world seems to have been turned upside down. If you cry and carry on it won't help them. Avoid quarrelling and laying blame.

7. Turn your attention on the children, not on each other. Be as cordial as you can under the circumstances.

8. Talk about what will remain the same. Kids will wonder if they will be moving, whether they will go to the same school, what will happen to pets and possessions, etc.

9. Reassure them that you both still love them. If possible, explain that they will still see both parents.

10. Reassure them that it is not their fault and nothing they did was responsible for the split.

11. Answer their questions as frankly as you can. If you don't know the answer, say so.

12. Be patient. Things do get better with time. Children are resilient. With your help, they will cope.

How Children Are Affected By It

If you have to divorce or separate, children will be affected in different ways. Some will be relieved because the constant tension at home will finally go away. Others will be distraught. A few will seemingly take it in their stride. Whatever reactions they show to us, I have found that most children are negatively affected by these three aspects of divorce or separation:

1. They are lonely and feel isolated. Attention and affection that would go to them is diverted away because parents are struggling with their own emotions and needs.
2. Children use a stable family life as a base and as a model for their future relationships. If this base is unsettled it can make them unsure and distrustful about forming close relationships with people.
3. Children are often used as part of the cannon fodder of disintegrating relationships. They are pulled one way and then the other by parents trying to gain their loyalty. They may be asked to prove their love by rejecting or vilifying one of their parents – an impossible choice for most kids.

If you can address these issues, it will help your children in the long run. Obviously, you cannot help breaking up the family base, but you can talk about it and help your child see that not all relationships end this way. If there is any way you and your ex can form a friendly or at least tolerable relationship, it usually helps the children enormously.

Reactions

Children react in different ways to family break-up. They may:

- withdraw
- cling to both parents
- become irritable
- become aggressive
- be sad and cry
- do badly at school
- blame themselves
- play one parent against the other
- grieve
- run away
- get sick or even try to commit suicide as a means of getting parents back together
- stop eating
- become angry

- feel guilty and responsible
- be bullied by other kids using this as an excuse
- feel bitter
- start acting out and refusing to obey

Some children will show none of these signs and will improve because the situation was so bad previously the divorce has made it better. Others will take all their pain inside so they can protect their siblings or their parent. To help make it better:

1. Tell your children as much as possible. The kids I've talked with really resented not knowing what was happening. One boy said that his parents presumed he wouldn't understand and didn't explain things. As a result, he imagined all sorts of things and worried unnecessarily. 'They thought that, since I was only five, I was too young.' Kids usually cope better when they aren't kept in the dark.
2. Answer their frequent questions. Children will ask the same questions again and again, but it is not to get attention or to drive you nuts. They need to be told for reassurance. Answer in a matter of fact way and don't get annoyed.
3. Spend as much time as possible with them and try to keep their routine as it was. If they are acting out, it is probably to test that there are still limits out there. Allow some leeway, but don't let them get away with things. If they do it will only increase their anxiety. They need to know you're still in charge. This will give them stability.
4. If things are not going well, get professional help. Sometimes it is too much for you and the children to cope alone. As I mention in the next chapter about grief, there are times when it is easier and safer to talk with someone outside the family. This is not a reflection on your parenting skills. The reality is that you might be too close to what's happening to be able to help effectively. Of course, you may wish to get help, too, through this difficult time. (See Where to Get Help, p. 314, for suggestions.)

Afterwards

You will have many things to work out regarding the children. I see far too many children who have parents who hate each other. They need lots of help and are lost little creatures. I suspect there are lots of children out there who have gone through the divorce and who don't need professional help precisely because their parents handled things so well. The parents may well hate each other, but somehow they have managed to put their own needs aside and help their kids. Maybe they are just good actors! In any event, try to make it as easy for your kids after the split as you can:

1. Try to agree access before the court battle, realising that seeing both parents is very important to most children.
2. Give children as much input as possible, depending upon their ages. One seven-year-old girl told me that she was furious because no-one asked her if it was all right for her to see her father only once a week. It was not all right, and she showed her anger by withdrawing from everything – school, home, friends. She came to my attention when she deliberately walked in front of a car to try to kill herself. Of course, this was an extreme case with other overlays, but so much could have been avoided had she thought anyone cared about how she felt and what her needs were.
3. Give them stability, even if it is in two separate places. Have a routine for each home, and make sure your children feel equally welcome in both your homes.
4. Seeing both parents is important so the children can make sure each parent is OK and coping. It makes them feel more secure and less stressed if both Mum and Dad seem to be happy, or at least getting on with things.
5. Bite your tongue when you want to criticise your ex. Children may agree with you now, but form a completely different opinion later on and then blame you for turning them against the other parent. You cannot win by undermining your children's love for their other parent.
6. Involve children, if they are old enough, in custody arrangements, but not in nitty-gritty details. I firmly believe that a

person independent of both parents needs to talk with children and find out who they think they would like to live with. I know the courts might decide against the wishes of the children 'for their own good', but it is time we stopped treating kids like communal property with no voice of their own. The CD player doesn't care where it ends up – the kids do, and usually with good reason.

7. Don't fight every time you pick up or drop off the children. If you can't stand your ex, then stay out of the way when he or she arrives to collect the children.
8. Don't ask children to spy on and report back on your ex.
9. Don't question children about what they did – tell them you'd like to know, but don't dig at them to tell you.
10. Accept the loss your children feel and sympathise with them, even if you wonder why you ever got involved with your ex in the first place.

All I can say to end this chapter is that children are often so badly affected by the break-up of families, it is worth doing everything in your power to try to avoid a split if possible. But if it isn't possible, don't despair. For some children, the divorce or separation turns out to be a blessing in disguise. Children can and do adjust to new situations. Some are happier either with one parent, or in a new step-family. And bad effects seem to get better with time, especially if you are sensitive to your children's needs. My friend Celeste says now that she wishes her parents had been more tuned in to how she felt about their divorce, but in the long run it was best for all of them. But Celeste was determined not to have her children go through what she did, so she and her husband have worked hard to avoid the pitfalls and to create a happy marriage and stable environment for their children. So far, they have succeeded wonderfully.

As to the question of step-parenting and merged families, there are zillions of books and articles about this and I suggest another trip to the library or bookshop. Best of luck!

31

HELPING CHILDREN COPE WITH GRIEF

Six-year-old Eric and eight-year-old Dennis lost their mother, Carmen, to cancer when she was only thirty-four. They and her husband, Robert, were devastated. Carmen was a friend of mine, a fellow teacher and one of the most beautiful and kindest people I ever met. After the funeral and the initial shock, Robert turned all of his attention to helping his children adjust to their terrible loss. But the children also made it their business to help their father. I'll never forget Robert telling me that one of the boys took his hand in the car on the way to the funeral and said, 'We'll get through this together, Dad.' And they did. But it wasn't easy for any of them.

Most children will experience the death of someone they love – grandparent, friend, relative, parent or sibling. I remember my first experience of death, when my great-grandmother died. I'll never forget having to approach the coffin and being lifted up to kiss her goodbye. She looked strange and cold and I started to wail. Nonetheless, I had to do as I was told. No-one comforted my sister or me, and we hid under a table and discussed how horrible it all was that she would never make us her delicious cakes again and how awful it was that we had to kiss her. Worse, we decided it wasn't fair that we were stuck inside, and we slipped outside to play. Were we callous and unfeeling or just working things out for ourselves, as kids often do? No-one took the time to tell us anything, so I guess we just handled it as best we could. Looking back, we were lucky that we didn't have the kind of trauma that Eric and

Dennis had – the death of someone young and vital to our well-being, such as a member of our immediate family.

We will return to helping children deal with the death of a person they know and love, but first let's turn to the question of dealing with the death of pets, something that affects every child who has ever had a pet of any kind.

Pets

It may seem insensitive to mention the death of parents or siblings and friends in the same chapter as the death of pets, but often the demise of a pet is a child's first experience of death. I certainly wish now that my first encounter with death had been with a goldfish or a gerbil or another pet, instead of a person. I think that my sons have been fortunate because their first experience of death was with their hamster, Hammy (such an original name, I know). This, at least, gave me the opportunity to help them learn about death in what I consider a fairly non-traumatic way, though they thought it was pretty terrible at the time. My youngest son found Hammy, and came running in crying that Hammy was dead because he had forgotten to feed him that morning. Not so, of course. Hammy died because he was, in hamster terms, old. My son didn't believe me and continued to say that Hammy would still be alive if he had fed him.

Help your children by:

1. Explaining

If your pet has died of old age, explain how all creatures have a time to be born, to live and to die. If possible, try to prepare your children in advance for the death of an aging pet, so it won't come as such a shock.

If your pet has died as a result of an accident or illness, talk about how some things happen that we can't change, no matter how much we wish we could. We will perhaps be angry and sorrowful and miss the pet, but there is nothing we can do except remember the good times and how lucky we were to have such a wonderful pet.

2. Arranging a 'Funeral'

We buried Hammy in a shoebox, complete with flowers and a moment of silence. Allow the children to organise the formalities, if they wish.

3. Talking It Over

Discuss the childrens' feelings and let them cry. Eventually, my son accepted that he wasn't responsible for the death of our hamster, but he was sad for several weeks. We talked about his sadness and how it was all right to feel that way. My son decided that Hammy was now a spirit roaming freely around the hamster universe, which made him feel better.

4. Considering a Replacement

Get a new pet, when the time is right. After Hammy, we decided that if we were going to have all this hassle, we might as well have a 'proper' pet. After several months of careful planning, we got a lovely chocolate-coloured Cocker spaniel. He is only five now, but I have told both boys how long spaniels usually live, and hope that we don't have to deal with his death for years and years to come.

Children's Reactions to the Death of Friends or Relatives

Although it is difficult and sad for children to have to come to terms with the death of a pet, it is far more horrendous to have to deal with the death of a person they know and love. Whether that death is accidental, sudden or due to a long-term illness, children will usually respond with denial, anger and shock.

Children's reactions will depend upon their age and the

relationship to them of the person who has died. Children under the age of five usually have difficulty accepting the finality and reality of death. They will use the term without understanding what it means. One four-year-old girl I dealt with wanted to know when her older brother was coming back from his funeral. She worried that he was cold and hungry, and wanted her mother to set a place for him at the table.

Under Fives

With children so young, explain death in simple, concrete terms:

1. Say that the person is dead, which means he or she won't be coming back.
2. Say how sad you are, and don't be afraid to show your own feelings.
3. Explain that it isn't anyone's fault, because young children sometimes think it wouldn't have happened if they had somehow acted differently.
4. Don't say the person has gone to sleep, or is away on holiday, or other euphemisms. You may find young children terrified to go to sleep or go away on holiday because they think they'll die.
5. If you have a religious belief, talk about what you believe has happened to the person who has died. If you think he or she is in heaven, or in the stars, or is a spirit, then use this belief to help your child.
6. Answer your child's questions – be direct and as honest as you can be. If you don't know the answer, say so.
7. Try explaining that death means not breathing or eating or feeling pain anymore. It also means not being frightened or worried or angry.
8. Encourage your child to talk about the person who has died, and especially to remember as many nice thing about them as possible.
9. Keep photographs of the person who has died, and help the child to remember what the person looked like, and how the person acted, laughed and talked, etc.

Be prepared for the young child's lack of understanding. He or she may ask to go out to play upon finding out someone has died, and then come in and ask where the person is. Or the child may ask the way to heaven, or even pack some belongings and set out to find the place where the dead person is. After a time, you may think that the child finally understands, only to have him or her saying that 'Mummy or Daddy has been gone long enough now, and when are they coming back?'

When I was five, a little girl in our class died in a fire. Though we were all told that the child was dead, several weeks later I asked her brother when she was coming back to school. He was only six or so and he just replied, 'Don't know.' Neither of us really understood what it was all about.

Fives to Tens

As children grow older, they have more understanding that death is irreversible. They are interested in what happens to people after they die, and may draw lots of pictures of tombstones and skeletons. When Carmen died, one of Eric's teachers became very concerned because he was drawing a picture of his mother in her grave. The teacher thought it was macabre and unnatural. On the contrary, it was a normal, healthy way for Eric to come to terms with what had happened. Eric's father accepted this and did not react with disgust or horror, as some parents have when their children depict death in this way.

When talking about death with children this age:

1. Give them as many details as they ask about what happened, and how the person died. They are not being weird by asking, they are trying to put the death into their own framework.
2. Tell them you understand if they try to deny what happened, but that it really is true.
3. Agree that it isn't fair and that you, too, wish it wasn't so, but that sometimes things happen which aren't fair.
4. Don't respond with anger if the child seems to be apathetic or doesn't seem to care. Sometimes this is the only way they can

cope for a while. If the child did love the person and this continues, think about getting professional advice to help the child
unblock his or her feelings.

5. Encourage memories, display photographs, talk about the
   person.

6. Don't be afraid to cry and show your own feelings. This will
   give your child permission to express his or her feelings, too.

7. Answer questions and try to put fears at rest. Children at this
   age realise that they, too, could die and it is frightening for
   them. This is especially true if a brother or sister has died.

8. If one of your children has died and another child asks for the
   dead child's room or belongings, don't be shocked or angry.
   This, too, is a natural reaction, and the child does not mean it
   in a cruel way. The child may be seeking comfort in his or her
   sibling's possessions, or be thinking that somehow this is a
   way of maintaining contact.

Be prepared for the child of this age to react with anger and aggression. But you may also be surprised at how empathetic and
supportive they can be. While this may be a way of keeping the
death at a distance from them, it can also be an excellent way for
them to cope. As Robert found with his children, they gained
strength by supporting him when he was low, just as he became
stronger by helping them. By all means, allow children to do something to help. Preparing tea, or adding their own comments to any
letters you might be writing, might help them and you. If the person who died is a parent or sibling, your child may wish to help in
planning the funeral or choosing the clothes for the deceased. Or,
if you are sorting out the person's belongings, it might be thera-
peutic to let the child help, if she or he wishes to. You could tell the
child you are about to clear the room, and give them the option of
helping.

Tens to Teens

Older children will respond to death with much more understanding, and will delve into the 'meaning' of life and death. If the death
is in the family, they may try to take on the responsibility of

dealing with the funeral, and of phoning people, in order to take the burden off others, such as parents. They may suppress their own feelings so they don't upset others, and they are very aware of how final death is.

When dealing with children of this age:

1. Give them as much detail as possible about what happened.
2. Allow them to help make arrangements.
3. Be willing to discuss the more abstract and philosophical aspects of death.
4. Beware of them becoming morbid about death in general and relating it to themselves. 'What's the point of living anyway, if we're all going to die?' type statements should be followed up and discussed, in case they are indications of suicidal thoughts.
5. Be prepared for them to be angry. One boy of thirteen when told his father had died, raged against his mother, saying it was her fault and he hated her. He didn't, but she was the safest person he could vent his anger and frustration at, though he was quite contrite later.
6. The child may react by going about his or her normal routine and showing not much emotion at all. This is one way of temporarily keeping the reality at bay. But it could also be that the child did not really like the person who died, even if they were a member of the family. One fourteen-year-old boy whose father committed suicide said that he was so relieved he wouldn't have to put up with his father's disapproval anymore, that he was glad he had died.
7. The child may react by doing badly at school, or playing up in an uncharacteristic way. For example, if a parent dies, a child may test the limits that the other parent or guardian sets. This is usually just to make sure that there are still limits, since the world as the child knew it has changed.

Specific Suggestions

When helping children to cope with grief, there are several things you can do to make it easier for them. If the person who has died is a friend of your child's, then at least you probably won't have the intense personal grief of your own to deal with, as well. If, however, the person who died is in your family, this often makes it more difficult for you to help your child.

If one of their parents has died, children will start to worry about the slightest thing happening to their remaining parent. They may ask questions like, 'What will happen to me if you die?' or become hysterical if you get sick or come home late. Sometimes, children have this reaction if the parent of another child dies. Three families from the school I was working at were killed in the Paris aeroplane crash of a DC 10. For months afterwards, children were not only continuing to mourn the loss of their friends, but many were fearful for their own families and parents.

If one of your children dies, it is the worst tragedy a parent can experience. But, far too often it also means that other children in the family also become casualties of the death of their brother or sister. They may feel that they should have died instead, or that the dead child is being turned into a saint who never did any wrong. That makes them feel angry, and at the same time guilty for thinking such thoughts.

Whoever has died, you may want to try some of the following approaches when trying to help your children:

1. Tell your children you know it is difficult for them to see you so upset, and that you know they are upset, too. Tell them you are trying to cope and that you love them very much.
2. Talk about the person who has died and try to remember the good and bad things.
3. Don't put the person who has died on a pedestal, or make your other children feel they must take his or her place.
4. Tell your children that it is all right to laugh and enjoy life, even if you can't join in at the moment. One nine-year-old I talked to said that his home had turned into a place of gloom

and dreariness – no-one was allowed to joke or laugh for fear of offending the memory of his sister.

5. Give your children permission to be angry that this has happened. Express your own anger, if you feel it is necessary and helpful. If the person died as the result of suicide or through an accident that seemed to be his or her fault, then it is a natural reaction to be angry with the person. If someone else was responsible, then it is also natural to be angry with that person. Bringing out these feelings can be an important part of coming to terms with the death.

6. Tell your children that you are glad they are here. Another child I counselled tried to commit suicide after his older brother died, because he felt that being dead was the only way to gain his mother's love. She, of course, did love him, but was beside herself with grief and could not reach out to him.

7. Give members of your family the right to grieve in their own ways. Just because someone is not crying all the time, it does not mean they are not grieving. Everyone grieves in their own way.

8. If it is likely that someone is going to die, prepare your children as much as possible. It may still be a shock when the person does die, but it will not come as a complete surprise.

9. If possible, allow your children to say goodbye to the person who is dying or who has died. This may depend upon your beliefs and on the age of the child, but I think it is easier to cope with death if you've been able to say goodbye. One mother shooed her children out of the hospital room just as their father was dying to save them from the pain. But they wanted to be with him and resented not being there at the end.

10. Keep to the routine at home as much as possible. When a death has turned the world upside-down, it is comforting for a child to have meals, bedtimes, etc., much as before.

11. Holidays, birthdays, and anniversaries may be particularly difficult, especially in the first year. Some families go away at these times, because they can't face being in the home where they are surrounded by memories of the person. Others stay put and fondly recall past holidays, or invite lots of people

over. Still others go to the grave of their loved one or have a religious service of remembrance. One family whose fourteen-year-old son died, said the first Christmas was so impossible that next Christmas they are going to volunteer to help in a soup kitchen for the needy. Give some thought as to how you are going to deal with these times, but also try to make them as fun as possible for the children, who will not want to think that every holiday is going to be hell from now on.

12. Get as much help and advice as you can from friends, from your children's teachers and from books. Poems like the one at the end of this chapter are often comforting if they fit in with your beliefs about death.

13. Seek professional help and advice for you and your children if you find you or they are not coping. Sometimes it is easier to talk with a counsellor, even if the person is a stranger. Children may feel more comfortable talking about their grief to someone who won't be hurt by their pain. It doesn't mean that children don't want to confide in their parents, only that an outside view and support may be more helpful at times.

14. Help your children find their own group of people to support them, as it might be too much for you to cope with everything. The list of people may include aunts, uncles, family friends, teachers and others.

15. Go out with your children. Do something different and fun together. Start creating new memories for them and for yourself.

16. Above all, don't try to shield your children from grief. You might think you are protecting them, but you aren't. They need to grieve and share in the sadness.

Putting it all into a nutshell, children will need your help and support to deal with grief, and they will respond best to honesty and lots of love and understanding – just like us adults.

By the way, Robert married one of his son's teachers and both boys have grown into wonderful young men of whom their father and stepmother are very proud. Carmen would have been proud of them too.

A Helpful Poem

Canon Henry Scott Holland wrote this many years ago, and I find it comforting. Perhaps you will, too:

Death is nothing at all . . . I have only slipped away into the next room. I am I, and you are you. Whatever we were to each other, that we are still. Call me by my old familiar name. Speak to me in the easy way which you always used. Put no differences into your tone. Wear no forced air of solemnity or sorrow. Laugh as we always laughed at the little jokes we enjoyed together. Play, smile, think of me. Let my name be ever the household name that it always was. Let it be spoken without effort, without the ghost of a shadow on it. Life means all that it ever meant. It is the same as it ever was. There is absolutely unbroken continuity. What is this death but a negligible accident? Why should I be out of mind because I am out of sight? I am waiting for you for an interval somewhere very near . . . just round the corner. All is well.

32

TEN PARENTS TELL THEIR WORST REGRETS

The perfect mother or father? I've never met one! We all make mistakes with our children. But we can learn from the things we do wrong and just hope that it hasn't damaged our children beyond repair. I know I was a much better mum by the time my second child came along. (Mind you, my older boy often tells me that I let his little brother get away with murder!)

Most of us eagerly devour 'expert' childcare manuals in the hope that we'll learn to avoid the pitfalls of parenthood. I read every one I could get my hands on and they did help, as I hope this one will. But I also think that chatting to as many other mums and dads as possible, and learning from their experiences, is invaluable. So, I am ending this book with words of wisdom from those who have been there. See what you make of other parents' regrets while bringing up their children.

1. Let Them Be!

'I loved it when people told us how well-behaved and angelic our children were,' says Kate, mother of two girls, now aged twenty-one and twenty-four. 'It's true, they were good – but at a price they are now paying. Both my girls are perfectionists, and worriers. I'm sure that's because I was always anxious about them making a

5. Tell Them They're Great

'I told everyone else how wonderful my kids were, but I never told them,' says Patrick, a father of two. 'I guess I assumed they must know it and I didn't want to make them big-headed. If anything, I underplayed my pride in them, which I now think was a big mistake. My compliments were always conditional. I'd say, "I'm pleased you've got a good mark in maths, but why isn't it higher?" or, "Well done for washing the plates, but why have you left the pans?" I wish I had praised them without reservation and told my kids that they were great.'

Praise Your Kids Often

I think we all love compliments. Nowadays, Patrick's daughters love to hear their dad say how much he thought – and thinks – of their achievements. The only caution is, don't send your adult friends into a catatonic state by going on and on about your kids. There's nothing worse than continually hearing how well someone else's are doing – especially if our own aren't as successful!

6. Ask for Help

'I was too reserved to ask for help,' says Liz, an awesomely competent office PA before she gave up her job to have children – now twelve, eleven and seven. 'I lived in a street full of people I knew and my parents were only twenty minutes away, but looking back at the early years I think it was pride that made me tell myself I should be able to cope on my own. As it was, I remember being constantly exhausted.'

Pride Mustn't Prevent

Liz is bright to notice that it was secret pride which stopped her asking for help. It's a pity, because it's important for children to know their grandparents, and that little bit of extra help might have relieved some of the early stress for her. Still, she finally saw the sense of not being Supermum and now has a network of other mothers and relatives who all help each other. She thinks the kids are a lot easier to live with; the funny thing is, they seem to think the change is in her!

7. Make Time for Cuddles

'They grow up so fast. Where did the time go?' Debbie shakes her head in amazement that the eldest of her four children has already left home. 'I miss the cuddles, the kisses on their little noses, the hands clasped tightly around my neck. I wish I'd spend more time giving them cuddles, and being there for them. You think you have all the time in the world and suddenly they are eighteen. I stopped cuddling when they were about five and starting school because I felt it would toughen them up.'

Show Your Affection
Hugging and cuddling children is one of life's greatest pleasures. We do have to hold back when our kids signal they are not in the mood for a cuddle. They'll push you away with an 'Oh, mum . . .' if it doesn't feel right and, of course, you should never embarrass them in front of their friends. But I reckon there is never a right time to stop showing affection. After all, we Mums and Dads enjoy – and need – those hugs as much as kids do! And holding kids physically close can actually make them more independent, because they'll feel secure in your love.

8. Trust Your Intuition

Linda, who has an eleven-year-old son, rang me at my office to ask advice. 'Gavin's been quiet and moody for more than a week,' she said. 'Yesterday, he told me he was fed up at school – though he wouldn't tell me why – and said he didn't want to go. I thought I had to make him face up to the problem, whatever it is, and go in to his classes. When he came home, though, he was in tears and he looked terrible. This morning he doesn't want to go to school again. I'm at my wits' end.'

We Know Best

Linda may have rung me for advice, but she didn't need me to tell her what to do. All I had to say to her was, 'What do *you* think is best for Gavin?' 'Well . . .' said Linda doubtfully, 'he's so upset I think he really might do something stupid, but he has to go to school.' 'Leaving school aside, what do you really think would help Gavin?' I asked. Linda paused. 'I really want to keep him home for a few days, get him to calm down enough to feel safe. I want to find out why he's so unhappy.'

Linda already had the answer. Her son's welfare was more important than forcing him to go to school. She rang back later to say that Gavin had finally blurted out the truth about a group of bullies at school. Thank goodness she hadn't forced him to go back into an intolerable situation. Her instincts told her what to do – protect her son when he was vulnerable. I told her she was lucky Gavin had shown some symptoms to alert her to the problem – some children don't, as I have seen all too tragically.

9. Don't Organise Too Much

'My worst mistake was that the children never had a free moment,' remembers Anna, the mum of two teenage daughters. 'They had swimming lessons, sports, trips to museums – anything going on in the community and they were signed up for it. I organised them to death. I thought that fun had to be planned and that children left to their own devices would stagnate. My kids don't have much self-confidence now, and maybe it's my fault if I have to prod them to do things.'

Use Imagination

Anna's kids might have had more self-confidence if she had encouraged them to come up with their own ideas, or just let things happen spontaneously once in a while. OK, there might be failures some days. But letting them have the freedom to find out what they want to do is how they will learn to organise themselves and become self-starters.

10. Write It Down

'If only I had scribbled down even a few of those great moments,' sighed Marilyn. 'The other day, my nine-year-old asked me when he first walked and I couldn't for the life of me remember. You think you'll remember everything your children do. I thought that every momentous event would be seared on my memory forever. Hah! When my eldest was only two, I already could not tell you when he walked, the cute little things he did or the date of his first tooth.'

Favourite Stories
Marilyn told me this when we were both in hospital – me with my first baby, she with her third. I took it to heart, bought a blank note-book and jotted things down. Sometimes I waxed eloquent; other times it was a quickly jotted, misspelt mess. Those books were my children's favourite bedtime reading for years! Even now, my teenagers will listen with rapt attention to a day in the life of them, aged three or four. So, Marilyn, wherever you are, thanks for telling me your mistake.

Happy Families

If you recognise yourself in some of these scenarios, don't worry. We have all made at least one of these mistakes, and perhaps much worse ones. But if anything touches a raw nerve, there's no point tormenting yourself with guilt. The good news is that it's never too late to change the way we do things and improve our relationships with our kids. Be positive, keep a sense of humour and stay cheerful – no child wants a woe-is-me parent! And be prepared to experiment to find the changes that might suit your family. Remember, kids are resilient and we can't go too far wrong if we tell them often how much we love them, and how lucky they are to have us as parents!

WHERE TO GET HELP

The following agencies and organisations can listen and give you advice about a variety of problems and concerns. Of course, you can always contact the police, social services and your GP. Someone in your religious community may also be able to help.

When contacting any of the listed organisations, you will need to use your own judgement about the suitability of their service or advice for your particular needs.

ABDUCTION (PARENTAL)

The Child Abduction Unit
The Lord Chancellor's Department
81 Chancery Lane
London
WC2A 1DD

Tel: 0171-911 7047/7094

If your child has been abducted from the UK, The Child Abduction Unit will give advice about what action you can take and what the British Government can or cannot do to help.

Reunite
National Council for Abducted Children
PO Box 4

London
WC1X 8XY

Tel: 0171-404 8356

A booklet entitled 'Child Abduction' is available from Reunite.

ABUSE

Child Protection Societies

These provide help and advice or referral information about protecting children from child abuse:

Irish Society for the Prevention of Cruelty to Children (ISPCC)
20 Molesworth Street
Dublin 2

Tel: 00 353 1 6794944

National Society for the Prevention of Cruelty to Children (NSPCC)

Tel: 0800 800500   24-hour telephone helpline

Children 1st, Royal Scottish Society for the Prevention of Cruelty to Children
Melville House
41, Polworth Terrace
Edinburgh
E11 1NV

Tel: 0131-337 8539

ChildLine
Freepost 1111 (no stamp needed)
London
EC4 4BB

Tel: 0800 1111

ChildLine is a 24-hour charge-free telephone counselling and advice service for children in trouble or danger.

Kidscape
152 Buckingham Palace Road
London
SW1W 9TR

Send a large SAE for a free copy of 'Why My Child?' a 28-page booklet for helping parents cope with the sexual abuse of their child or children.

AIDS

Your GP or paediatrician should be able to give you advice and can arrange for testing, if necessary.

For free leaflets and booklets, contact your local health education unit, which is listed in the directory under the name of your Health Authority.

You can also contact:

Health Information Service   Tel: 0800 665544

Health Literature Line   Tel: 0800 555777

These lines are run by The Department of Health.

ALCOHOL

For help with dealing with alcohol abuse contact:

Alcoholics Anonymous
PO Box 1
Stonebow House
Stonebow
York
YO1 2NJ

Tel: (01904) 644026

Al-Anon/Al-Teen
61 Dover Street
London
SE1 4YF

Tel: 0171-403 0888

For family, friends and children who have a relative affected by drinking problems.

ANOREXIA/BULIMIA/OTHER EATING DISORDERS

The following organisations will give advice and/or therapy for those suffering from eating disorders (and their families):

Eating Disorders Association (EDA)
Sackville Place
44/48 Magdalen Street
Norwich
NR3 1JU

Tel: (01603) 621414

The National Centre for Eating Disorders
11 Esher Place Avenue
Esher
Surrey
KT10 8PU

Tel: (01372) 469493

BEREAVEMENT

The Compassionate Friends
53 North Street
Bristol
BS3 1EN

Tel: (01179) 665202

Helpline: (01179) 539639   9.30am to 5pm, Mon. to Fri.

A nationwide (and international) self-help organisation of parents whose child of any age, including adult, has died through accident, illness, murder or suicide. A postal library and leaflets are also available.

Cruse
126 Sheen Road
Richmond
Surrey
TW9 1UR

Helpline: 0181-332 7227   9.30am to 5pm, Mon. to Fri.

Offers counselling for all bereavements.

BULLYING

ChildLine

Tel: 0800 1111

24-hour freephone for children to discuss problems, including bullying.

Kidscape
152 Buckingham Palace Road
London
SW1W 9TR

Tel: 0171-730 3300

Send a large SAE for a free booklet about bullying and other information about anti-bullying schools programmes.

Telephone counselling for families available on Tues. and Weds. from 9.30am to 4pm.

CONTRACEPTION

For advice on contraception, pregnancy, or abortion contact:

Brook Advisory Centre (for young people)
Head Office
165 Grays Inn Road
London
WC1X 8UD

Tel: 0171-713 9000   9am to 5pm, Mon. to Fri.
     0171-617 8000   computerised 24-hour helpline

Family Planning Association
2–12 Pentonville Road
London
N1 9FP

Tel: 0171–837 5432

COUNSELLING

These organisations offer counselling on family and other problems:

British Association of Counselling (BAC)
1 Regent Place
Rugby
Warwickshire
CV21 2VT

Refers people to qualified counsellors. Send A5-size SAE for list of counsellors in your local area.

Samaritans

Tel: 0345 909090

Samaritans are trained volunteers who talk with people about problems in confidence.

Family Service Units
207 Old Marylebone Road
London
NW1 5QP

Tel: 0171-402 5175

Provides family counselling in branches throughout England.
Ring to obtain number of your local branch.

Youth Access (formerly NAYPCAS)
Ashby House
62A Ashby Road
Loughborough
Leicester
LE1 3AE

Tel: (01509) 210420

Provides names and addresses of local free counselling services
to young people. Telephone, or write enclosing an SAE.

DIVORCE/SEPARATION

National Family Mediation
9 Tavistock Place
London
WC1H 9SN

Tel: 0171-383 5993

Helps couples (married or unmarried) going though a separation or divorce to make joint decisions about a range of issues,
with particular focus on arrangements for their children. For
information ring or send a large SAE for leaflets.

National Step-Family Association
18 Hatton Place
London
EC1N 8RU

Tel: 0171-209 2460   office
Tel: 0990 168388   counselling helpline: 2pm to 5pm, and
                       7pm to 10pm Mon. to Fri.

Offers support to all members of step-families and those who work with them. Send a large SAE for information pack.

Relate Marriage Guidance
Little Church Street
Rugby
CV21 3AP

Tel: (01788) 573241

Provides advice for couples (married or unmarried) who are experiencing relationship problems. For the telephone number of the Relate office near you, check your local directory under Relate, or ring the national headquarters for a referral. Send a large SAE for leaflets.

DRUGS

Doctors, Social Services, the Police and Citizens Advice Bureaux should be able to advise about drug centres. The National Drugs Helpline has been set up to provide help and leaflets:

The National Drugs Helpline
PO Box 5000
Glasgow
G12 9BL

Tel: 0800 776600,   24 hour helpline

These leaflets are available in English and several other languages:

- Drugs Misuse: a basic briefing
- Drugs: a parent's guide
- Solvents: a parent's guide

- Drugs and Solvents: you and your child
- Drugs and Solvents: things you should know
- A Young Person's Guide (for 8 to 12 year olds)

The Department of Education and Science and the Welsh Office also produce leaflets and booklets about drugs available in English and Welsh from:

Welsh Office
Information Division
Cathays Park
Cardiff
CF1 3NQ

Adfam National
5th Floor
Epworth House
25 City Road
London
EC1Y 1AA

Helpline: 0171-638 3700 10am to 5pm, Mon. to Fri.

National helpline for the families and friends of drug users, confidential support and information.

Families Anonymous
Unit 37
Doddington & Rollo Community Assoc
Charlotte Despart Avenue
London
SW11 5JE

Tel: 0171-498 4680

Families Anonymous self-help groups are for those affected by drug abuse or the related problems of a relative or friend. It is completely independent, non-professional and anonymous.

FAMILIES

Exploring Parenthood: The National Parenting Development Centre
4 Ivory Place
Threadgold Street
London
W11 4BP

Tel: 0171 221 6681   10am to 4pm, Mon. to Fri.

Provides professional support and advice to all parents who experience problems from time to time. Easy access to professional advice and support.

Family Rights Group
(England & Wales)
The Print House
18 Ashwin Street
London E8 3DL

Tel: 0171-249 0008   advice/helpline 1.30pm to 3pm, Mon. to Fri.

Promotes partnership between families and childcare agencies in England and Wales. They offer confidential advice on the telephone or by letter.

Gingerbread
16–17 Clerkenwell Close
EC1R 0AA

Tel: 0171-336 8184

Offers support, information and social activities for one parent families

National Council for One Parent Families
255 Kentish Town Road
London
NW5 2LX

Tel: 0171-267 1361

Write or telephone for practical literature regarding issues such as housing, separation, getting back to work, etc., or for a referral to a local help agency.

Parents Anonymous
6 Manor Gardens
London
N7 6LA

Tel: 0171-263 8918 Answerphone – gives telephone numbers of volunteers who are on duty. They aim to give a 24-hour service.

Parents Anonymous offers a listening service plus help and support to parents who are experiencing problems with any issues regarding children and young people.

Parent-Line
Endway House
The Endway
Benfleet
Essex
SS7 2AN

Tel: (01702) 554782   office

(01702) 559900   helpline: 9am to 6pm, Mon. to Fri. 12 noon to 4pm, Sat. After hours number supplied on answerphone.

Provides support for parents under stress, therefore maximising a family's capacity for its children.

Parent Network
44–46 Caversham Road
London
NW5 2DS

Tel: 0171-485 8535

Programmes to equip parents to feel supported and encouraged whilst doing the most important job of raising children.

GAMBLING

Gamblers Anonymous & Gam-Anon
PO Box 88
London
SW10 0EU

Tel: 0171-384 3040   24-hour helpline

Gamblers Anonymous is a self-help group of men and women who have joined together to do something about their gambling problems. Gam-Anon offers friendship, practical help, comfort and understanding to families of compulsive gamblers.

UK Forum on Young People & Gambling
PO Box 5
Chichester, West Sussex
PO19 3RB

Contact name: Paul Bellringer
                       Tel: (01243) 538635

Offers advice to parents and young people with gambling problems. Also offers advice to young people addicted to video games.

LEARNING DIFFICULTIES

The Dyslexia Institute
152 Buckingham Palace Road
London
SW1W 9TR

Tel: 0171-730 8890

Carries out assessments of children in centres throughout the country and operates a national teaching network. For further information and or copies of their leaflets, ring or send an SAE.

LEGAL ADVICE

Advisory Council for Education (ACE)
1b Aberdeen Studios
22–24 Highbury Grove
London
N5 2EA

Tel: 0171-354 8321   2pm to 5pm, Mon. to Fri.

Gives advice by telephone or letter about all aspects of the education service. Also publishes handbooks and information sheets for parents.

Citizens Advice Bureau

Telephone numbers listed in local directory.

Will give details of services available and advice on how to get help.

Education Law Association
Lawn Cottage
Lodge Lane
Salfords
Surrey
RH1 5DH

Tel: (01293) 822923 office hours

Gives names and addresses of solicitors throughout the country who specialise in education law.

PUNISHMENT

End Physical Punishment of Children (EPOCH)
77 Holloway Road
London
N7 8JZ

Tel: 0171-700 0627

National campaign to end all physical punishment of children. It provides leaflets and posters. Send a large SAE for a free copy of their No Smacking leaflet.

SAFETY (PERSONAL)

Kidscape
152 Buckingham Palace Road
London
SW1W 9TR

Kidscape offers practical leaflets, posters and books on children's personal safety, including *Keep Them Safe* – a booklet with suggestions for teaching five to eleven-year-olds ways to stay safe. Send a large SAE.

SUICIDE

ChildLine

Tel: 0800 1111

ChildLine is a 24-hour freephone for children to discuss any problem, including feeling suicidal.

Kidscape
152 Buckingham Palace Road
London
SW1W 9TR

Kidscape has a free leaflet entitled *Suicide and Young People*. For a copy, send a large SAE.

Samaritans

Tel: 0345 909090

The Samaritans run 24-hour helplines staffed by volunteers who listen to any problems, including depression and suicidal feelings. They also have some drop-in centres.

TELEPHONE NUISANCE CALLS

Nuisance Callers is a leaflet giving guidance on how to deal with abusive or nuisance telephone calls and what BT can do to help. Available free from BT Customer Service.

Tel: 0800 411423.

VICTIM SUPPORT

Parents Against Injustice (PAIN)
10 Water Lane
Bishop's Stortford
Herts
CM23 2JZ

Tel: (01279) 656564

Gives advice, counselling and support to parents and others when a child is mistakenly thought to be at risk or to have been abused.

Victim Support Scheme
National Office
Cranmer House
39 Brixton Road
London SW9 6DZ

Tel: 0171-735 9166

A nationwide network of support groups offering practical help and advice to victims of violence and crime. You can find out the number of your local branch by either contacting the office listed above or by looking in your local directory.

INDEX